BALKAN VILLAGE

Rila Monastery, sacred to Bulgarians for six centuries

BALKAN VILLAGE

by

IRWIN T. SANDERS

With Original Photographs by the Author

THE UNIVERSITY OF KENTUCKY PRESS

Lexington : 1949

Dedicated

to

My Mother

FOREWORD

THE EUROPE of headlines and newsreels and newscasts is a Europe we Americans know all too well. It is the Europe of swiftly maneuvering armies, umbrellas of planes, and scorched earth. Its air is filled with noisy propaganda, whispered intrigue, and the cries of starving children. This was the Europe of tottering dictators and victims restive for the day of liberation.

There is another Europe whose foundations are laid far in the past of people working a well-loved land, of peaceful rivers carrying barges laden with fruit and grain, of families of storks returning from Egypt, as they have for a thousand years, to nest in the same protected spots. This is the Europe I have known and loved as I saw it from a tranquil village clinging to a Bulgarian mountainside, in the shadow of a twelfth century monastery.

No one village can typify a whole region, yet the faithful account of the everyday life of this Balkan village through the 1930's does reveal something deeper than the picturesque or the spectacular. It reveals the timbers out of which generations of rural Europeans have constructed their lives. And it reveals further the stability, the weakness and strength of a rural community where change comes not so much through violence as through the slow, inevitable processes of time. The prewar Europe of Baba Dragana's children, living out their patiently laborious days in the rhythm the seasons set for them, was to me the Europe that seemed permanent.

Yet in the Balkans today an irresistible force is meeting an immovable object—and both are being changed by the impact. Communism, with its dynamic drive for power, its sense of mission, and impatience for reform, is charging against the Balkan peasant mass, a mass which heretofore has preferred tradition to science and familiar ways of the past to what we moderns choose to call efficient living.

Dragalevtsy, the village described herein, brings this struggle into focus. It reveals the nature of that Balkan peasant mass wherever it is based on private ownership of home and fields; the travail of this village since the war reveals something of the kinds of forces now at work.

My sympathies go not to the extremists of either side—not to the revolutionaries of the moment nor to the devotees of the past—but rather to the millions of men and women and even little children who are caught, trapped, wedged in by the impact; people whose one desire is the opportunity to earn their daily bread, the chance to laugh and love and to close their eyes at night without dreading the thought of waking on the morrow.

IRWIN T. SANDERS
December, 1948

ACKNOWLEDGMENT

THIS BOOK has really been in process since 1929, the date of my first contact with the Bulgarian peasant and his interesting manner of life. Since that time many people have helped me gain the background out of which this book has grown. The people of Dragalevtsy themselves deserve a special tribute for their patience and co-operation; some of the government officials in Sofia provided basic statistical data; while my colleagues at the American College of Sofia aided me greatly in understanding the rural folk of Bulgaria. Dr. Floyd H. Black, President of the College, did much to facilitate my research and trips of investigation, and Dr. Heinrich Schneider, now of Cornell University, aided me in a search for German source materials. The late Professor Dwight Sanderson, of Cornell University, guided me through much of my research, even to the point of visiting me in Bulgaria. Dr. C. E. Black of Princeton University, Professor C. Arnold Anderson of the University of Kentucky, Mr. Clayton E. Whipple of the Office of Foreign Agricultural Relations, Washington, and Dr. William Kling of the United States State Department have made many valuable suggestions. But I am more deeply indebted to my wife than to anyone else, especially for her constant interest in this task and her competent help.

The editors of the *Journal of Applied Anthropology, Rural Sociology, Sociometry,* and *Social Forces* have kindly permitted me to reprint material originally appearing in their publications.

CONTENTS

ILLUSTRATIONS

MAPS AND TABLES

APPENDIX TABLES

BALKAN VILLAGE

CHAPTER I

THE PEOPLE AND THEIR VILLAGE

WINTER had begun. The first snow of the year had fallen. It covered the muddy streets of the village, softening the nakedness of the fruit trees which stood lonely in the bare yards. The wind from Mount Vitosha came whistling down the empty lanes, sending both man and beast to seek protection and warmth. The animals huddled in their thatched folds and shelters; the women and children crowded on the little stools near the fireplace at home. The fall sowing of wheat was in. The fields, wind-swept and snow-laden, were deserted, seemingly forgotten by the men and women who had spent so much time with them during the past months.

One ordinary day followed another. Every morning the water buffalo had to be groomed until they shone; the oxen had to be cleaned after the night in the dirty stall; these, as well as the sheep, had to be fed. Usually the animals received their meager rations before ten o'clock. Shortly thereafter the men, wearing their dirty-gray sheepskin coats, their brimless lambskin hats, and their pigskin sandals, congregated at the taverns to relieve the monotony of their daily routine. At noon they plodded home to a lunch of beans, looked after the cattle once more, and gave commands to their womenfolk. The rest of the day was spent at the taverns in drinking and talking, interspersed with long, easy silences. After the evening meal, the cattle were fed again. Then the men dropped off to sleep along with the rest of the household.

The winds and enforced idleness of winter were not alone responsible for the apparent sluggishness on every hand. Slow motion was characteristic of Dragalevtsy life in general, but especially of the bodily movements of the people. *Ima vreme* (there's plenty of time) was either a practical philosophical tenet which explained their lack of hurry or else it was an expression frequently used to rationalize their casual manner. I never saw a peasant with a watch.

These quiet people of Dragalevtsy, whose way of life is not very different from that of peasants throughout the Balkans, are more than just Bulgarian peasants who arose in the seventh century from a dash of Tartar added to a predominantly Slavic mixture. They are a special breed of Bulgarians called *Shopi,* a term originally meaning boorish. That is, a *Shop* was a bumpkin. Some authorities say that this term was derived from *sop,* the long staff which the men of this area carried. Since those living in the *Shopsko* area, or the immediate vicinity of Sofia and Mount Vitosha, are in general more conservative than villagers elsewhere in Bulgaria, the word *Shopi* also carried the idea of backwardness and mental simplicity. Among the many attempts to explain the special physical characteristics of these people, the most plausible theory is that of descent from the Pechenegi, or Mongolian tribesmen who infiltrated into that section of Bulgaria and nearby eastern Serbia in the eleventh century. Historians deal none too kindly with these Pechenegi; nor do the *Shopi* receive many compliments in contemporary accounts. Even their physical appearance is considered unattractive by many other Bulgarians.

From faces naturally swarthy, further darkened and weather-beaten by sun, rain, and biting winds, the small round eyes of Asia stare through one without giving an inkling of the impression registered. In the thin-lipped mouths of the young the teeth are gleaming white; beneath the drooping mustaches of middle-aged men teeth show yellowish in a rare childlike smile; and toothless gums accompany the gray stubbly beards of the old. Straight, prominent noses lend ruggedness rather than beauty; the customary clipping of the scraggly black hair of the men reveals wrinkled, leathery necks; the hair of the women is worn in braids down the back, and hangs from beneath a kerchief that covers the top of the head. Here, too, age is clearly marked. The glossy, thick braids of the girls all too soon become, with advancing years, dull and thin and are often pieced out with other, brighter hair. The men are of medium height. Because their shoulders are so broad and their chests so powerful, their short, sturdy legs seem out of proportion. The women, slightly shorter, walk erect unless stooped by age. Hands seldom gloved in winter are rough and dirty and calloused. I often thought that one of the strangest things about death was the way it quieted the hands of these simple folk, who, although reserved in demeanor, constantly gestured when they spoke.

I grew accustomed to the mannerisms of the people as well as to the flavor of village life by slow degrees. At first I was attracted most by the gala occasions, or the spectacular. There was the annual Christmas *horo* (folk dance) which provided the first break in the monotony of winter. On a comfortably mild Christmas Day old women and little children, the first to arrive in the main village square, sat in twos and threes waiting for the dancing to begin. Girls in their Sunday best, with necklaces of gold coins flashing in the sunlight, passed through the square and sang as they walked. They were bareheaded, since they could not yet wear the married women's head kerchief. As they drew closer, the blotches of rouge, the tremendous earrings, belts laden with clinking silver pieces, and heavy bracelets showed that the girls considered this no ordinary holiday. They formed a line, side by side, and began the dance after persuading the gypsy musicians to strike up a tune; one by one the boys who had come out of the taverns joined the moving line: one step to the right, one step to the left, then three steps to the right, kicking high as they stepped. As the dancing progressed, many married women participated, while the married men looked on with condescending interest. The little children, dressed like miniature adults, gathered on the fringes of the crowd to imitate the dancers. Gossiping groups formed, buzzed, and then dissolved to form anew.

A commotion arose in the center of the square as two young men fought over the cane which was carried by the leader of the *horo*. The leader was supposed to pay the musicians for the dances he led, in exchange for which he could direct the dancers in a serpentine movement, always in step with the music, so that they wound in and out with a "crack-the-whip" at every major bend of the line. To the peasant, the boisterous physical activity gives an exhilaration little else can induce. In fact, some of the "young blades" at this *horo* were so carried away with animal spirits that they performed six or seven steps to the prescribed two or three, tiring themselves out to the plaudits of those close by.

To the old-timers, however, the modern version of the traditional dance was a sad commentary on the state of things. They thought the young people too soft. After I had been watching the *horo* for some time an old man hobbled up to me. I had seen him shaking his head and muttering to himself, so I asked him, "What do you think of it, *dedo*?" He grunted, "It's all right for the young people to have a little fun, but they aren't as strong as I used to be when I was young. I used to hoe corn, harvest wheat, and come back to dance all evening. The young people can't do that now. And I wasn't as healthy as my father used to be."

The village registrar, Bai Angel, told me why there had been a declining interest in the *hora,* especially those which used to occur around the neighborhood fountains. About seven o'clock the people used to go to the pasture to get their animals. If the animals were slow in coming, then the people danced the *horo* there in the fields. When the animals had been taken home, and after the girls had finished up their housework, they went with jugs to one of the three fountains in the village and there danced again until eleven o'clock. In 1924 more fountains were installed in the village, thus tending to break up the larger groups which gathered around the three original fountains. The girls preferred to carry water from the fountains nearest their homes, and no longer attended the evening *horo.*

Tavern life was another, less colorful way of passing the bleak winter days. In the four ill-ventilated *kruchmi* the men gathered to discuss the harvest and to argue over the news read aloud from yesterday's newspaper. Some man sought his godfather, or the godfather of a recently christened son or daughter, and invited him to have a drink of *rakiya* (plum brandy) or wine. Sometimes men who had completed a business deal drank to clinch it. Men who had been in the army together told the same tall tales of adventure over and over again, re-creating those experiences which lifted them for a while out of their limited village environment. There were seldom any fights, because the frequenters put an end to disagreements before they got

"Their round completed . . . the milkmen began . . . to retrace the long uphill journey from the city's outskirts to the village." *See page 5.*

". . . in front of Bai Penko's tavern on the northern side of Renaissance Square." *See page 8.*

"The priest could look past the modern school building . . . to the church just beyond." Sofia is in the background. *See page 8.*

"Yurdan, the leading tailor . . . and his wife Zdravka were a unique couple." *See page 14.*

out of hand. The fact that not all patrons of the tavern drank liquor was shown by the comment of one of the villagers:

"I come to the tavern chiefly for the newspaper. I have a strong will, drink little, and know when to stop. The young men when starting the temperance association asked me to be president but I couldn't give up coming here for the newspaper. The small coffee house across the square has only room enough for five or six people and there's no point in going there. Many blame me for going to the tavern, but they have no interest in finding out what is going on in the world."

One advantage of visiting the tavern included the announcements that the town crier always made there as well as out in the square.

The tavern keepers, however, had no illusions about their standing in the public estimation. All of them were of the same peasant stock as their patrons, but had sold some of their land in order to set themselves up in business.

"If the people of the village took a vote, the majority would favor shutting up all the taverns. The people don't like us," was the tart comment of one tavern keeper. This dislike sprang from the indebtedness of so many people to the tavern keepers, as well as from the strong feeling many have toward the social consequences of excessive alcoholism.

There were, however, a number of men who had to miss the morning session at the Dragalevtsy *kruchmi*. They were the milkmen. Each morning while it was still dark eight tiny donkeys left their yards, pattered down the slope just outside the village, and followed the straight gravel road five miles to Sofia. They were accompanied by their prodding masters who kept an eye on the two or three large cans of milk which had been strapped onto the wooden saddles. These donkeys long ago learned to swallow any pride they might have had, for each morning, with monotonous regularity, they were overtaken by the high two-wheeled horse-drawn milk carts used by the remaining thirty Dragalevtsy milkmen. Once in Sofia, the majority of the milkmen covered their routes, knocking at the doors of the regular customers and waiting patiently for a container into which to pour a quart or so of milk from the large cans. The round completed, most of the milkmen began at once to retrace the long uphill journey from the city's outskirts to the village.

Sometimes I overtook these men outside the village and fell in with them. *"Dobra stiga"* ("Well-reached"), I said; and they answered, *"Dal ti bog dobro"* ("God has given you good"). The amenities observed, I then asked about other matters. "How far is it from Sofia to your village?" Always the answer came in terms of "walking hours" and never in kilometers, the accepted measure of distance in Bulgaria. When we would encounter those going in the opposite direction we stopped our conversation long enough to say, *"Dobra sreshta"* ("Well-met"). When I chanced to inquire about the size of Dragalevtsy, the usual answer was, "About three hundred houses." If I wanted to know how many inhabitants this would mean, I multiplied the figure by five, the size of the average household. (The difference between this crude estimate of fifteen hundred and the 1934 census figures of 1,669 persons meant little to the peasant.)

No, Dragalevtsy was in no sense of the word a large village, as Sofia savants used to point out to me when they asked where I saw material enough there for a book. Theirs was the loss. An old village with more than sixteen hundred people teems with life. The stuff of which its days are made is rich and lasting; the intricate crisscross of vigorous personalities and deep-rooted folkways proved a never-ending drama for which nature usually provided a superb setting.

The meadows were lush from the spring rains, some of the fruit trees were in bloom, numberless tiny silver streams spread a glittering net down the side of Vitosha, and a veil of green leaves lay over all the red roofs of the village. Against such a background, a group of peasants made ready for their pilgrimage to Rila Monastery. Such an occasion was as truly an outpouring of joy as was the departure of the Canterbury pilgrims in Chaucer's day. The clanging of the church bell summoned the friends and relatives of the departing pilgrims to the incense-filled church. Inside, before the iconostas, dark and gilt, the priest read a prayer and led the little flock of people to the edge of the village, to the beginning of the outside world, where the travelers, dressed in their brightest, newest garments, were speeded on their way. The friends and relatives loaded them with money and presents of clothing, food, and wool, which the pilgrims were to donate to the great and holy monastery. The whole ceremony of leave-taking was made a part of the bright landscape by the flowers everywhere—on the dress of the pilgrims, fastened to the gifts, and carried in huge bunches. Upon their return a few days later the dusty pilgrims were met at the outskirts of the village and escorted home through the blue twilight by those eager to hear of every adventure during the days and nights in the great mountains, whose jagged walls have protected Rila Monastery for hundreds of years.

Formal piety, as shown in pilgrimages, was only one of the major characteristics which these Bulgarian villagers possessed. The Dragalevtsy people, especially the men, were predominantly literate. Bulgaria, despite what seems a forbidding Cyrillic alphabet, has the highest rate of literacy of all Balkan countries, a fact which can be attributed to the tendency to regard education as a panacea for individual and social ills. While only 44 per cent of the women over fifteen years of age could read and write, 92 per cent of the men were literate. Of course, I often came upon groups of peasants crowded around a friend slowly spelling out a newspaper article aloud, but these little clusters of attentive listeners originated because of the scarcity of newspaper subscribers, not necessarily because of illiteracy.

The Dragalevtsy people were also law-abiding. During the first three years I knew the village, and informants said that the record went much farther back than that, no Dragalevtsy peasant had been taken to Sofia for imprisonment. There was no local jail, nor any need for one. This was not a sign of the inefficiency of local police, but rather an indication of the peaceable and honest traits of the people.

In many other characteristics the villagers shared what have come to be known as the universal "rural virtues," for theirs was an agrarian way of life. More than three-fourths of the family heads were peasant proprietors. In addition to these, there were two other occupational groups: the intellectuals and the artisans. Despite their small number, the intelligentsia, as they were called by the peasants, were the most influential group in the community. Whenever the

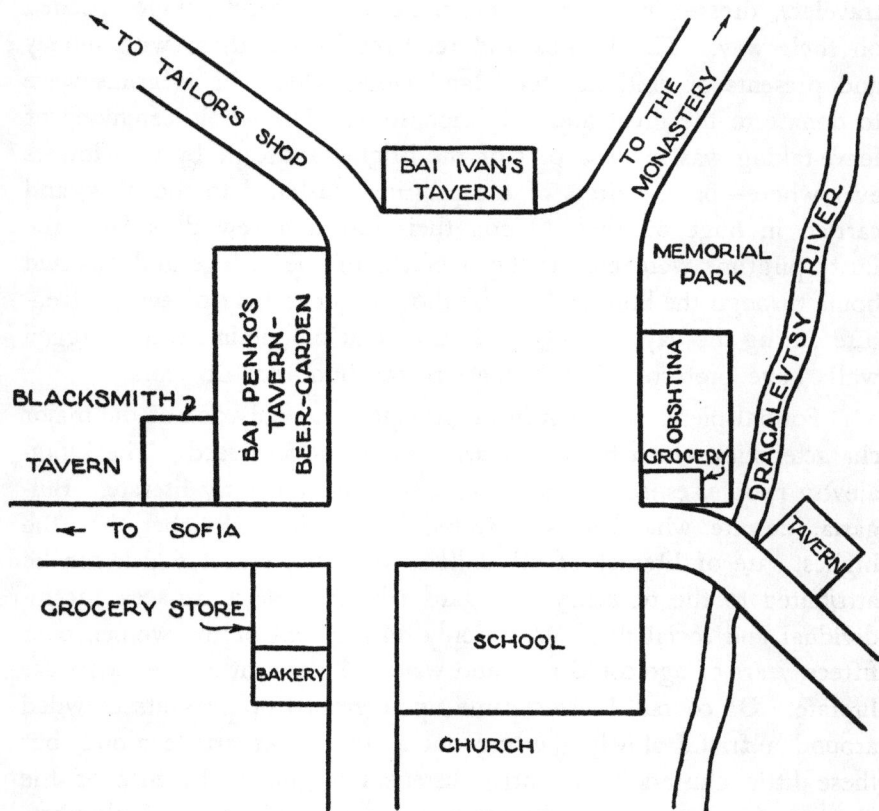

Renaissance Square, the focal point of Dragalevtsy's communal life

weather was agreeable I was sure to find several of them playing
cards in front of Bai Penko's tavern on the northern side of Renaissance
Square, where the winter *horo* was held. Even though they sat en-
grossed in their game, they could still keep an eye on what was happening in the village, since this square was the focal point of community life. The mayor, for instance, could watch the Obshtina, or
municipal building, across the square, as well as all traffic that entered
this rocky plot of ground on its way to the city of Sofia below or to
the monastery higher up Mount Vitosha. The priest could look past
the modern school building, flanking the western side of the square,
to the church just beyond. The village doctor's husband was near in

case his wife needed him, although he invariably grumbled in his native Russian upon being called away from the game. A fourth hand during the summer was a reserve army officer whose intense love for German efficiency and ideology and whose contempt for the "ignorant, unreliable peasant" became bywords in the community. Peasants sitting on the porch of Bai Ivan's tavern on the eastern side of the square could observe with seeming indifference the intelligentsia at play, distracted though they were at times by the fervent temperance lectures delivered by the tavern keeper's daughter-in-law whenever she placed a glass of *rakiya* in front of a customer.

These intelligentsia proved to be interesting people. The mayor had a good education, completed by the study of law in Russia. His father had been a priest in Boyana, a village just four miles to the west, so the mayor, himself a *Shop*, knew the workings of the peasant mind. When he was sent to the village as mayor back in 1934, after the *coup d'état* of that year abolished all elections and deprived many local officials of their jobs, he issued a flowery proclamation which contained such thoughts as these:

> Therefore, as I take up my duties, desiring greatly to use the small abilities that I possess for the economic and cultural uplift of the villages included in the commune entrusted to my care, I wish to express my good feelings of loyalty and friendliness and attachment to the population and to certify that I am ready to work for the uplift of our commune and to be the loyal conveyor of its economic and cultural interests and needs.
>
> Imbued with the idea that we are all members of the same family, sons of mother Bulgaria, let us forget the recent past of shameful partisan struggles and begin to live as genuine brothers—Bulgarians filled with mutual love, patience, harmony, respect, and good will.
>
> Let us do our duty to these beautifully situated villages, perched on the slope of Mount Vitosha, and make them attractive gardens, with culture, and places of merriment and songs.

The people soon learned that the mayor when excited talked so rapidly that he failed to enunciate clearly, and they always enjoyed mimicking this mannerism. They did not particularly resent his management of their affairs, despite the fact that he had been sent by the central government which gave local communes no choice in the matter. The mayor was happily married to an attractive wife, who dressed *po modata* (in the latest fashion) and kept her children so neat and proper that they contrasted vividly with the peasant urchins who ran up and down the unpaved streets.

The mayor was charged with maintaining law and order with the help of the *strazhar* (police officer), the field policeman, and the forest policeman. The second wandered from field to field to see that cattle did not stray unattended onto strips where there were growing crops; the forest policeman prevented the purloining of wood from the forest lands used by Dragalevtsy people. The mayor also acted as local justice of the peace, and was ex officio member of the school board, health board, and any other village organization he considered worthy of serious attention.

But the mayor, although he enjoyed the spotlight, had to share it with the village priest. For five centuries, while the Bulgarians were subject to the Turks, the priest was often the only person in a village with any formal education. He not only interpreted the laws of God, but the laws of man as well. The Bulgarian monks and priests helped keep the feeling of Bulgarian nationality alive during those dark days, and thereby eventually aided in the achievement of national independence in 1878 at the conclusion of the Russo-Turkish War. Since traditions die slowly in a Bulgarian village, the position of the priest is still very high, although few people attend religious services and fewer people observe the rather rigid fasts of the Eastern Orthodox Church. However, the priest is an essential officiant at christenings, weddings, and funerals. Without him the peasants have no way of meeting life's major crises.

Father Sava was the *sveshtennik* or priest in Dragalevtsy. He wore with dignity his long black gown and high brimless hat, his uncut red hair in a knot at the back of his head, and a long auburn beard. I never failed to marvel at his wide range of interests. One day we would poke around his beehives; the next day he would show me his favorite photographs and competently discuss the relative merits of American and German cameras. But it was after I learned of the man's romance that I began to see him in a clearer light. The young lady whom he wanted to marry was the daughter of a priest who flatly decreed that his daughter could marry no one but a priest. (Not only are priests well provided for financially, but they can marry only once. This means that they supposedly take exceptionally good care of their mates.) Sava had already completed the commercial gymnasium, had studied for two years in a school for leaders of co-operatives, and planned to attend the university. In order to comply with the demands of his sweetheart's father, however, he interrupted his educational plans long enough to prepare himself for the ecclesiastical examinations, which he passed with credit. He was then assigned to the Dragalevtsy parish. Meanwhile he had married the young lady of his choice. Soon thereafter he obtained leave of absence from his church responsibility in order to complete his work in Finance at the Svoboden (Private) University in Sofia. He was highly respected by the people whom he shepherded and was vitally interested in their welfare.

There were often two or three kibitzers while the intelligentsia played cards. These were lesser officials interested in advancement, or well-to-do peasants who wanted to hobnob with the controlling group. None of these hangers-on had been westernized to the point of wearing a tie, and some of them still wore the heelless, pointed pigskin sandals.

Oddly enough for a Bulgarian village, the veterinarian and physician were both women, who constantly found the patriarchal traditions stumbling blocks to the winning of village support. The medical doctor was a Russian who had spent part of her childhood in San Francisco, but returned to the University of Petrograd for her medical training. After the Revolution she left Russia with her family.

The only other "educated" people in the village were the teachers, eight in number, selected for their posts by outside school authorities rather than by the villagers themselves. Four of the eight had been born outside the pre-Hitler boundaries of Bulgaria, in territories which irredentist Bulgarians sought to recover permanently. Maria, for example, was from Dobruja, which was then a part of Rumania; Anna and Georgi were born in parts of Macedonia which were turned over to Greece and Yugoslavia, respectively, after the first World War; while Dimiter was from the section of Thrace which Bulgaria was forced to surrender. Since the teachers had such backgrounds it was no wonder that adorning one of the classrooms was a sign, "NEMA MIR DOKATO NEUILLY" or "There will be no peace as long as the Treaty of Neuilly is in force."

The director of the school was a vigorous woman with splendid preparation for her task. She told me on several occasions how disappointed she was that her teachers took so little interest in helping the peasants improve their way of life. They were supposed to spend Sunday afternoons visiting the homes of their pupils in an effort to advise parents in matters of child care and standards of hygiene. Actually, the teachers, being all too human, preferred to spend the week end in Sofia rather than reform the unenthusiastic adults.

The intelligentsia were usually seen in their glory at some great occasion such as the celebration of an important holiday. The event which caused most excitement during my six years of residence in Bulgaria was the birth of Prince Simeon, heir apparent to the throne of his father, King Boris. The exercises which were held in Dragalevtsy four days after the royal birth in 1937 showed how the intellectuals worked hand in hand, since the school, the church, and the state were so closely allied.

The crowd had to wait at least forty-five minutes for the priests from the monastery who were to help Father Sava with the liturgy of the *vodosvet,* or consecration of the holy water, whose sprinkling gave official religious recognition to the closing of the school year. Then the mayor began to speak the high-sounding phrases which the villagers loved to hear. He told them how significant for Bulgaria was the birth of Prince Simeon.

June Sixteenth [he said] will be written in golden letters in the history of Bulgaria. June Sixteenth marks the day when an heir was born to the throne of Bulgaria. Our school house has no name, so I recommend that we petition for the right to call our school "Prince Simeon II." The first Simeon who reigned a thousand years ago was called Simeon the Great. I feel sure that Simeon the Second will likewise go down in history as Simeon the Great.

In honor of this great occasion, the Government has decreed that the marks of every student will be raised, so that no one will fail in any subject. [Hurrah!

"But the mayor, although he enjoyed the spotlight, had to share it with
the village priest." *See page 10.*

"Most of the houses in Dragalevtsy were one-storied." *See page 22.*

"The hearth or stove was the focal point of the barely furnished living room." *See page 23.*

Hurrah!] That's right; nobody will fail. No pupil will repeat the class next year! [Hurrah! Hurrah!] All deportment marks likewise will be raised and anyone who has been expelled from school will be accepted back on probation. The government is cancelling over a billion leva in unpaid taxes and is freeing thousands of prisoners . . . .

Before he finished he led the children, and such adults as would join, in further cheers for Prince Simeon, for King Boris, and for Queen Iovanna. After the school choir had sung the national anthem and the "Hymn to the King," all filed inside for the official gradua- tion exercises. There were more patriotic songs and at least twenty declamations with such titles as "Three Days at the Battle of Shipka," "To our Teachers," "A Prayer to God," "I Like the Priest," "I am a Temperance Girl," and "Nature." Displays of the children's hand- work, as well as these recitations, brought some recognition to the teachers who had worked behind the scenes.

The director in her remarks thanked the mayor and the priest profusely and the parents casually for the help they had rendered during the past year. When she was about to present the diplomas, such bedlam broke loose that few could hear the compliments she paid the brightest pupils, who had received as special awards from the mayor books on war and religion. The exercises concluded with the presentation of a large bouquet from the pupils to the school director, who politely accepted the flowers on behalf of all the teachers.

The intelligentsia just described had more importance than their village duties seemed to indicate. They were the channels through which the national state, the national church, and the national school system expressed themselves. No member of this select group was Dragalevtsy-born. Their high status rested not only upon the in- fluence they wielded as representatives of powerful institutions, but also upon the fact that they were educated. Education, along with the patient accumulation of land and money, was one sound way of raising one's social position, and those who had persevered in its pur- suit received due honor. As one father said to his son upon sending him to school: "If you don't study you will plow, sow, and work in the fields, and where will you get then?"

The artisans, though few in number, comprised a third occupational group. Just because their knowledge and special skill raised them above the ordinary peasant, these artisans in no sense of the word walked in the rarified atmosphere of the intelligentsia. In 1937 the people of Dragalevtsy supported one blacksmith, one full-time and two part-time tailors, a cobbler, and a barber. Of course, the six or seven Dragalevtsy men who went to Sofia every day to ply a skilled trade were enumerated in the census but had little connection with the economy of the village. The few tradesmen were identified more with the agricultural group than with the artisans.

One of the most picturesque characters in the village was Iliya, the smith. Dark-complexioned, sturdy of frame, with his stolid face weighed down by enormous mustaches, he was far too forbidding in countenance to attract the village children to his small establishment behind Bai Penko's tavern. In fact, customers often had to look for him in the tavern, where he consumed record-breaking quantities of liquor. In his sober moods he and his two apprentices occasionally worked fourteen hours at a stretch to finish up some much-needed job. The three of them combined wagon-repairing with blacksmithing, working at the lathe almost as frequently as at the anvil. However, frequent preoccupation with hinges, wagon bolts, horseshoes, plowshares, and wheel rims gave Iliya a fair claim to being a *kovach*, or smith. So did his master smith's certificate hanging on the wall.

Yurdan, the leading tailor, was another artisan. He and his wife Zdravka were a unique couple in that they were the only Dragalevtsy people to become involved in divorce proceedings within recent years. To be sure, Zdravka withdrew her petition for divorce soon after it reached the high church court, which, rather than civil bodies, then decided upon all matters pertaining to marriage. Yurdan had a small but well equipped workroom attached to his trim little house. Although Dragalevtsy-born, he worked for twelve years in Sofia as an apprentice and *maistor,* later becoming the first tailor to set up business in Dragalevtsy.

I often went to converse with Yurdan and Zdravka, for I found them both loquacious and inclined to be objective in their views of village life. I questioned them in particular about the peasant costumes, which always seemed picturesque to me, a foreigner. It was Zdravka who told me how the women made their garments.

"Women's clothing is made chiefly by hand and of homemade cloth. In the homes we have very few sewing machines, which only the young girls know how to run. Most of the outer garments for men are made by the village tailor. All of us can do the traditional embroidery patterns which make our dresses so pretty, but we do not have as much embroidery now as formerly; the old women cannot see to do it and the young people want modern things."

Then Yurdan told what clothing the peasants bought:

"The women buy *zabradki* [pieces of cloth for the head]; every once in a while they also buy some flannel or silken goods, and shoes. The old women wear *kozhusi* [sheepskin coats], for which they provide the hides or buy them ready-made. Men also have to buy these *kozhusi* in addition to headwear called *kalpatsi* [pointed brimless caps], or cheap cloth caps. Many men buy ready-made suits, especially if they are unmarried, for use on holidays. Even they, when working in the fields, go back to the more durable homemade garments which do not tear so easily. They also buy some shirts and sweaters, or *shubi* [short overcoats with fur inside], and shoes. In general the tendency of the younger people is toward city dress."

I asked them why everybody dressed so much alike. Both of them chuckled and told me about the time the daughter-in-law from the wealthiest peasant household, who had spent some time in Sofia, tried to appear in a distinctive style at a Sunday promenade, only to find that the next Sunday many other girls were wearing the same innovation. Zdravka concluded from this incident:

"No, there is not much individuality in dress, for whenever someone gets something new the others copy it. Especially the young unmarried girls try to buy or to make something new so as to attract attention. But all the rest, as soon as they see it, won't take time to eat until they have made the same thing so that the one possessing it will not feel that she is in a higher position than others. It is this which makes the richer girls most angry."

This led to a discussion of how changes of style had come to the village. This is what Yurdan said:

"Since the World War there has been much change. Men stopped wearing their narrow white trousers which belted below the hips because they saw during the war that pants that belted above the hips were better. The women changed to lighter clothes because a woman from Vladaya [another village] came with others to visit here, married a Dragalevtsy man, and settled here. Other women saw that the clothes she wore were more convenient and began to adopt the new style."

The tailor's customers brought their own cloth. Five or six of the more fashion-minded young women brought dresses from other villages to be copied. A girl before marriage accumulated about twenty black *sukmani* (jumper dresses), all of the same pattern. She wore out about three of these a year. The men had one black and one rough everyday suit.

Much of the cloth was dyed at home by the peasants with the use of commercial dyes. Black was the universal color for men except in the case of the old style white trousers. If any man deviated from this fashion, people said mockingly, "You are a gypsy," thereby reminding him that he had better act like other people or run the risk of additional social disapproval.

Shoes in Bulgaria were definitely a sign of social rank. *Tsarvulin* or "sandal-wearer," once a common term for farmer or peasant, has been somewhat displaced by *selenin* or "villager." As a matter of fact, most men in Dragalevtsy continued to wear the pigskin sandals, whereas all self-respecting village women possessed a pair of cheap western shoes. Comically enough, they frequently walked barefoot and carried these uncomfortable badges of status. Just the same, these shoes periodically needed the services of a cobbler, who in Dragalevtsy happened to be the youngest married son of Bai Milush, a highly respected peasant proprietor. Three sons, their wives and progeny comprised part of the twenty people living in Bai Milush's patriarchal dwelling. As the land which will someday be divided up among the sons was limited, each son agreed to specialize along some particular line: the oldest was the dairyman, the middle son was the crop expert, and the youngest married son (and, incidentally, the most delicate in health) was a cobbler, whom the family agreed to send to a trade school in Sofia. Because he drove in his wooden pegs with the best of them, he was building up a profitable business in the village.

Barbers stayed only a short while in Dragalevtsy. One from Sofia opened up a shop on the main square with high hopes, but his white coat and swanky airs attracted only a few intelligentsia and summer residents, and practically none of the peasants. The barber that seemed to enjoy the most popularity during his erratic visits to the village frequented the taverns. When his services were in demand, he pulled the victim's chair to a corner where he set to work in view of the general public. His mellow tenor voice, none the worse for his imbibing, brought him more trade than his ability as a barber.

Other artisans were even more itinerant than the barbers. The *maistori* (contractors, master builders) came to the village whenever a building was to be put up. One day in the fall of 1934, upon arriving in Renaissance Square I was amazed to see a shirt and a flag flying atop the highest beam of the then unfinished Obshtina, or municipal building. I heard a powerful voice calling out:

"Half a gallon of wine from Ivan Stoynov! May there be as many blessings in his house as there are ants in the field; may his joys be as numerous as the leaves on the trees."

The voice paused for a minute or two, perhaps for the owner to sample the wine, but soon rang out again substituting "two pairs of stockings" for the "half a gallon of wine" in the chant about the ants in the field and the leaves on the trees. I soon learned that the villagers had chosen this day to carry out the traditional practice of bringing presents to the master builder for distribution to his workmen, who were dutifully acknowledging the gifts in the accepted manner.

The tinsmiths usually were gypsies who spent a few days each year in Dragalevtsy. In spite of their low social position they performed a useful task in keeping the pots and kettles serviceable year in and year out.

My growing acquaintance with the people and the work they did helped me to sense the atmosphere of Dragalevtsy life. But I soon began to feel, with the peasants, the dominance of the great mountain

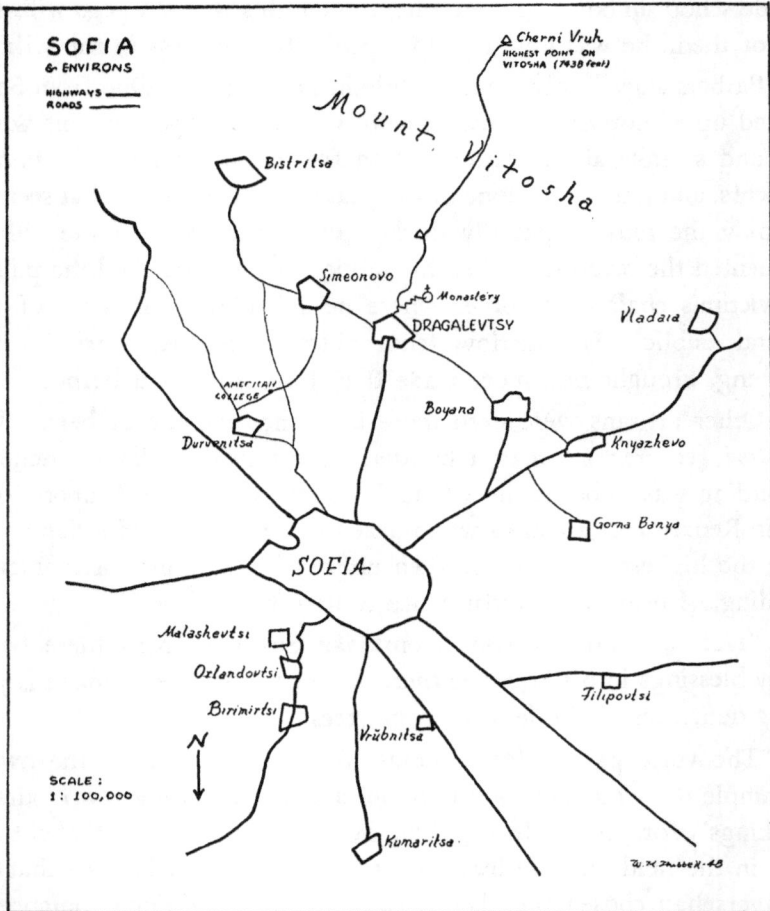

on whose side the village lies. That huge, partly naked mass of
diorite which is Mount Vitosha rises majestically with barely per-
ceptible foothills out of the broad Sofia plain to a height of seven
thousand feet. The side of the mountain toward Sofia is twelve miles
long, and is brightened in spots by the brilliant patches of the red-
tiled houses of the principal villages. Farthest to the west, nearest
to Sofia, is Boyana, where many of the peasants have sold their farms
to real estate agents, and thus have earned the contempt of their landed
Dragalevtsy neighbors two miles to the east. Dragalevtsy, partly up
the slope, lies between the fields which fan out below and the scrubby

trees above, pitiful reminders of a once-proud forest. A hurried mountain stream called Dragalevtsy River passes through the village and, in doing so, turns the grist mills and assists with the washing of clothes.

A mile to the east of Dragalevtsy is Simeonovo, a settlement decidedly run-down at the heel. It was here that I spent a busy morning trying to explain to two villagers that the earth was really global rather than flat. Farther on around the shoulder of the mountain is Bistritsa, where the people are said to sing as they dance the *horo*:

"There is no city more populous than Sofia,
There is no river more majestic than the Iskar,
There is no mountain more lofty than Vitosha."

This is an accurate illustration of ethnocentrism, or the belief prevalent among most people that they, and they alone, are the center of the universe and God's chosen children.

My usual approach to the village was across the unfenced fields and up the mountainside. Sometimes I came along the dull road from Sofia. By either way, the great mountain, changing color from hour to hour, was a rest to the eyes. The way across the fields led one gently into the village through patches of vegetable gardens and clumps of overhanging fruit trees. Upon entering the village from the direction of Sofia I passed the cemetery and then was closed in between whitewashed walls which lined the curving streets. Animals also felt much at home in these streets. Just before sunset the village goatherd headed the two hundred animals in his care toward the settlement. Into Renaissance Square they trotted, a capering mass of gray, black, and white. At each street several goats detached themselves from the rest to run unguided into their respective dwellings. The same scene occurred when the pigs came squealing home. At other times of day peasant girls passed by carrying washing to be pounded on rocks and dipped into the icy water of Dragalevtsy River. Hikers, many of them, lounged around Bai Penko's, or tramped through the streets obviously amused at the manners of the peasants.

Few things were as dependent upon the weather as the state of the village streets: muddy beyond description in the autumn and spring,

dusty in the summer, icy or slushy in the winter. The refuse from
most of the houses flowed through little trenches into the ditches along
the streets, thence to be carried, if enough water could be diverted
from Dragalevtsy River, to some place below. Fortunately, blasts of
fresh, pure air rolled down from the mountain most of the time.

While all of the mountain villages had the same kind of streets
as Dragalevtsy, it alone had electricity. These other villages disappeared from the sight of men as soon as shadows stole up the mountainside, but Dragalevtsy burst into view at dusk as electric lights from
street and dwelling shone against the dark background of Vitosha,
vividly revealing the location and size of the village. (Electric lights
were first used there in 1928.) The lights of the village used to go
out one by one as bedtime approached, and at ten o'clock even the
street lights were off, leading one to the conclusion that the street
lights were as much for adornment as for public safety.

Frequently I had to leave the village alone after dark to return
to the American College, where I taught and lived during most of the
year. Invariably the peasants, still under the sway of a custom wise
enough in Turkish times, argued that sensible people never left the
village late at night.

"But what is there to be afraid of?" I asked.

"Oh, but one never can tell."

"Are there bandits around?"

"Thank God, no."

"Will I run into wolves?"

"No, not at this time of year. But there are sheep dogs."

"If sheep dogs are all I have to worry about, I guess I had better
be starting," I told them.

They would then reply:

"*Gospodine* [Mister], you are a brave man," but I could tell
from the way they shook their heads when they spoke that they considered me more foolhardy than brave.

Once away from the village I turned to look at the irregular
string of beads of light that was Dragalevtsy and thought of the
people with whom I had talked during the day and of their homes,
around which centered their simple hopes and unpretentious dreams.

CHAPTER II

THE HOUSE BECOMES A HOME

A LTHOUGH I had been studying Bulgarian peasant life for three years before concentrating upon Dragalevtsy, I never ceased to marvel at the home life of these people. Their quiet, satisfied way of taking their marriage partners for granted, the manner in which they treated their children, and the brief courting days of the young invariably fascinated me. Therefore, I started at the beginning to learn.

"How do you build a house?" I asked, eager to check my observations with their frequently droll explanations of why they did as they did.

The seriousness with which the peasants replied showed that building a house, although it cost only five or six hundred dollars, was a tremendously important undertaking to the Dragalevtsy family. The "new house" was discussed for a year or two in advance by the members, who also consulted kinsmen and neighbors before eventually deciding as to the type of dwelling desired. Before they could begin any construction the villagers had to get a permit from the Department of Engineering in Sofia, which sent out an engineer to "draw up the line" and to offer the choice of two or three plans. The government in requiring this permission sought to do away with the long, unhygienic, old-style type of home which the peasant would traditionally build. The fee for the services of the engineer was about a dollar and a half.

The family members next began to gather the materials. They piled up wagonloads of stone, and purchased sand, lumber, brick, and tiles before they called in the master builder *(maistor)* from outside to tell him what kind of house they wanted and to agree verbally about details. If all the materials had been gathered ahead of time, the house went up quickly, perhaps within three weeks. The skilled labor was furnished by workers brought into the village by the *maistor*.

A brief ceremony accompanied the completion of the simple stone foundation. The priest sprinkled holy water on the new construction, and the chief guests signed their names on a parchment which was then placed in a bottle filled with olive oil and wine and thrown into a deep hole later to be filled in as part of the foundation. Food and drink were served to the guests.

Most of the houses in Dragalevtsy were one-storied, though the slope of the land often made possible a room just below the first floor. The inner wall, made of crude mud brick, was covered inside and outside by mud plaster, which was whitewashed when dry. As soon as the roof beams were in place, before the colorful red tiles were added, a cross was tied aloft to stand guard, as it were, until the house was completed. The houses, on the whole, impressed me as being small and low, so low in fact that repeated bumps finally taught me to keep my head down upon entering a room. Only one-third of the homes had as many as three rooms. Almost half of the homes had wooden floors; the rest were of clay, packed to the hardness of concrete by the tread of bare and sandaled feet.

Soon after occupying the house and scrubbing it very clean, the family fasted one week in order to insure success and good health. The following Sunday, after the morning church service, two priests, the neighbors, relatives, and specially invited friends arrived to dedicate the home. For an added fee the priests substituted the more efficacious oil for the ordinary holy water; they read passages from the Gospels; swung their smoking censers; and displayed the other sacred objects called for by the ritual. A festive meal followed. The family was now at home.

These various ceremonies, perfunctory though they sometimes were, heightened the significance of the home and showed the close alliance between the formalized religion and family life. In other words, moving to a new home was a major undertaking which occurred not more than once or twice in a lifetime. Such an event called for solemnity and the benediction of the priest.

The hearth or stove was the focal point of the barely furnished living room. When winter came the small fires burned steadily, but slowly as though undernourished. For fuel, people in Dragalevtsy used small branches brought from the village forest up on the mountainside, though a few bought coal from the mine at Pernik. No longer did they burn cow dung. Older people of the family felt that fire was sacred because it could bring on great disasters; therefore, it should not be treated lightly. The aged would never think of spitting in the fire, and gravely deplored this disrespect of the young. This attitude is perhaps an ancient survival of the days when the Bulgarians were sunworshipers.

The walls of the homes were pierced by comparatively few windows, which were small and were kept tightly shut during the winter to keep out the "dangerous" night air. The rest of the wall space was brightened somewhat by gaudy calendars decidedly patriotic in theme. The iron bedsteads or the heavy wooden beds which lined the walls contrasted strikingly with some homemade cradle or trundle bed reserved for the succession of young. A kneading trough stood near the door, usually covered to serve as a table. The only other table was a low circular *sofra* around which people ate seated on three-legged stools. I once asked a peasant:

"Why do all of your little stools have three legs instead of four?"

"Far back in the past people used such stools and so we use them also. And I guess they are easier to be made and also are cheaper; furthermore, some people think that they keep a better balance since on a three-legged stool there is one less leg to wear down and become uneven than would be the case with a four-legged stool."

I have not been able to discover any flaw in this example of peasant logic. The same woman once explained to me why the people use the *sofra,* which is two feet high:

"This height was chosen through the ages because if it were lower, people would have to sit on the dirty floor. If it were the height of a regular table such as people have in the taverns, the three-legged stools would be too short. Therefore, the height of our table and the height of our stools are intimately connected."

No home was really furnished until it had a small wooden iconostas which contained an icon, a picture of the Virgin or a saint. The iconostas was usually placed in the east or southeast corner of the room. In case some disaster befell the family, they found out to which saint the unlucky day belonged, and got a picture of him for their iconostas. Thereafter, on his name day they did no work and used holy water in the house. In the *kandilo,* the small lamp before the icon, they burned olive oil during church time and on the eve of holidays. In case the family had used holy water at home in the hope of curing some sick person, the flowers with which the water had been sprinkled were placed on the household shrine.

Usually there were a number of small implements or articles scattered about the room. A two-edged axe might be leaning against the door frame, and old clothes or bed clothes hanging from a long thick pole in a corner. I often saw in common use small baskets obtained from the gypsies. For pay, the gypsies asked the purchaser to fill the basket with beans or wheat, which they retained. The peasants themselves, especially the shepherds and goatherds with much leisure on their hands, made the very large baskets or hampers used for carrying hay or straw. These baskets stood in the entryway or hung under the eaves.

Only a few of the Dragalevtsy homes had a washstand, but even for these the water had to be carried from the nearest fountain. Over and over again the peasant women would say:

"We would like to have running water in our houses because it would help us a lot and make our life a little easier. But we don't have the money, and all this needs much money for installing a water system in the house, and also we would have to pay quite a high tax· to the Obshtina. Anyway, the fountains in the village are sufficient and it doesn't take us much time to go and get water."

The water was carried from the fountains either in clay vessels called *stomni* or in the more modern large copper vessels called *mentsi.* The long sticks on the ends of which the water vessels were suspended were called *kobilitsi.* The water from the fountains was used only for preparing food and drinking, and the water for the animals came from the little brooks in the street. Maintaining personal cleanliness was very difficult indeed. Not only did the villagers have to contend with the problem of carrying water but also with the lack of privacy in their crowded dwellings. One peasant said:

"We have no public bathhouse in our village, so only the wealthier people can take baths, because they are able to go to the nearby villages two or three times during the summer and make use of the mineral baths. In general, we do not bathe in fall, winter, or spring. If we bathe in the summer at home, we use a wooden tub and warm water. Sometimes when the weather is warm, men and women [of course, separately] bathe in the river. When the women are bathing there must be someone to guard against their being seen by others. Regularly at least once a week we wash our heads with soap and hot water, and also wash our faces and hands in the morning, but not necessarily with soap. No, we do not wash our hands before every meal, nor do we ever wash our teeth."

Throughout Bulgaria it was a common courtesy to say to a friend who had just emerged from a bath, *"Chestito banya"* or "Congratulations on your bath." However, if one dreamed of bathing, the villager would tell him that some trouble, perhaps death, was imminent.

I was surprised to find that some of the poorest homes had electricity. The occupants explained:

"Oh, we find electricity cheaper than petroleum lamps provided we use small electric bulbs. Those who do not have electricity in their homes know of this advantage but have never saved up enough money to put in the wires."

And there they sat on a winter's night: the older women doing fine, closely stitched embroidery, the girls knitting, and the man perhaps reading a newspaper. The only illumination in the whole room, except for the flicker of the fire in the sheet metal stove, was a fly-specked twenty-watt bulb swinging from the ceiling.

The two or three large kettles hanging over or resting on the floor beside the stove, the knife and fork rack on the wall, and the few pottery dishes stacked on the kneading trough called my attention to the peasant's food habits. This was the way the people described their diet:

"The villagers generally feed themselves well. Of course, it depends upon how rich the family is. But usually we Dragalevtsy people do not think much about the money we give for food and drink. We are not stingy. The people here eat beans, potatoes, rice, cheese, milk, and meat. We do not use tea as food, for it is only water and does not satisfy us."

Here is what another informant added:

"Indeed there is variety in the diet throughout the year. During the summer months we use mainly vegetables produced at home or bought from the market. In the winter we eat potatoes, beans, and conserved foods [chiefly pickles]. Meat, milk, and rice are eaten throughout the whole year. We eat few eggs because we sell most of our eggs in Sofia. Since so many of us keep cows we naturally have begun to give our children milk to drink. We all are very fond of *kiselo mleko* [Bulgarian "sour milk"], which we eat with a spoon during the winter. In the summer it is thinned with water and mixed with garlic, walnuts, and chopped cucumber and is the dish [called *tarator*] that we most prefer on a hot day in the field. Since most of our dishes are stews we use a great deal of bread, which is baked by the women once a week in the ovens standing in the yards just for that purpose."

I had seen a number of large vegetarian restaurants in the city, but the peasants dismissed this Tolstoyan influence in a sentence:

"The people of Dragalevtsy are not so foolish as to eat no meat, for how can man be strong and able to work if he does not eat meat?"

In spite of this point of view the fact remains that the diet is largely vegetarian except for the traditional pig at Christmas, a lamb on Saint George's Day (May 6), milk, and cheese.

Food is served either on a *trapeza* (a piece of cloth on the floor) or on the *sofra,* the low table previously described. It was a rare experience to have one's first meal with a peasant family. To begin with, there were no individual plates or dishes; instead, one satisfied his hunger from the nearest dish from which three or four others might be eating. If a chicken had been boiled, the spoons struggled for favorite pieces of fowl; if there was chicken broth, even of a particularly delicious flavor, vinegar was added in quantity to make it palatable to peasant taste. If the bread supply gave out at the table, the diners sat calmly without eating until the new loaf was brought in, for it was almost impossible for them to eat unless holding a piece of bread in the left hand. Dunking was the approved method of disposing of the juice of a stew. When eating, one was apt to get a greasy coating on the lip; the accepted technique was to scrape this off with a piece of bread already on its way into the mouth. Forks and small spoons were used only when there were guests. But why should table manners not be simple and direct?

"Knives for everybody are not used. There is one knife at the table, but people use their hands, for we peasants say, 'For what did God give the fingers to man if he does not use them to feed himself?' "

As for the preparation of the food:

"Usually it is the duty of the oldest woman in the family to prepare the food, because she knows the best how to cook and she can cook most deliciously of all. In case she is sick, then her daughter-in-law or her daughter cooks. If there are not such, then the man cooks." Here my informant sniffed and added scornfully, "Of course, in such a case dry food is eaten chiefly, but even the men can cook at least some of the dishes."

I asked another woman who really "knew her place," as a Dragalevtsy man would say, whether men could cook:

"Of course, men can do everything woman does, but woman cannot do everything men do. Who cooks for those men that are shepherds or work in the forests but they themselves? Men do not need women half as much as women need men. Yet we all recognize that cooking is for the women, not for the men."

No matter what time of day I entered a village home the *domakinya* (housewife) with unfailing and genuine hospitality offered me food or drink. I began to wonder when the people had their regular meals and found that some homes had no regular mealtimes; instead, people got up and took a piece of bread or anything else available whenever they were hungry. In most families, however, about nine o'clock in the morning a meal called *ruchok* was served to all; at about two, dinner was served, and two hours after sunset the people gathered for supper. One villager put it this way:

"When we work in the fields we eat five times daily: as soon as we reach the place we have a light lunch *(zakuska)*, at nine we have the *ruchok,* at one dinner, at five another *zakuska,* and in the evening after finishing work we have supper. We older people don't eat between meals but let the children do so if they are hungry."

From time to time during my stay in the village I tried to teach the tavern cook some simple and uncomplicated western dish to vary the biting peasant food. She tried faithfully but unsuccessfully to comply. After one such hopeless but courteous attempt she read me a little lesson in village menus:

"We Dragalevtsy people are pretty conservative in everything and have added no new dishes to our menu. The western combinations which people eat in Sofia are tasteless and slimy. If one doesn't use lots of salt, hot pepper, and vinegar, then the food has no taste at all."

Beverages other than milk and wine made little appeal. Wine was much in evidence on holidays or when there were guests. An average village home would use from 250 to 300 quarts of wine a year. Most of the *rakiya* was drunk either at the taverns or on festive occasions. In commenting on the liquor consumption of the village one man said:

"We are not such fools as not to drink wine, for the wine is transformed into blood and gives strength to man."

Someone has said that a house does not become a home until it knows a birth, a wedding, and a death. In other words, it is more than plaster walls, crude furniture, and steaming food. It is even more an association of memories deeply rooted in family crises.

A frequently recurring crisis in Dragalevtsy was childbirth, which always took place in a home, never in a hospital. Usually it was the home in which the couple lived, for only rarely did the wife return to her paternal home for the event. When a woman learned that she was pregnant, she told the fact only to her own mother and to her husband, embarrassment preventing further disclosure. The mother-in-law learned about it a month later, for in the words of one of the older village men:

"She always looks at the undershirts of the daughter-in-law that are to be washed, and so draws the conclusion that leads her to ask the younger woman in the conventional phrase, 'Something's going to happen, isn't it?' The daughter-in-law becomes very embarrassed and does not say anything until the older woman assures her that it is something perfectly natural and something which she herself has experienced. Then the daughter-in-law will answer, 'Well, I don't know. Maybe there is such a thing as you suggest.' So pregnancy," concluded this informant, "is considered rather immoral and women are embarrassed to tell the others about it."

Because of the shyness and innate modesty of the Dragalevtsy matron, remarkable traits in view of the crowded living conditions, I found it helpful to supplement and check the information given by men in this connection. Miss Petrana Peneva, of the American College, rendered invaluable aid in interviewing the women.

No special prenatal care was given to the mother in spite of the efforts on the part of the doctor to get such women to come for advice. The villagers know that the mother-to-be must not bend much nor lift heavy things. They also told her not to jump over a dog, "because the child would then have a hoarse voice or no voice at all." Generally she was given whatever she asked for on the grounds that "if she is not satisfied, there is danger that the baby in her will die." One day I attended a carding *sedenka,* which was a gathering of about twenty women in one of the homes to help the hostess card her wool. I noticed that one woman, obviously pregnant, tasted the stew being prepared for dinner in the entryway each time she passed it. I was given two reasons for this: "She better than anyone else present could judge the correctness of the seasoning" and "If she did not taste of the food each time she passed, she would have a miscarriage." Yet custom did not allow the expectant mother to eat fresh fish because "the nose of the baby will be closed [adenoids]"; nor could she drink from a pail of water for fear that the baby if a boy would be born with swollen sex organs. But, other than these practices and prohibitions, little fuss was made over the expectant mother. No special prayers were said for her nor were any special services held. "The woman is born to be a mother. She knows it and, as her duty, should not expect anything from the others."

Before the birth of the child, swaddling clothes were prepared, and a cradle and wooden tub were bought. The mother herself was not supposed to sew because it was believed that this would make the baby dumb. In fact, nobody went to any trouble at all to provide an elaborate layette, for that would really seem to the peasants like tempting fate. One of the men asked me, "Who can tell whether it will be a boy or a girl, and most important, who has unnecessary money to throw away in vain, for the baby may die?"

At the delivery of the baby, all the young people were sent away, and only the old people and the midwife remained with the mother. "The business of the relatives is to give courage to the mother, and in case the delivery of the child is painful, the midwife massages and carefully pulls the baby out."

The peasants much preferred the midwife or *baba*, to whose old-fashioned ways they were accustomed. To be sure, they called in the village doctor if the case seemed very complicated or if the woman fainted in labor. Dr. Chirkova has encountered many interesting superstitions and folkways in her village experience; these she included in her annual reports to the District Health Office. For instance, since the baby is supposed to be born on straw, in conformity with the birth of Christ, some deliveries occurred in mangers where the doctor was quite apt to find the baby blue with cold. There were instances of women who kept the pains secret from everyone, especially the husband, for they did not "want to add to his troubles." Some of these women even went so far as to remain alone during the childbirth, cutting the cord with a sickle and tying it with their own hair. Such instances, however, were exceptional.

Many deliveries were made with the woman standing, but when labor seemed to be difficult those in attendance put a rope beneath her breasts, tied it to the ceiling, and swung her "in order that the baby might be born more easily." To lessen the ordeal still more, the *baba* moistened the lips of the woman with an herb called "The Hands of the Holy Virgin," which had been put into a bowl of water. It is assumed that the Virgin will render direct aid.

Should the baby appear to be in the wrong position for delivery those attending put the mother in a rug and swung her until the baby came into the "right" position. Normally coffee or wax was used on the navel "so it will stay there one week without falling." Furthermore, the mother was supposed to drink some of the water in which the baby was washed and to which a clove of garlic had been added "in order that the mother's milk may come sooner."

"After the baby has arrived the children are told that the stork has brought a little brother or sister to them through the chimney and they are very glad about it," was the way a proud young father phrased the matter in the course of our conversation about the arrival of his son.

The taboos of childbirth did not cease with the birth of the child. Since the woman was considered unclean for forty days she had to remain at home and was not allowed to attend the christening of her own child. At the end of this period she went to the church for a special purification ceremony at the hands of the priest.

If the child had a birthmark, many peasants assumed that the mother had stolen some object which touched her own body where the birthmark appeared on the child. Any serious abnormality in an infant was explained by the *babi* on the grounds of too close kinship of the parents to each other or the occurrence of conception on Tuesday, Thursday, or Saturday night, each of which is supposed to be kept free of intercourse because Wednesday, Friday, and Sunday are holy days. As one would expect, the latter taboo is of little importance nowadays; it is simply recalled as a convenient way of explaining something out of the ordinary.

Some of the more ignorant peasants rubbed the head of a very sick infant with urine or, if the baby was born with a "closed nose," a cure was "effected" by putting a small fresh fish tailfirst up the nose. Afterwards the fish was put under a stone.

To keep the mother from fainting during her convalescence the family surrounded her with incense smoke and burning feathers both morning and evening, and gave her holy water to wash the baby's face and her face. Should some member of the family have returned after dark he could not enter the room where the mother was lying. She herself was not allowed out after sunset, but if she should have to go, "she takes a burning coal with tongs out with her, after leaving a broom near the baby to use in defending himself against the devil."

The baby's clothes were taken from the line before sunset. They were first held over the fire before they were put on the baby. During the whole first year the clothes were not turned inside out, nor were they pounded when washed by the customary *buhalka* (paddle). If this should be done, the baby might be afraid of thunder. Furthermore, the water in which the baby had been bathed could not be thrown out after sunset.

If a child became sick, "the first thing was to warm him, for he might have caught cold." Then he was given some home remedies prescribed by the *babi*. If the child did not then recover, the parents tried everything they knew, hoping that after some time "everything bad would pass away." In case the child grew worse, they called some of the neighbors or some old woman to come to see him. Only in very serious cases, when the peasants became convinced that nothing could help the child, would they carry him to the doctor. The reason for taking the child to the doctor was to save the extra fee charged for a home visit. Finally, "if God has given the child some more days to live, then the child will recover; if not, then his days are finished and God wants to take the child." (It is no wonder, then, that in Bulgaria 123 out of every 1,000 infants born in 1941 died during their first year of life. Although this represented a decline from the 1938 figure of 144, it still is more than two and one-half times the rate in the United States, which was 46 in 1941.)

The care given to a sick adult differed somewhat from that given to a sick child. When a person had been ill for a long time, his relatives went to the priest for holy water called *babina voda* (old woman's water) by the less respectful peasants. Sometimes the family let the sick person drink some of this water, but this practice was falling into disuse, "for the young people do not believe in it." I was told that very few believed in the curative power of the icons; but if a sick person should happen to, he was carried to the church to kiss the icon.

"For fuel, people . . . used small branches brought from the village forest up on the mountainside." *See page 23.*

". . . we use a great deal of bread, which is baked by the women . . . in the ovens standing in the yards. . . ." *See page 26.*

"The procession . . . was led by a boy carrying . . . boiled wheat to be placed on the grave." *See page 38.*

"Many times we carry clothes to the river . . . where we pound them with the *buhalka.*" *See page 39.*

Prayers were also believed efficacious. As soon as a person became sick, his people prayed to God to help him and cure him. In addition, the priest prayed for the sick individual in the church (or in the home if the sick person could not go to the church) asking God to cure his servant from such and such a sickness and to give him peace. Candles were burned when the prayers were being said, but the burning of these candles was not supposed to have any curative power. "This service is performed more for the old people and although it is said to be *vetur rabota* [plumb foolishness], yet many times it helps the sick to recover. Nowadays people do not believe in God and this is why many people die, and also that is why life in general is as it is, so heavy."

In looking for the causes of illness the peasants also turned to the Almighty who, it was formerly believed, sent sickness as a punishment upon individuals for wrongs they had done. While many people in 1937 had the same attitude, there were some who accepted the germ explanation. But even some of these, if a sickness dragged on and on, suspected that God might be meting out some punishment, germs or no germs. Here was the way they so often put it: "And God has the right to punish the people, for now they have begun not to believe in him and not to listen to him. Now the people are forgetting God and are with the Devil."

The villagers knew the names of only a few diseases and classified all illnesses under one of these few. The worst disease was the "plague" (typhoid fever), then tuberculosis, *sharka* (pox), scarlatina, and finally, "a bad cold." The doctor used a more scientific classification in listing the causes of death. Her report for 1936 showed that thirty-three people died within the year. Diseases accounting for four deaths each were tuberculosis, nervous disorders, and pneumonia; those accounting for two deaths each were scarlatina, whooping cough, diphtheria, cancer, heart disease, old age, and childbirth (mother); those causing one death each were childbirth (infant), typhus, erysipelas, bronchitis, diarrhea, digestive ailment, and accident. Her scientific approach did not necessarily mean that the doctor's recovery percentage was very high, because patients were brought too late for proper treatment. Therefore the peasants said: "And

many times the doctors cannot help. They cannot give a second soul
to the sick. If he has some more days to live, he will live; if not,
he will die. Doctors are not God and even the doctors die as well."

In keeping with this fatalistic attitude toward sickness, the peasants accepted death as simply as they would any life process. Before
I began my study of Dragalevtsy I was already familiar with the
peasants' conception of death. One account which had proved helpful in gaining this understanding appeared in the *Bulgarian-British
Review* back in 1931, and was written by Mrs. A. Vessova. She said
in part:

"Death to these people is not considered the end; it is but the
continuation of the earthly life in another sphere—the invisible world.
The bounden duty of the family is to prepare the dying for their long
journey so that they will not have to roam disconsolately in the dark-
ness without finding their way to their new surroundings. Of the
dying person they repeat to one another that he or she is now a
traveler. Their first duty is to light a candle which they place above
the head of the patient, so that they may not see it, should they happen
to be conscious. Should the patient be allowed to die without lighting
this particular candle, it is considered by the villagers to bring great
discredit on the family. The meaning of the candle is that when the
soul starts upon its long journey it has to pass through dark passages,
and the candle will light the way.

". . . As soon as the neighbors hear the announcement [of the
death] they immediately throw away all the water found in the house,
and proceed to the fountain to replenish all their vessels. The same
procedure takes place in the house of the deceased. There is no clear
explanation for this custom or its real meaning, but it is supposed to
symbolize, as do other customs, that as the water flows smoothly and
evenly, so the voyage of the soul will be made smooth and easy.

"The peasants believe that though invisible the soul continues
to keep the form of the body which it has just left. For this reason
the deceased is laid to rest in his grave in his ordinary clothing. Led
by his or her angel, for they believe that every human being at his

birth receives a guardian angel, the soul of the deceased after leaving this world starts first to visit all the people and places where it has been when on this earth. This journey, no matter how great the distance may be, must be completed in forty days. If the departed has lived most of his time in his village, and only occasionally has gone to neighboring towns or villages, the journey will be an easy and pleasant one, but if he has traveled great distances the journey will be tiring and rough. It may be that this belief has been responsible for keeping the peasants so firmly attached to their land and village, and preventing them from migrating to new lands. . . .

"The soul has started on its journey, while the body is still in the house, being mourned by the family and the neighbors. The members of the family throw grains of corn or wheat into the coffin. They also believe that there is a great river to be passed and if the deceased has no money he will be unable to cross, and his journey will be impeded. Another peculiar belief is that the neighbors send through him messages to their departed, firmly believing that he will deliver them."

Investigation showed that these statements held true generally of Dragalevtsy but needed to be supplemented. For one thing, the villagers had definite ways of foretelling death. They said, for instance, that there were as many stars in the sky as there were people on earth, and that there was a particular star for each person. When a star fell to the ground, someone was said to have died and his star to have gone out like his soul. If the star merely moved from one place to another, then its particular earthly representative had changed his residence. Many peasants also believed that "stars with tails" (meteors) foretold some great misfortune to be sent by God. Usually they were thought to signify war "because before the Balkan War and the World War there were such." But there were even more specific ways of predicting death in any given locality. When the owls cried at sunset toward a house or when a hen crowed, death was sure to follow soon. Certain dreams indicated the coming of death. Bai Angel, the village registrar, told me that a soldier could be practically certain of death if he dreamed of a snake. He supported this belief with the story of an officer in the first World War who lined up his men before a battle and went down the ranks to shake hands with the soldiers and told them that he would not return from the fight. He was sure of this because he had dreamed of a snake during the night. Sure enough, he was killed in the action that followed.

If a person dreamed of a wedding or that he was leading a *horo,* death was probable; or if he dreamed of having a tooth pulled, the same held true. If he dreamed that he saw a deep black hole (similar to a grave), someone connected with him would die; if it was white inside, somebody else would die; if he fell into the hole, he would die.

In Dragalevtsy there were certain old women who considered themselves specialists in the preparation of the body for burial. They were "priestesses of superstition" who saw to it that all the pagan rites were carried out before the priest arrived to conduct the funeral. Their presence at any crisis showed the duality of the peasants' view of the universe.

God was thought to be the force symbolizing the Good. The priest was His representative and should be given due respect; furthermore, he should be asked to perform all of the customary ceremonies such as the sprinkling of holy water in every room of the house at Bogoyavlenie or Epiphany on the nineteenth of January. Keeping on the good side of the priest meant keeping on the good side of God, whose favors one needs both in this life and the next.

Inasmuch as they believed in a principle of Good at work in the universe, it was logical for the peasants to believe in a principle of Evil which could do them harm, with or without the consent of the Good. Some parts of the church ceremonies, such as spitting over the child at the devil during the christening, were directed at nullifying the efforts of the Evil One. Seeing that the church concerned itself chiefly with the Good, the peasant in his naivete felt compelled to do something to ward off the Evil, and thus perpetuated many primitive customs which startle both educated Bulgarians and those westerners who are not familiar with the equally primitive customs found within certain areas of their own supposedly civilized lands.

The intermediaries in this "cult of the Evil Eye, Devil, Bad Luck" were certain old women, called *babi,* already described in the account of a village birth. These women showed people how to keep the Evil Eye away. They advised mothers whose babies were only one or two months old to make a spot on the baby's neck beneath the ear, using axle grease from the wagon. The spell of the Evil Eye could be cast by one who was envious or of an evil heart. That is why I soon stopped complimenting babies or animals, for the frightened look that came into the mother's or owner's eyes on occasion showed me that mine must seem an envious heart. Such envy was supposed to cause sickness in the object admired. Then a *baba* who was old and ugly, with crooked teeth, pale and wrinkled face, and sunken eyes, was called upon to perform a magic rite *(baiane).* Water was put in a pottery bowl, an incantation was read, and live coals were dropped into the water. Some people suggested that an Evil Eye might be kept away by hanging an onion or garlic over the house, or by wearing blue beads. A few people were said to dye good animals in order to distract the attention of people from their good qualities.

Along with the belief in the Evil Eye was the belief in vampires. No cat or dog should ever be allowed to jump over a corpse before burial, or that person would become a vampire and return to plague his friends and relatives. In some Balkan villages, when it was suspected that a person might be or become a vampire, a stout stake is driven through the heart of the corpse upon interment. But there were no such stakes in the Dragalevtsy cemetery.

Funeral ceremonies could not be extensive since the body had to be in the ground within twenty-four hours after death. One of the last funerals I attended was that of an old woman whom I had interviewed on one occasion. When the priest arrived he found the room filled with about twenty people, two-thirds of whom were relatives and one-third neighbors. The body dressed in the best holiday costume was placed on a black, rough wooden coffin with some white flowers, dahlias, and fruit such as oranges and apples. Around the head and under the chin was a white band. The room became blue with incense smoke through which the black cover of the coffin, standing against the wall, could scarcely be seen. The chanting of the priest was constantly interrupted by the wailing of the women.

At the conclusion of the service in the house, four men bore the coffin into the yard as the wailing continued. All the sons and daughters carried under their arms new garments which their mother had left for them. The procession, which formed in the yard, was led by a boy carrying the boiled wheat to be placed on the grave; another carried the flower-decked grave marker on which the name, date of birth, and date of death had already been inscribed; a third boy carried a bowl of fruit, and a fourth a cross. The priest came next, wearing over his right shoulder a pair of socks, a gift from the deceased woman. Following him, with the covered coffin, were the four pall-bearers, each with a kerchief pinned to his coat. A relative carried a loaf of special bread and was followed by the other relatives near the coffin. Neighbors came next. The women wore black kerchiefs tied with a loose knot instead of the customary tight knot.

The procession moved through the gateway into the street, leaving behind the homestead where the woman had come as a bride, where each of her children had been born, and to which her husband would return a lonely widower. As we moved up the street the husband said to me, "Well, we're putting the old woman away." He was stoical, resigned, but deeply grieved. On the way to the church the procession stopped at each crossroad, symbolic of the Stations of the Cross on the way to Calvary. There was a brief ceremony in front of the church door after which the coffin was carried inside and put on chairs in the center of the church. On the small table at the head of the coffin there were a large pan of bread and bottles of liquid. Early in the ceremony everybody burned candles around the coffin; at a given sign these candles were taken away. At the end of the cere-mony all performed the "last kiss," kissing the icon which rested on the body and the hand of the deceased.

The body was taken to the cemetery where quite a few super-stitious practices were carried out in the presence of the priest, but without his "noticing" what was being done. There were no pro-fessional wailers at the funeral; but two women loudly mourned for the infant each had recently lost and constantly asked the departed one to deliver messages to their children. Only the close relatives made any show of grief, while all the rest maintained a dignified silence.

Thus the house became a home. Birth and death took their turn, so that every square foot of the small dwelling held its special memories. Over in that corner Ivanche was born; that stool by the bed was the one great-grandmother sat on many hours each day until her death at 102 years of age. She was the one who told the children the fascinating stories about dragons, who were "human beings like the rest of us but had wings in their armpits." She always enjoyed telling the legend about the lazy woman back in the days when people did not have to bring wood home from the forest in a wagon but simply tied the wood together in a bundle, whipped it, and sent it home by itself. It seems that the lazy woman was not content with this simple expedient, but after tying the pieces of wood together sat on top the bundle in the hope it would carry her home. God became so angry at this presumption that He forbade the wood to go home any longer under its own power. Henceforth it had to be taken home in a wagon.

Not far from the iconostas was a faded photograph, the only one in the room, of Peter and his bride Tsveta. Peter was the oldest son, and soon after his marriage in 1917 left for the army, never to return from the battlefield. Tsveta of course was married again, three months after his death, to a man from Bistritsa who needed an efficient housekeeper.

But not all of the life at the homestead took place indoors. The walled-in yard was also the scene of many family experiences. In fact, so many of the household processes went on outside in warm weather that the grass was completely worn away. I once asked a woman doing her washing out in the yard where she preferred to do that job. She replied:

"Clothes are washed with soap and hot water, and since we do not have special places for washing we do it in the living room in bad weather, or in the yard in good weather. Many times we carry the clothes to the river, but even there we heat water for rinsing. We pound the clothes with the *buhalka* [heavy wooden paddle] and wash not only our underclothes, but our outer garments as well, with the exception of the leather *kozhusi* [jackets]." She also volunteered information as to wash days: "We wash twice a week: on Monday and Wednesday, or on Wednesday and Saturday."

Many of the yards still had the threshing floor, reminiscent of Old Testament days. This could be located by a forlorn post which seemed to be serving no useful purpose. In the fall great quantities of drying wool hung from the clotheslines; and a little later the family piled in the yard the winter supply of wood from the forest.

The eaves of the house, deep as they were, sheltered such things as strings of drying peppers and ears of corn; milk utensils hung beneath them practically the year round; even the scythes and wooden hayforks found frequent lodging there. Storks nested in the trees and chimneys. With the coming of the warmer weather the sheep left their folds in the yards for the pastures, and the shepherd took with him his wattled shelter, which he moved on sleds across the grassy meadows.

In many yards a heavy, large-wheeled wagon stood near the primitive sheds for the animals and the ever-present strawstack. If the peasants were unusually superstitious, there would be dabs of blue paint on the wagon to keep the Evil Eye away. When the weather was nice there were usually children at play in the yard. Upon seeing a visitor they added their lusty shouts to the ominous barking of the dogs. They chased the dogs away from the gate by throwing sticks and stones at them, and at the same time warned the visitor to be on the alert. Far too often the dogs sneaked up behind to nip an ankle of the unsuspecting visitor.

The yards had few flowers, because chickens of a nondescript variety pecked freely throughout the premises. One or two scraggly trees, from which the children shook most of the fruit before it had time to ripen, stood in a corner wistfully seeking to give a touch of beauty to the scene. In the spring the blossoms of such trees made the village bright, but when the fruit and leaves were gone the bare, black skeletons of the trees fitted in only too well with the poverty and sternness of village life. Poor land, inefficiently tilled, contributed to this poverty. Although the peasants worked hard in their fields, they had little cash on hand after selling their crops and paying their debts. Home improvements were postponed from year to year, but the hard work kept on just the same.

To describe a home, as this chapter has shown, means describing a miscellany of life activities which center there. Not only are shelter, furnishings, and the littered yard a part of the story, but also practices of cleanliness and health, religious ceremonies, food habits, the peasant's philosophy of life, childbirth, and finally death. But fascinating as Dragalevtsy home life proved to be, I soon learned that it had to take its place alongside the peasant's love for his fields. This attachment to his land and fondness for his home were the twin clues to the understanding of the peasant's limited universe.

CHAPTER III

LAND, LABOR, AND MONEY

A PEASANT'S life in spring and summer centered around the narrow strips of earth which surrounded the village. If the scene of labor was distant from the village, the tired workers who had been at their tasks since sunup often spent the night in the field rather than trudge the long way back home. In the middle of the morning, at noon, and again in midafternoon, the toilers stopped long enough for food, sometimes only bread and salt, and a little sleep. The burning noonday sun sifted through the leaves of the solitary tree beneath which the people sprawled. Fragile rays danced upon tired faces, old-fashioned costumes, a hand raised to brush away a fly, and oxen chewing lazily. Like animals the peasants worked, like animals they slept; but when harvest time brought an end to their toil they experienced the joyous satisfaction of work well done.

The average farm was about eighteen acres in size and was composed of sixteen separate and widely scattered strips. (See Table 10, Appendix I.) This land sold for a comparatively high figure because of its nearness to Sofia, but not because of any superior quality. In fact, most of the soil was sandy and gravelly, with a mixture of heavy clay.

In addition to a house in the village and his land, the peasant also owned a few animals and agricultural implements. The work animals numbered fewer than two for an eighteen-acre holding, and the plow was the only large implement found on every farm. More than any other joint operation, plowing had the flavor of an antique ritual. At dawn a slow procession moved from the village. The distant Balkan range loomed vaguely blue far across the Sofia plain, and the golden dome of Alexander Nevsky Cathedral in Sofia shone in the thin, clear light of morning. Behind the village, the slopes of

Vitosha and snow-covered Cherni Vruh, its peak, looked raw and wild. Against this background a trio of woman, ox, and man was repeated over and over as the households fell into line. The woman came first, leading the moon-eyed oxen which drew the crude wagon with the wooden plow inside. Behind them walked the man who was to guide the plow. He carried a long staff to poke the oxen when they grew sluggish at their task. With the stately pace set by the animals, the peasants walked as gravely through the hush of early morning as though they were moving to some pagan altar rising in the dewy fields. Time slipped back for me countless centuries when I saw the first spring plowing, for small boys had hung the oxen with garlands as though these animals had been meant for sacrifice.

As the days passed, this picture had its variations. Black buffalo, with a cruel crocodile look on their faces, sometimes replaced the oxen; occasionally the woman was busy about something else and the man plowed alone. If the beasts got off the track, a flood of abusive language burst forth from the exasperated peasant. The sound of the language and the pitch of the voice were even more effective than the meaning. Not only in Dragalevtsy but all over Bulgaria, slowly and laboriously the heavy earth was broken with endless patience, for almost three-fourths of the plows had wooden shares, and oxen outnumbered horses four to one.

After the seed was in the ground the peasants left the responsibility mainly to God, but partly to the field policeman and his routine patrols. To ensure God's benevolence the village had a special day for a religious procession through the fields: the first Thursday after St. George's Day (May 6). Once the constant beating of the church bell coming from a strange direction attracted my attention to a spot about one mile east of the village. There was Father Sava, the priest, in his official regalia, accompanied by several boys carrying the church cross, the bell, a flag, and large icons. From forty to fifty villagers followed in a winding line. The procession stopped to pray for rain in several places where there had been insufficient rainfall. Later I learned that on one occasion the party had climbed almost to the top of Vitosha in order to fulfill to the letter their mission of encircling all of the fields owned by the Dragalevtsy people.

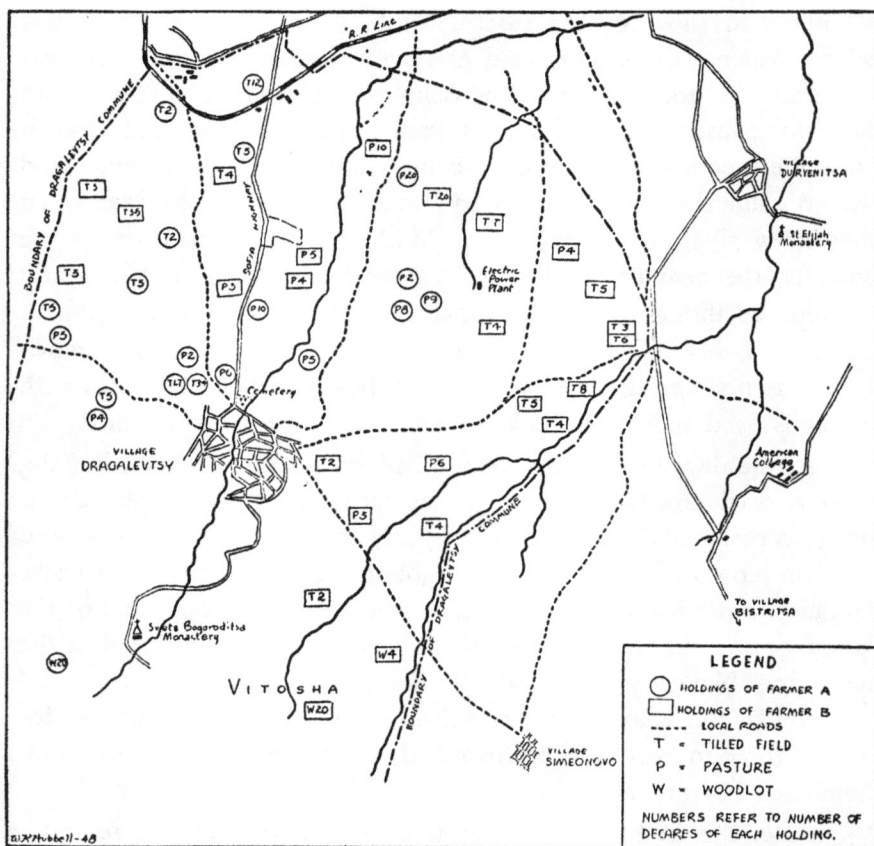

Map of holdings of two Dragalevtsy farmers

Should drought be very severe, say in midsummer, the villagers asked for another procession and additional prayers to do more effectively what the May procession had failed to do. The need for such ceremonies was explained to me one day by a tavern keeper: "While the people know in their minds that wind keeps the rain away from their fields, they believe in their hearts that the cause of drought, like that of sickness, is the sinfulness of the world today for which God is punishing the people."

The chief bread-grain used in this region was called *smes,* a mixture of wheat and rye. It was sown by hand from a bag slung over the shoulder. In late July harvesters came from other villages to help at least one-third of the families (the others harvested their own grain) to cut the grain with sickles and place the stalks in little piles. An old man, expert through years of practice, then made up the sheaves by tying together a bundle of stalks with the longest stalks taken from a previous sheaf. He used a round, pointed stick about fourteen inches long to make the grain compact and to tie the knot ingeniously.

Most of the grain was threshed by the hoofs of animals, usually horses, on the packed, earthen threshing floors near the house. The Karakachani, a band of Wallachians from the village of Yakoruda in the Rhodope Mountains, brought about fifty horses to the village at threshingtime. A peasant paid the equivalent of a dollar a day for the service of a team. The grain was placed in the center of the floor, near a pole to which the animals were hitched. Around and around the pole the horses walked until the rope's length was used up, whereupon they reversed their direction. Much grain was threshed by the machine owned by some of the wealthier men of the village, which was beginning to supplant the old-fashioned threshing floors. Some of the families still winnowed the grain by tossing it in the face of a stiff breeze, but many others had access to a separating machine in the neighborhood.

But this *smes,* or wheat and rye mixture, was not the only crop raised. Quite a few of the homes had garden patches, either in the yard or on the edge of the village, where peppers, mealy potatoes, cabbages, and tomatoes were grown. The white beans from Dragalevtsy were said to be the best in this part of Bulgaria.

Some families grew sunflowers in order to sell the seeds for oil. Pumpkins from the cornfields were prized for use in a soggy pumpkin pie called *banitsa.* Fruit raising was decidedly underdeveloped, but the trees that were properly cared for produced very well. Straw for the animals was frequently borrowed or purchased from the wealthier peasants who had a surplus from the threshing.

The crop second in importance to *smes,* however, was corn. Of considerable interest were the groups of women who hoed the cornfield first in one direction, and a week later in a different direction. Varying in number from three to fifteen, these groups did more than merely chop weeds and loosen the soil; they also afforded an opportunity for visiting and conversation. A day or two ahead of time the woman needing help broached the matter to those whose assistance she wanted in her cornfield. She was careful to include only those women who would work in a congenial manner, shunning those known to be gossipy or quarrelsome. At four in the morning on the day of the hoeing the hostess had to go to the home of each guest.

"Anka, Anka," she called above the barking of the menacing dogs. Anka came to the door to greet her walking alarm clock with a cheery *"Dobro utro"* ("Good morning"). Since Anka owed the visitor two days of work for having helped with her cornfield, she readily accepted, hurried about her household tasks, and was ready to leave for the fields by six o'clock. Young women received many invitations because they could better withstand the summer heat. Occasionally, young men, upon hearing that their sweethearts were to be invited, asked the hostess the night before to call them along with the others in the morning. In the field all day long they had a wonderful opportunity to hoe next to the girls of their choice and "to tell secret things and to speak what they shouldn't."

Each woman brought her heavy, semicircular hoe and her own bread, but the hostess provided the vegetables and other food. Sometimes the people were paid in cash for their work, but more often the work was repaid in kind. The oldest maiden was "at the post." She apportioned the number of rows and kept the workers from getting in each other's way. She set the pace as the workers moved in a line, side by side, across the field. Her word was supreme, and even the hostess kept quiet, although she might think the girl was giving poor directions. The hostess watched the time and told the group when to stop working for the three meals she served. The girl "at the post" gave the signal to resume work, but she did not urge others to work until she saw that the group sentiment favored it. If one woman was not ready to start, the others began anyway. But the niceties of etiquette were always observed: the hostess, who was profiting from the work, invited the group to stop to eat; a guest, who was directing the group, rather than the hostess, suggested that they take up work once more.

I spent many hours in the fields chatting with these women. There was a hypnotic rhythm of sound and color in their work as the line of black-clad bodies, and white headcloths, swayed forward together through the thin green blades. In the high altitude everything was sharply defined: the red-roofed village two miles away, the puffs of white cloud infinitely high in the blue, the strong harsh peasant voices close by. While the women worked they sang old folk songs about beautiful heroines and the brave Krali Marko, a legendary Balkan hero who carried out prodigious feats against the Turks, or of peasant girls knitting gay stockings for village boys. The songs were usually romantic and often were cheerful in theme; but now and then one was moved by a haunting sadness deeper even than that of the Negro work songs. Hour after hour I used to hear the unhappy music rise in its bizarre cadence; day after day for three weeks the corn was hoed in one field after another. Week after week the sun beat down on Vitosha and the Sofia plain, while summer burned itself away. The corn grew waist high, then shoulder high, and finally yielded the golden ears to the strong brown fists of some boy or girl at the autumn cornhusking *sedenki*.

Early July was the haying season. Each sunrise would find most of the villagers out in the fields. Some of the men with their sharp scythes cut the hay in even swaths, letting it lie as it fell, to dry in the parching sun. Others would load the cured hay onto the wagons fitted out with ladderlike sides. As the wagons rolled through the village streets they were greeted by the little children who had had to stay at home with their aged grandparents or great-grandparents. The haystacks, whether left in the field or dressed near the house, were weighted down by lines to which heavy stones had been attached.

One could not be with the peasants long at haying time, or indeed at any other time, without sensing their feeling of close dependence upon the weather. In fact, I soon found myself sharing this feeling, although I remained somewhat dubious of the infallibility of the signs by which they "read the weather." They believed, for example, that it would rain if the crows bathed in the river, if the sun set or rose behind a cloud or was surrounded by a circle, or if the oxen dug the earth with their horns in the springtime. When the moon was surrounded by a dark circle, the weather would supposedly change to rain if it was summer and to snow if winter. Rain would also follow if the stars shone brightly, the sky was red in the morning, or the middle part of Vitosha was foggy. But the surest sign of bad weather was the sight of pigs carrying straw to the sty at sunset. Yet good weather alone did not ensure good crops. The human element was of utmost importance.

Bulgaria had, according to prewar figures, the largest labor supply per decare in Europe, with 5.8 workers available for 100 decares (25 acres) of land. Italy came next with 4.7, then Poland with 4.3, but Great Britain had only 0.7. In spite of such a surplus of labor the people had not begun to cultivate intensively. An increasing number of young people therefore had to seek a living from sources off the farm. Such intensive cultivation, however, would require radical changes in farming practices. Not more than thirty Dragalevtsy families saved liquid fertilizer, although the rest did haul wagonload after wagonload of manure from the stables to the fields late in the winter to be dumped in piles awaiting later spreading. There was very little harrowing, and what was done took place in the spring after the rains.

The cornfields were plowed under at once after the harvest and were immediately sown with grain. If the field had produced *smes,* the stubble was plowed under to lie fallow for one or two years. The fallow fields were plowed once in the spring, once in the middle of the summer, and again in the autumn just before the grain was to be sown.

What might be considered a Bulgarian counterpart of our Thanksgiving feast occurred at the time of this fall sowing of grain. Early in the morning the woman arose quietly to bake one large and two small loaves of bread, and to catch a young rooster which she handed over to her husband just before he was ready to start to the field in the oxcart. What followed was the observance of a pagan fertility rite. With the dignity of a priest performing an ancient sacrifice, the

"Plowing had the flavor of an antique ritual." *See page 42.*

". . . harvesters . . . cut the grain with sickles, and placed the stalks in little piles." *See page 44.*

"The cornhoeing groups . . . also afforded an opportunity for visiting and conversation." *See page 46.*

"The patriarchal system . . . won out" (a father and three married sons living together in a one-room house). *See page 62.*

stopanin, or male head of the house, killed the cock and held its twitching body over a bag of grain seed so that several drops of blood would fall upon it. He then drove slowly to the field to prepare the ground for the sowing, meanwhile eagerly awaiting the arrival at midmorning of the *domakinya,* his wife, dressed in her most beautiful costume and bearing a pan containing the boiled cock, meal, and bread. The family group made a tour once around the field, whereupon the man solemnly broke the bread and, before sitting with the others in the middle of the field to feast, gave pieces of the bread to the oxen. The peasants called this the "sweetest meal of the year" and delighted in having friends from a neighboring field join them in the repast. Summer's hard work was at an end; the harvests were plentiful; the peasants were deeply grateful.

Life in these scattered fields of Dragalevtsy was hard and laborious, but to the peasant, life without the fields would not be worth living, for these narrow strips of land were his children growing under his painstaking care. The land was his companion and friend, as he shared with it the thoughts and dreams of a starlit summer night, with a cloak for a pillow and dew for a blanket. Land meant more to the peasant than money in the bank; it meant more than food on the table; it meant life itself.

Some years ago I heard a Sofia University professor say in a lecture that the Bulgarian peasant was more devoted to his work than to his religion. "There are more songs dedicated to labor than to saints," he added. Because I wondered about the truth of this statement in respect to Dragalevtsy, I polled village opinion. Here are some of the questions I asked, with representative or characteristic responses:

Nowadays, which do people enjoy most: working in the field or sitting in the tavern?

"People work to get bread. They can't earn money enough to save. Some prefer to work in the fields because we quarrel when we are in the *kruchma.*"

"Most of the people prefer to be in the tavern, though there are some who go there to do *pazarluk* [arrange a business deal], drink a little, then leave to do their work again."

"I prefer to work in the fields than to sit in the tavern."

Why do young people want to become artisans and do not want to become farmers?

"They want easier work. Field work is heavy. If they work inside, they will live longer, the wind won't beat in their faces, they won't remain in the cold."

"It's better to work inside than out in the weather."

"If one is an artisan, one won't become hungry. There will always be work to do. But in the fields things are not so sure. Work is easier as an artisan than as a farmer. The money is only of minor importance."

Do people of Dragalevtsy, like the heroes of old folk songs, love hard work more than easy work?

"They prefer easy work. Fifty years ago people liked the harder work, for there were few occupations. Now parents don't control their children. A son sees his father at one tavern and he goes to the other. If his father comes to the second tavern, then he goes back to the first. Formerly people had big fields and had to do much work. They prided themselves on the amount of work they could get done. They were healthier, because they didn't smoke and drink so much. The one who could work the most was the most honored. Now the fields are small. There is little work to do in them, and so people get out of the habit of working hard."

"They like easier work now. Everyone looks for something that is light. It was not so fifty years ago, but the change came about especially since the war."

"They love easy work. Formerly there were more animals, more fields, less people, and therefore more work."

With what adjective would a Dragalevtsy peasant prefer to be described: industrious, rich, influential, wise?

"Now all want to be rich and will lie to become so. There is no one who wants to be industrious. They sit in the tavern and say, 'Let those who are foolish work.' There is no shame nowadays. Formerly a man was ashamed to be seen away from his work. Furthermore, people prefer to be influential than wise."

"People would rather be rich, but think it necessary to be industrious in order to be rich. It is better to be influential than wise."

When I pursued the attitude toward money by further questioning I received such replies as these:

"When I was young I could work and get money, but now I can't, so therefore I think more about it. I sent my son to be a soldier and have to do everything all alone."

"Prices are now higher, money doesn't go so far, and therefore has to be watched carefully. Formerly people didn't have to buy so much. Now there are many who want to get more and more money."

The position of the wealthy man was described as follows:

"Rich men have lots of influence, even more than the priest. The priest is a good man and people listen to his advice, but when they go to Trayko Danev [a wealthy peasant] they take off their hat and ask for money. They give him wine to drink and roast lamb to eat because he is rich. Before the war what the priest said was thought to be what God said. Now he can't get anybody to go to church and stand for five hours hungry. It's a punishment. During the World War our people went many places—Salonika, Serbia, Bucharest—and saw how people lived; they then agreed that life in the village was too hard and not for the likes of them."

Education, which ordinarily was held in very high esteem, had yielded ground to commercialism. Villagers were beginning to prefer money to education, and said:

"In Sofia there are many unemployed educated people, and so if I have money, I'll be better off than if I had education."

Many of the villagers considered it highly desirable to have a government pension, and so valued jobs with the state railways, state telegraph system, or postal service.

An intelligent woman once summed up for me the peasant's attitude toward labor and money in this terse fashion:

"Most people work because they want money. Everyone looks for money."

Although the peasant considered money of greater importance than formerly because he was becoming more and more a part of a money economy, he really handled very little in the course of a year. The annual income for a family of four or five was less than two hundred dollars, an amount that came into the family coffer in driblets and was paid out as slowly as possible. After the autumn market or the sale of a cow, the peasant was flush with money, but when he had bought the necessities which he could not produce for himself (kerosene, shoes and other articles of clothing, rice, salt, and some hardware) he was little better off financially. If a member of the family worked outside the home, his wages were a considerable help, especially when some of the many taxes were due.

I asked nine young men, picked at random, about the money they earned. Their monthly income varied from the meager equivalent of $6 a month earned by a twenty-five-year-old servant and an eighteen-year-old shepherd to $66 earned by a twenty-year-old milkman. There was only one who kept more than half of his earnings for himself. He explained apologetically that the reason he did not turn these over to his father was that he had to pay board and rent in Sofia, where he worked.

Very few Dragalevtsy people accumulated savings in the bank. They preferred, like people all over Bulgaria, to invest money in real estate. The city people did it because of the security of investment, whereas the peasants, especially in Dragalevtsy, were more interested in possessing land for its own sake.

The great majority of the peasants were in debt, though many debtors were also creditors. Those specializing in field crops preferred long-term loans, usually for fifteen or twenty years, with land as security, while sheep owners usually sought short-term loans of three or four months. One village merchant, to whom many peasants came for advice, estimated that 70 per cent of the loans were taken from banks and 30 per cent from individuals. The government had done much in the past through periodic moratoria to reduce the amount of indebtedness.

Another feature of the economic system in Dragalevtsy was the way the work was divided up, chiefly on a customary basis. There was, for instance, a traditional division between the work of men and women. Certain duties which an American man performs without hesitation, a Dragalevtsy man would think far beneath him. Furthermore, he would use the term *zhenska rabota* (woman's work), and in this one phrase express a feeling of masculine superiority handed down through the ages. To be caught at woman's work was the same as being caught wearing a petticoat. Since the chief labor was agricultural, most of the customary division of labor centered about the work of home and field:

IN THE HOUSE

Cleaning and sweeping: all the women.

Setting the table: daughter or daughter-in-law.

Cooking food: mother or mother-in-law.

Making bread: daughter or daughter-in-law.

Getting the water: children and unmarried daughters.

Taking care of fire: usually mother-in-law. Often anyone. (Depends on who feels cold.)

Spinning thread: all the women.

Weaving cloth: daughter and daughter-in-law.

Cutting out and sewing together garments: undergarments—wife, for her own children and husband; outer garments—village tailor.

Washing clothes: wives for their immediate families; unmarried daughter for herself and parents.

IN THE YARD

Caring for chickens: the old man or old woman.

Caring for oxen and buffaloes: both men and women.

Caring for horses: men.

Caring for pigs: women.

IN THE FIELD

Caring for animals in the pasture: the children.
Plowing: the father or oldest son.
Sowing: the father or oldest son.
Hoeing the corn: unmarried daughter or housewife.
Harvesting the grain: the whole family.
Threshing the grain: the whole family.
Saving the seed for next year: no one in particular.

AT THE MARKET

Selling butter, eggs, poultry, vegetables: the housewife.
Selling sheep, pigs, and other animals: the men.
Buying the necessities from Sofia: the men.
Buying necessities in the village: the women and children.
Keeping the cash box: the father; in rare cases, the mother.

It can be seen that children as well as the adults shared in this specialization of labor. The chief occupation of those below sixteen was the care of the animals. During the pasturing season these children spent more time in the fields than in the village. Because their pastures joined they were able to get together for group games and still keep a watchful eye upon their animals. The work they were called upon to do was not dangerous, but it was time consuming. Many famous men who grew up in the villages looked back upon this pastoral experience as a childhood heaven-on-earth. Some of the old men, recalling the days when the large joint families (*zadrugi*) still existed, told of being sent with the animals up the mountains a long way from the village. For a month they were absent, seeing no one but a few strangers who happened to pass by. But those distant pastures were no longer available to the peasants, so they kept their animals (and children) close to the village.

Whether this seems exploitation or not is a matter of definition, but custom did decree that there should be no idle hands in the village economy, even to the extent of keeping small children occupied. To be sure, the attitude toward labor was changing, but the love of the land persisted, and owning land meant working that land, at least in

Dragalevtsy. In general, though the division of labor was traditional, the specialization of occupation was increasing. Though unemployment was absent from the village, this in no way implied that all had the kind of work they wanted. It was astounding enough that even in times of world depression all did have a way of earning a living.

In Bulgaria, as in most countries, property passed from parent to child. There too the laws governing this transfer were very complicated. However, as a general principle in the villages sons inherited twice as much land as daughters. Usually the sons received equal amounts, but a father while still alive could divide the land, taking an equal share for himself, which he later gave to his favorite son. Quite often a sister said when the time of division arrived: "Why should I take land away from my brothers?" and forfeited her claim. In some cases she would sell her share of the estate cheaply to a favorite brother. If she was married, however, her husband could insist that she take what was her due and might even go to court to pursue the case. Every year there were a few Dragalevtsy people involved in long-drawn-out lawsuits originating over the division of inherited land. More often than not, lawyers' fees used up a great part of the value of the property.

A heavy inheritance tax accompanied any such transfer of property from the father to his children. One man at work in the hayfield took time off to tell me of the arrangement being worked out in his family:

"Our father, who is still living, told us three brothers to divide his property equally among us. We have not made the division officially as yet, because if we did we would have to pay an inheritance tax amounting to about four hundred dollars. We divide the land by lot. We take strips of land, both meadows and fields of equal value, and draw lots for the strips. Of course, our father has kept some of the land for himself, but we shall divide that among the three of us after his death."

The most serious conflicts in the village arose when there was disagreement over the division of a patrimony. Brother turned against brother, and whole families became involved in the dispute. There was also conflict over the location of boundary stones. At first I could scarcely believe my eyes when I was shown how the peasants distinguished their fields. Taking some landmark such as a tree, a bend in the road, or a stream, the peasants marked off their strips by small piles of stone. Fences and hedgerows were impracticable because the strips were too small to justify the expense of enclosure. Since every farmer possessed several strips, possibilities of conflict over the boundaries were numerous. The wonder is that there was so little trouble, in view of the fact that every foot of the strip must be utilized if the farmer was to make any profit.

Animals too proved a source of dispute. The oxen, for instance, strayed into an unprotected field and did considerable damage to the growing crop. The person incurring loss often took the matter to the mayor for trial in his magistrate's court. Once an effort was made to have all funds collected from such disputes turned over to the local *Chitalishte,* or Library Association, but this received little public support. For some time there was very bad feeling between the shepherds and the dairymen over the question of pasturage. The *Obshtina,* or local government, passed an ordinance that grazing should be done on one's own land and the common pasture abolished. The shepherds, accustomed to roaming over a considerable area in a day's time, were violently opposed to the new measure; those possessing five or six head of cattle naturally favored it.

Other types of conflict also arose over animals. The widow Zdravka, in explaining to me why she was not on good terms with her neighbor Dimiter, brought another case of disagreement over livestock to my attention:

"Just before St. Peter's Day, Dimiter's dogs fell upon my sow as she passed his yard on her way home from pasture. The pig, which was to bear young the next day, became frightened and fell into a ditch. I immediately went to the veterinarian who told me that the pig's young would be stillborn, and sure enough, they were. I went to the priest and the mayor to ask for justice, but Dimiter told them that he didn't let his dogs out and the accident wasn't his fault. Since he was a man, nothing was done to him and I can't do anything about it myself."

When I asked her if she and Dimiter had quarrels about other things, Zdravka answered:

"We don't quarrel for I keep quiet, and he only speaks to me 'between his teeth.' "

Poultry was a source of much ill feeling among neighbor women. Whenever a hen or rooster strayed into the garden next door there was apt to be a verbal battle, the effects of which fortunately wore off within a few days. There was one woman, however, who had not spoken to her next-door neighbor for three years because of harsh words uttered about a straying hen. "May her chickens be homeless," cursed the other person in describing the incident.

In case the women quarreled over such things as chickens, overhanging branches of a fruit tree, or the return of a borrowed article, the men were inclined to treat the whole incident lightly and speak of it as "woman's business." On the other hand, if two men had a serious dispute, their families behaved distantly toward each other, either because of actual antipathy or because of paternal command. From the standpoint of social interaction, therefore, a serious row between two men was more of a strain on the social structure than was a quarrel between two women. It was apt to last longer, involve more people, and have larger issues at stake.

A visit to the village courtroom convinced me that money was also the basis for much misunderstanding. The court records were full of cases of men who had argued over financial matters until one of them haled the other into court. Most of these disputes were settled by the mayor, but many people left his courtroom still dissatisfied. Because the Dragalevtsy peasant was penurious, every lev was cherished and spent only when absolutely necessary. Such frugality was a virtue from one point of view, but it became a vice when it led to disruptive conflict.

This increased emphasis upon money permeated even the family relationships. One woman exclaimed:

"Relatives don't even lend sewing machines to one another without payment. I have a sister-in-law who has a machine, but she won't let my daughters use it unless I pay."

But day in and day out co-operation was much more common in the community than conflict. Conflict was more colorful, it varied the ordinary routine for participants and observers, and it brought to the surface many causes of minor irritation. The character of village life, however, called for continued interchange of labor, implements, and even work animals.

At breakfast one morning Bai Penko told me that I had better go down to the school meadows if I wanted to see something interesting. The dog days had come. The peasants would do no work of their own during three of these days because of their firmly rooted superstition that fire would later destroy whatever they did. If they should use these days for getting in their own hay, it would probably burn during the autumn. Some imaginative leader had taken advantage of this traditional idleness by proposing that every family send a member down to the school meadows to mow and stack the hay which was later to be sold for the benefit of the local school. The villagers obliged with the mental reservation that it was no concern of theirs if the school's hay burned before it could be sold to the commission merchants.

Even before I had finished my pale cocoa made of sheep's milk, some of the tavern faithful began to drift in. It was already hot outside, so hot that the men rejoiced because they did not have to go down to the meadow in the broiling sun. One patriarch had trouble persuading a daughter-in-law to represent the family, but she had agreed to go if he would buy her the pair of new shoes he had been promising her; another said his son wanted to go because he thought it would be more fun down there than hanging around the house. Such remarks as these spurred me on my way.

I had gone only a hundred yards before I caught up with a housewife headed for the meadow, a wooden pitchfork over her shoulder. She was not looking forward to the toil ahead of her, because she wanted to work in her vegetable garden, dog days or no dog days.

Even before I reached the group I saw them hard at work. Rows of men were wielding scythes, rhythmically and unhurriedly advancing together without leaving an erect blade of grass between them.

Women, their kerchiefs loosely drawn over their heads, turned the swaths of hay that had been curing. The younger people, displaying an amazing amount of energy and enthusiasm in such sultry weather, collected the dried grass first in small piles, next in larger piles, and then several joined forces to scoot these heaps of hay across the field to the nearest stack. This scooting was the center of the day's hilarity, for it was always accompanied by shouts of triumph ("Look what a big pile we have"), and warning ("You'd better get out of our way; we're coming"). The scoot usually ended in several youngsters taking a terrific tumble, but they did not seem to mind falling in the sweet-smelling new-mown hay.

The large stacks conveniently placed around the forty-acre meadow were dressed without a wasted movement by men who remained on top and were lifted higher as the stack grew in size. By the end of the afternoon some of the stacks had grown so large that the men on top had to be helped down.

A little before lunch time the priest and the mayor came strolling across the fields swinging their canes like true intelligentsia. They exchanged friendly comments with all the people they passed. They continued on across the meadow to a tavern on the Sofia road, returning eventually with two jugs of *rakiya* and a bag of fruit for those who spurned brandy.

Lunch time was quiet except when some boy played a trick on a dozing neighbor and got an angry protest in exchange. The only shade was directly next to the stacks, so most of the people had to endure the sun even while they rested. Trees were a mile away. As the afternoon wore on, the desire to get a big patch finished overcame the natural fatigue setting in. The captains, appointed by the mayor to control the activities of the people from their respective neighborhoods, stirred up the spirit of competition, and the stacks grew larger and larger. At length all the cut hay had been piled and we began to leave the field as the sun was setting behind the mountain. The towering stacks stood motionless, symbolic of that co-operation which is the heart of communal life everywhere.

CHAPTER IV

THE GOOD OLD DAYS

THE DRAGALEVTSY of 1937 had much in common with the Dragalevtsy of the past centuries. The dances, the homes, and the
farm practices proved that. The differences were also marked. For
instance, a crude but efficient means of population control in the
good old days was the killing off of the old people when they had
passed the period of active usefulness. That at least was the theme
of an old folk tale still current in the village. "It so happened that
one spring the people discovered that they had saved no grain for
sowing. The king sent men everywhere in search of grain, only to
see them return empty-handed. One son, who at considerable risk
to himself had kept his aged father alive, secretly hidden in his home,
told him of the people's distress. The old man said: 'Tell the
people to go to the ant hills for grain.' Some of the men followed
this suggestion and found the grain they were hunting. When the
king learned that an old man had told them where to look he ordered
that the aged should not be killed for their disability but should be
kept alive and respected for their wisdom."

Just at what time this story became a part of the folklore was
difficult to determine, because of the numerous racial mixtures which
the people represent. The Pechenegi, according to all accounts, might
have been the ones who practiced this parricide. They got themselves
into the history books by driving the Magyars (the modern Hun-
garians) westward from what is now Russia in the latter part of the
ninth century. For about two hundred years more they, allied first
with one prince and then with another, raided tribe after tribe and
lurked near important trade routes. In 1091 the Pechenegi who had
survived previous setbacks were finally destroyed by the Crusaders
under Peter the Hermit, and little was heard of them after that.

One account in the *Encyclopaedia Britannica* describes their nomadic existence and the camps they formed out of rings of wagons. "They wore long beards and mustachios, and were dressed in long kaftans. The food of the wealthy was blood and mares' milk; of the poor, millet and mead. They were originally 'magicians', i.e., fire-worshippers; but a form of Islam early became current among them, and the nation was temporarily converted to Christianity in 1007-1008. They were the most dreaded and detested of all the nomads." They were disagreeable in other ways too. But when the writer goes on to describe the *Shopi* of today, the descendants of these Pechenegi, as "despised by the other inhabitants of Bulgaria for their bestiality and stupidity but dreaded for their savagery," I wondered how much he was letting historical antecedents influence his description of the present. He goes on to say: "They are a singularly repellent race, short-legged, yellow-skinned, with slanting eyes and projecting cheekbones. Their villages are generally filthy, but the women's costumes show a barbaric profusion of gold lace." The *Shopi* then have quite a reputation to live up to—bestial, stupid, savage, ugly, filthy, and barbaric in their tastes. Some of these definitely do apply. My version of the *Shopi* necessarily includes some positive as well as negative traits, for I have lived among them and have learned to see their good as well as their bad points.

But I must admit that if one looks to the Bulgarian ancestors of the *Shopi* for the origin of the parricide story, he will also find forebears capable of such a deed. According to Henry N. Brailsford's *Macedonia* the Volga-men, or Bulgarians, "were polygamists, owned slaves, and were accustomed to military discipline. Like the Turks they shaved their heads and wore pigtails. They burned their widows and indulged in human sacrifices." This is not a pretty picture, but one which bears marked resemblances to the accounts of the tribes in western Europe before the spread of civilization to that area.

The killing of feeble parents has been a common practice among nomadic peoples because of the difficulty of caring for the aged and infirm when on the move. The mention of grain in the story quoted above would indicate that the tribe had settled down, and that parricide was by that time an out-of-date practice no longer linked with the precarious economic existence of a wandering people.

But it was a far cry from the cessation of the killing of aged parents to the "Honor thy father and mother" of the Decalogue, which later became a part of the Bulgarian family system. The peasants had another story to explain this dramatic change:

"In the olden days, when fathers died the sons would drag the bodies with a hook to a stream or gully and push the bodies in. One day a middle-aged man returned home from disposing of his father's body in this way, but failed to bring back the hook. Whereupon his own son in greeting him said:

" 'But, father, where is the hook? What will I use when I drag you away?'

"This made the father thoughtful, then remorseful. It was then that he retrieved his father's body and gave it a proper burial. Since then sons have been more respectful."

At any rate, whatever may be the explanation, the patriarchal system with its respect for and obedience to the father won out. Contact with Byzantine culture until the coming of the Turks must have reinforced the Bulgarian father's right to dominate his family. He became more fully acquainted with the *patria potestas* which had been too strongly entrenched in the Roman family system to be forgotten by the Byzantines. Likewise, the patriarchal emphasis of the Old Testament and the Pauline epistles of the New aided in the continuance of male supremacy. It is fascinating indeed to observe the response that the Slavicized Bulgarians made to the Byzantine culture in general. First they opposed cultural assimilation by force of arms; more than once the armies of the Bulgarian kings thundered at the gates of Constantinople in Bulgaria's proud golden age (about 900). Military expeditions, however, proved inadequate, with the result that the Bulgarian leaders sought to build a Slavic culture to rival that of the Greeks. It was this new culture which kept the feeling of national uniqueness alive among the Bulgarians, while other tribes upon entering that region became so thoroughly absorbed into the Byzantine Empire that they ended as curious names of the past with no modern representatives.

Then came the Turks in the fourteenth century to begin a reign which lasted five hundred years. It was in this period, termed by Bulgarians *Igoto* or The Yoke, that Dragalevtsy was supposedly founded.

A pregnant sow was the beginning of it all. At least, so the villagers said. Two or three hundred years ago this particular sow ran away from home and grunted up the mountainside to bear her litter in the brush. Baba Dragana, a widow who owned the animal, after a long search found her on the spot where the village church now stands. Since the old woman could not carry the animals back to her village, just south of Sofia, she built a small hut where she was. She liked the place so much that she decided to stay; finally she persuaded her former neighbors to join her. The Turks who robbed them in the village on the highway, she argued, would not harm them on the mountainside. Besides, there was an ample supply of delicious water near her new shelter. The ten families who joined her began to call the settlement Dragalevtsy in honor of Baba Dragana, and the name has remained to this day.

Baba Dragana was also known for her fiery patriotism, as well as for "eternal beauty, strength, and power," if we are to believe an old folk song. This beauty was noticed by the Turkish Pasha in Sofia, and led to frequent meetings between Dragana and him. Years passed. Dragana lost her beauty but retained her strength and power. One day a Bulgarian shepherd, wounded and beaten, stumbled into her yard. Before he died three days later Dragana learned that Turkish shepherds, enraged because his animals had entered their pastures, had fallen upon him. This was too much for Dragana. She called her sons about her, armed them with pitchforks, and sent them out to avenge the death of a fellow countryman. Blood for blood. A few days later their yard was surrounded by Turkish soldiers who promptly bound the sons and carted them off to Sofia for a summary trial before the Pasha. Death was their sentence. But just before the execution the bold Dragana appeared to ask indignantly if the Pasha knew what he was doing. "These are your sons that you are about to put to death," she said. "If you do not believe me, see how much they resemble you." Confused, the Pasha looked at Dragana's sons, saw the resemblance, and called off the death sentence.

This story, in addition to its glorification of Baba Dragana's love of country at the expense of her morals, gives us a picture of government under the Turks. Despite the claims of some Bulgarian historians, Bulgaria was not badly off before the end of the seventeenth century. It was during the eighteenth and nineteenth centuries that Turkish rule became oppressive in its efforts to stamp out the spread of revolts owing, in no small measure, to the spread of national consciousness among the subject peoples. As a matter of fact, Bulgarian historians deplore more vigorously the actions of the Greek clergy who arranged with the Sultan to collect all religious fees from the people. Whereas the Turks were little interested in mass conversions to Mohammedanism, the Greeks were said to be desirous of so Hellenizing the Bulgarians that they would lose their sense of nationality. These Greek priests, however, had so much contempt for the villagers that they made little effort to influence the peasant population.

This period of bondage to the Turks and the Greek priests must have made the family and the village community much better integrated social units. Struggle with an outsider tends to do that. The peasants put higher walls around their yards so Turkish soldiers would not be attracted by something seen while passing. Girls who went to a friend's home for an evening spinning bee spent the night there rather than risk the possibility of capture by the Turks on the dark way home. Even today this custom persists, perhaps because Dragalevtsy youths occasionally steal their brides. Certainly Turkish influence did nothing to weaken the man's authority; at the same time it probably strengthened monogamy because of the unpleasant association of polygamy with things Turkish.

Many of the older Dragalevtsy residents with whom I talked looked back upon the Turkish rule as preferable to their present lot. They said that they were seldom disturbed by the Turkish officials unless they molested the Turks or were forced to contribute men and materials to the Sultan's army. Of course, the Turkish tax collectors also made their regular visits, at which times many peasants conveniently arranged to be away from home. The villagers occasionally joked about the peasant who climbed a tree to escape the tax collector and had to remain in that uncomfortable predicament for many hours before the visitor left. But the Turks did recognize the traditional form of village government, or government by elders, and let the heads of the zadrugas, or large joint families, run village affairs to their liking. Most of the time, the head of the zadruga had to accept the responsibility for the deeds of all members of his family group.

These zadrugas were little principalities guided by a *stopanin,* usually the oldest male. His word was law; he distributed the work among the men, bought the necessities, sold the produce, and represented the zadruga before the outside world; therefore, the zadruga usually bore his name. Whenever a son, brother, or nephew of the *stopanin* married, he brought his wife back home to become a member of his zadruga. The wife of the *stopanin,* known as the *domakinya,* managed the housework. She kept the women busy making bread, cooking, washing, spinning, and weaving. Everything was owned in common. Work too was done in common, and whatever one earned outside was turned over to the *stopanin* for the common treasury. In return, all the members got clothes and food, which in those days were about all they expected to have.

After the death of the *stopanin,* the members met to select the next most capable male as their leader. At times, the *domakinya* took over the position of responsibility. Such was doubtless what happened in the case of Baba Dragana, or her prototype, since the ending of the word Dragalevtsy would indicate that it had been settled by a zadruga. The old joint family comprised married cousins descended from the same ancestor, with the result that it sometimes numbered as many as one hundred people.

When the older Dragalevtsy peasants talked to me of the zadruga, which persisted as late as 1880 in their village, they showed that wistfulness for the past which runs through the works of many Bulgarian writers. The zadruga was supposed to be a source of plenty and happiness to its members. One aged peasant listed for me the advantages of this joint family over the modern family. First of all, he said, it had great economy. The members had only one lamp, one stove, and one of everything, but now the same number of people living separately require many of each thing. In the second place, there was obedience. The young people respected the old. This made for efficiency, since the *stopanin* was like "a general in the army, directing the young." Finally, he concluded, all the people worked together and could earn more, thus becoming richer.

Even under the Turks the zadruga was passing from the scene because it was too unwieldy to adjust to the economic and social changes taking place. Contributing to its decline was the spirit of independence which stemmed from the French Revolution and eventually reached the Balkans. Greeks, and then Serbs, drove the Turks from their midst and established national independence. In Bulgaria and Macedonia, still under the Turks, the *haidutsi,* or guerrillas, went to the mountains every spring on Annunciation Day to spend the summer warring against their Mohammedan masters. It was this same tradi-· tion which the Yugoslav guerrillas followed in their resistance to the Nazis. This spirit of independence and the other influences from the West led one zadruga member after another to ask for a division of the common property. Usually the older men, brothers or cousins to each other, secured their shares and then established semi-patriarchal families of their own which consisted of their own sons and their sons' families. What had been common land now became the property of the individual families living in dwellings of their own. But more important sociologically than the smaller size of the individual family unit was the changed basis of authority in the family circle.

In the zadruga the head had been an overseer who achieved his position on the basis of age, ability, and special influence in the community at large. He constantly had to exercise care to keep in the good graces of the zadruga members upon whose assent his office was dependent. In this way the patriarchal pattern, although it ran through the zadruga system, was tempered by the control vested in an elected as opposed to an hereditary head. The father of an individual family, on the other hand, felt that his right of dominance was God-given. He, allied with God, invested himself with the lordship and so held his own in spite of personal unworthiness and in spite of dissension and revolt of the subject children. The father was a *paterfamilias,* with a unique concentration of power in his hands. If his grown children did not submit to his control, then they could leave his house but had no means of removing him against his will. Death alone could do that.

Such was the family situation in Dragalevtsy with the coming of liberation after the Russo-Turkish War in 1878. The changes which have occurred in the family since then have been related in no small degree to the political fortunes of Bulgaria. The Bulgarian constitution was drawn up in Tirnovo in imitation of the constitutions of the West, and made Bulgaria a constitutional monarchy with a national parliament. Unfortunately, the new frame of government disregarded many traditional practices of the peasants and sought to impose upon them foreign ideas and strange governmental processes.

In April, 1879, Alexander of Battenberg, who was an officer in the Prussian army and the favorite nephew of Tsar Alexander II of Russia, was elected Prince over the country. In September, 1885, Bulgaria united with Eastern Rumelia, an area which had been placed back under nominal Turkish control by the Treaty of Berlin. Prince Alexander, because he did not collaborate sufficiently with the Russians in their desire to make Bulgaria completely subservient to Russia, was abducted from Sofia and forced to abdicate in 1886. Then the Bulgarian leaders shopped around Europe for another Prince, and finally in 1887 chose Prince Ferdinand of the Saxe-Coburg-Gotha line. He did much to make Bulgaria a stronger state, but he showed poor judgment in ordering Bulgarian troops to attack Serbia, thereby starting the Second Balkan War in which Bulgaria suffered catastrophic defeat at the hands of her former allies in the First Balkan War. In 1918, because he had been a party to the alliance of Bulgaria with the Central Powers in the First World War, he was forced to abdicate in favor of his son Boris.

From her inception as a state Bulgaria tried to make a success of representative government. Men were urged to vote; in fact, they were fined the equivalent of five dollars if they failed to vote. But in spite of the dream of Young Bulgaria at Tirnovo, in spite of her

vibrant youth and living hope, her fling at democracy failed, primarily
because ballots were given to peasants who were not being taught the
meaning of citizenship in a national state.

Those interested in democracy have much to learn from the story
of government in Dragalevtsy.   At the outset the informal rule of
the elders, which had been recognized by the Turks, was replaced by
a commune or *obshtina* with regularly elected officials.   At first these
units included a number of villages.   By 1890 the increase in population necessitated the breaking up of the larger *obshtini* so as to include
only two or three villages.   In other words, the pendulum was swinging
back in the direction of greater local control, the swing being further
accentuated after the First World War.

Political parties grew like mushrooms in Bulgaria.   In 1930 the
country had more than sixteen significant parties; in the village of
Dragalevtsy, with its total population of about sixteen hundred, there
were six important parties with recognized leaders and platforms.   To
be a party leader in the village meant added prestige; to be one in
the city or on a national scale meant power.   In order for a Dragalevtsy
man to become a local party leader he had to be acquainted with important people in Sofia.   Even though he had only one influential
friend in the city, he could persuade this man to come out and help
organize a party.   Other peasants were invited to the organizational
meeting and officers were elected.   Naturally, the one who took the
initiative would be chosen to an important post.   Because of the
multiplicity of parties and the intense strife among them, many people
throughout the country breathed a sigh of relief when the authoritarian
government, which came into power on May 19, 1934, abolished by
decree all political parties and started the practice of appointing university graduates as mayors in villages.   This meant that the head
of the government in a village was not dependent upon the will of
the populace but had to produce results satisfactory to the officials
over him.   The breakdown of the party system was associated,
especially as far as the conservative peasant population was concerned,
not only with forces outside the village but also with the failure of
popular education to develop into "a bulwark of people rule."

The attitude of the peasants toward government dates from the days of Turkish rule, when the chief aim of a citizen was to deceive the tax collector. The same spirit was still prevalent in Dragalevtsy in 1937. Furthermore, government had taken such a large share in the affairs of daily life that the peasants had come to feel that government, rather than individual effort, should introduce any reforms or improvements. Typical attitudes were the following:

"In general we have enough sense to know that government is necessary, but we do not expect any favors from it except to keep peace and order and to settle disputes."

"Government exists primarily to collect heavy taxes for the purpose of paying high salaries to high officials."

"Laws are things to be written in books and not to be obeyed. There are so many laws that we don't know them. The officials don't even know them. So we don't have much faith in laws."

While these political changes were occurring, things were happening to the large individual family which had come into being with the breaking up of the zadruga. Some of the forces had already been at work before the Liberation but became more evident with the westernization of the country. The impact of westernization was shown by the fact that the Bulgarians still said when they were going to western Europe, "I am going to Europe." That is, psychologically they still felt identified with the Near East, although they were more and more exposed to the material achievements of Euro-American culture. Education, whatever may have been its shortcomings, had spread rapidly and brought many individualizing tendencies; there had been an increase in commerce, which made it difficult for large family units to be as self-sustaining as formerly. The wars also, by quickening social mobility, proved harmful to the large families. One of the younger men listening in on a group of old cronies in their endless discussions of the good old days summed up the change:

"During the war [1915-1918] and after, people traveled more to other places and saw how people lived there, so we have become more modern and started dividing our estates according to the fashion. We can now live more quietly and peacefully by living separately."

A daughter-in-law especially disliked to live as a stranger in her husband's paternal home subject to the will of the parents-in-law. Time and time again I heard this opinion clumsily but definitely expressed:

"The large families started to break up after the wars. The chief reason for that was the daughter-in-law. Many of them come from different places and even if they come from the same village, they begin to care more for their own children and to make things for them without the knowledge of the others with whom they are living. This brings trouble among them and so they quarrel. Then they talk to their husbands; finally the brothers, although they love one another, have to separate in order to be at peace."

Ordinarily most men felt that conditions were better before the separation, though the women were more content apart. Ill will and distrust also grew up between the members of the family when some of them who worked as day laborers failed to hand over their entire earnings to the common treasury. In the villages around Sofia several brothers rarely lived together with undivided possessions after the death of their father as they would have done in the days of the zadruga. During 1935, a record year for the division of families in Dragalevtsy, there were 9 cases of estates being broken up, 3 of them the result of the separation of son and father and the remaining 6 involving the separation of brothers. When a large family divided, the younger brother usually remained in the old homestead and assumed the care of the parents.

This change from the large patriarchal family to the small conjugal family was having consequences which few of the peasants realized. For one thing, in comparison with the larger group, the conjugal family, which consists of parents and their unmarried children, has a short life. It ends, in a sense, with the death of one of the marriage partners. This especially affects the rearing of children, who in the olden days grew up with such a bevy of cousins that a special middle name was useful in identifying each child with his particular parents. More specifically each child received a "small" or given name selected by his godparents; as a middle name he automatically added to his father's given name an *ev* or *ov* ("the son of") or, if a girl, an *eva* or *ova* ("the daughter of"). As a last name he would take the larger family name of his father's kinship group. Thus an outsider could immediately place each child not only in the family group as a whole but in the small conjugal group as well. Students of child development have often pointed out the advantage to the child of growing up with a number of intimate contemporaries, as well as having several adults ready to serve as substitute parents whenever occasion demands.

But the change need not be viewed as entirely unfavorable. The smaller family unit was bringing about a more intimate relationship between members, breaking down the formalism between parents and children, and encouraging democratic living.

The good old days, if we are to believe the elders of the village, differed not only in the degree of governmental autonomy in community affairs and a patriarchy in which the young respected the old: occupations too were of a different order.

"Half a century ago there were very few educated people, the chief of these being a priest from the monastery and a teacher. The mayor was an ordinary peasant elected by the town council of twelve people. There was a swineherd, as well as other herdsmen, and five merchants, plus a tanner. Practically all of the people were farmers. There was no dairyman; there was no doctor. All dentistry was done by Turks who remedied an aching tooth by pulling it out. We raised no horses, and an itinerant gypsy smith did all the necessary iron work."

When I asked another man about occupations half a century ago, he added this information:

"It was 'simple business' fifty years ago. There was a teacher for boys in the first and second grades; there was no village tailor, and the single tanner had little work. A priest from the monastery ministered to the people on occasion. We had no tax collector and an illiterate mayor took all the taxes and kept the account on a *rabosh*."

(Here I steered the conversation off the subject of occupations long enough to find out what the *rabosh* was. It was similar to a practice of the Exchequer in twelfth-century England in which accounting was done with pieces of notched wood. Each family had a small piece of wood fitting into another piece kept by the mayor.

The notches in the wood told the financial status of the family as far as the tax money was concerned.)

"There was no barber because shaving and haircutting were done in the home or else by neighbors. When we began to use iron in the wagons, *maistori* came from outside. They also began to help in the building of simple houses. Until their arrival the houses were of straw with no bricks or tiles."

Even half a century ago there were a few young people who wanted to give up agriculture and become artisans, chiefly because there was not enough farm work for all members of the family. But the real shift in the young people's attitude toward farming as an occupation occurred in the 1920's along with the increased importance of the school.

"Formerly we were simple people," my informant concluded. "Now the situation is very different. Many go to study, to be officers and to be priests. Many finish the fifth and sixth class in Sofia. Now young people with ambition can be what they want to be."

One old woman in comparing the present with the period of her childhood said:

"The school is largely responsible for the change. Dragalevtsy would have been the same now as it was fifty years ago if we had had no school. The young people read and write, the discipline is more severe, and the youngsters have to go to school."

Whenever I wanted to stir up a lively discussion at the tavern, or with a group of women spinning thread, or with farmers out in the field, I could rely upon one question to do the trick: "Was life better fifty years ago than it is today?" The oldest person usually led off; after that, the discussion became a verbal free-for-all. Nothing was ever proved to anyone's satisfaction, but it was readily apparent that changes had taken place. The good old days in the opinion of some stood for the best that life had to offer, but others were glad that conditions of half a century ago belonged to the past. Perhaps the village drunk spoke words of wisdom when he finally got the attention of the group long enough to say: "Everything is better now but it is also more difficult." The more I think over that statement the more I feel that the drunk should have been a diplomat.

CHAPTER V

THE COURTSHIP AND WEDDING

WHENEVER I asked a man or a woman "How did you come to marry?" the response was always the same. After an embarrassed laugh, the person would say, "Oh, it's so long ago. I have forgotten. I have not had time to remember such foolish things." Then would come a quick look at me from dark eyes that never seemed to lose their brilliance even when the broad face was sagging, deeply lined with the years. "You really want to know?" First it came haltingly; then soon the man would drop the harness he was mending or the woman would lay aside her distaff to give undivided attention to the story. I needed to do little prompting. My interruptions were usually questions about attitudes toward courtship or marriage in general.

There was never any self-pity, even among those women who had been stolen. Even for them something bright had flashed across their days. And for all—"It was so long ago, I thought I had forgotten. There has been much work." From all their reminiscences, stripped of their meager romance, there emerged the village conception of marriage.

Marriage was expected of young people in Dragalevtsy and was an affair which they usually handled in a matter-of-fact way. The peasant youth did not trouble himself as to whether he should or should not marry. He simply concerned himself, sometimes much and sometimes little, about whom to marry.

A woman who had not married by her twenty-fifth year was considered an old maid. People began to wag their heads and ask: "Why doesn't Vesela marry? She's a nice looking girl. There must be something wrong with her about which we do not know." As a matter of fact, in 1937 there was only one peasant girl over twenty-five unmarried in Dragalevtsy. Because she had a physical deformity her parents had given up all hope of marrying her off since they knew she would be unable to attend properly to her housework and field work. During the first World War there were two old maids in the village who had not been chosen for marriage because each of them had a goiter. A doctor with the German forces cured the goiters and these two unmarried women became desirable prospects, one of them marrying a priest's son in Sofia, one of the highest prizes a village girl could capture in her matrimonial venture.

Since public opinion made life miserable for unmarried women, even a girl of independent temperament looked upon marriage as an inevitable event, especially if she stayed in the village. With men it was different. They could choose to remain unmarried and not lose prestige in the community. People only said: "Well, Asen simply doesn't want to marry. He's a bit shy of skirts, you know."

The young men to whom I talked were outspoken in regard to those qualities which they looked for in choosing a mate: good health, industry, efficiency in the house and field, and proper care of the person. The girls, on the other hand, had little to say regarding the qualities they wanted in a husband. They seemed willing to accept whatever luck brought them. But marry they must.

There were many ways in which the husbands and wives had become acquainted with each other. If both had been born in Dragalevtsy, as was the case with a little more than half the couples, they were already aware of the other's characteristics either through personal acquaintance or hearsay. Many of the married couples had played together as children while tending the cattle in the sun-drenched pastures, only to become distant until most of the adolescent period passed. Then began frequent meetings at the fountain at sunset, shy flirtation at the *horo* and *sedenki,* or rambling conversation on the way to and from the Friday market. At the *sedenki,* held by the young people in various girls' homes on winter evenings, games involving forfeits were played. At one *sedenka* I attended, the girl giving out the penalties sent a couple obviously in love to the dark outdoors "to see what the weather was like." A few minutes later she sent a second couple out to see where the first had gone. All four of the young people came back giggling with excitement. Only in some rare instances had shyness kept the young couple apart in the village until matchmaking elders brought them together on the wedding day.

Old and young alike agreed as to the importance of the *sedenka* as a boy-meet-girl occasion. Even some of the intelligentsia with a nostalgia for the simplicity of their early years in the village talked fondly of these groups in which young people whiled away many hours in common work and merriment. The *sedenka* was the Bulgarian counterpart of our pioneer cornhusking and quilting bee. There, romance as it existed in the hearts of the peasant boys and girls came to the surface and was expressed in such simple acts as the giving of a flower, the kissing of a hand or cheek. These groups, which met in fall and winter, consisted early in the evening only of girls who had been especially invited by the hostess one or two days ahead of time. Two or three hours before the *sedenka* was to begin the girl doing the entertaining had to put on her heavy *kozhuh* and again tour the neighborhood to extend a formal invitation to each guest. When the girls had gathered they immediately began to spin, since work was the pretext for coming together. Sometimes the guests brought their own work, and sometimes they assisted the hostess in carding or spinning her wool. If spinning was the order of the evening, each girl was supposed to average about a pound of rather coarse thread.

As the door was usually locked after the girls were inside, the boys, whose arrival was announced by the barking dogs, had to knock for admittance. The hostess then asked who was knocking, and one of the boys told his name.

"The girls and even the hostess know with which boys he associates and if there is any one of them who is undesirable to some or all the girls, then none of the boys is allowed to enter. Usually, however, if they open to the boys, they will open to all; but if they are not in a good mood [very rarely] then they do not open to any."

A gust of cold, fresh air accompanied the boys' entrance, and activities inside ceased until they had made the rounds, shaking hands with those present. After much squeezing and adjusting each boy found a place to sit, usually next to the girl known to be his favorite.

The coming of the boys might or might not stop the work. Quite often the girls were able to accomplish a great deal in spite of the boys, but usually the entertainment which began soon after the boys arrived distracted the girls from their task. There was much singing. Someone struck up an old ballad and others joined in. Then, after a few more ballads, someone ventured a popular song. I once asked a young woman whether she ever sang any modern songs (knowing well enough that she did). She replied:

"Yes, the Dragalevtsy girls know almost all the popular songs. They hear the boys singing them on the street or at *sedenki* and then ask some boy who is a relative to write down the words. If they see that the song is not appropriate, they will not sing it. They always learn the words of songs and never whistle or 'murmur' [hum]."

I wondered to what extent the patriotic songs in the school were replacing the folk songs. Here is what informants at one *sedenka* said:

"As soon as a girl leaves the school, she does not sing any of the songs learned in school, but starts singing again the old songs that she has learned from the old people. The boys, however, continue to sing the songs, chiefly military, learned in school."

No instrumental music was taught in the school, but the radio was beginning to have some effect on the peasants' choice of music. One man listened to the radio fifteen days, stopping almost all other activity, in order to get the words of a jazz song then popular. These he sang with great gusto to his admiring friends. Many of the young people were becoming ashamed of the old songs and told me that they were out of date. The new popular songs that they learned were contained in *Pesnopoiki* (songbooks) bought for a few cents on market days.

The singing of some particularly lively tune at the evening gatherings might lead to folk dancing in which both the boys and the girls took part. The very foundations of the house seemed to shake as the feet shuffled in time to the music. Parlor games of various sorts, quite similar to those played at a rural church social in America, were frequently played at these *sedenki*. This meant that the girls laid aside their spinning entirely and what started out as a work-bee became entirely a social gathering.

Usually after midnight, the singing at the *sedenka* began to decrease in volume, conversation became dull, and the boys sensed that it was time to go. After their departure the hostess often served refreshments such as a soggy cheese pie *(banitsa)*, and the girls might or might not spend the night. The courting aspect of the gathering was emphasized by the fact that none of the married people of the household, except the mother of the girl acting as hostess, could be present. Even she was absent much of the time in some of the homes.

It was at these *sedenki* that I collected a number of village proverbs, which were a real conversational aid to young people somewhat tongue-tied in mixed company.

"A kind word opens an iron gate."

"God gives but does not drive into the stall."

"A wet person is not afraid of rain."

"Listen much, speak little."

"Short are the legs of a lie."

"Stretch out your feet according to your quilt."

"I am telling your daughter so that daughter-in-law may hear [speaking indirectly]."

"After the rain, a raincape."

"Every pear has a stem."

"Give advice freely but not money."

"The thirsty carry water."

"A dog that barks much puts a wolf in the stall."

Within recent years the *vecherinki* provided young people other means of getting acquainted. The purpose of a *vecherinka*, or evening entertainment in the schoolhouse, was not to get any work done, but to raise money for some worthy cause. The villagers bought tickets to a program of music or drama, provided by both imported and local talent. Auctions and lotteries were features of most *vecherinki*. After the program was over the people joined in dancing: first, for an hour or so, they danced the native *hora*, to be followed, when the old folks

went home, by village versions of western dances. It was a strange
sensation on these occasions to see fifty young people trying to do
the fox trot, when it was obvious that not more than five couples were
experienced at it. But those who knew were patient with the novices.
The excited faces were flushed not with the interest in learning a new
step but rather with the daring of the dance's embrace. I asked quite
a few of my acquaintances how they felt about these dances. Most of
the older people who had seen the modern dances and many of the
younger people considered them very immoral. In the words of one
of these conservatives, "The boys especially are eager to learn a
modern dance so that they can do very immoral things, which are very
sweet for the young."

Although these evening entertainments had less importance in
the social life of the people than the *sedenki* or the promenade, the
villagers were proud of them as a formal medium of recreation in
imitation of what one would find in a city. It was a new experience
for many men to buy a ticket and be shown a seat; and such new
experiences were dear to a peasant heart if they did not take him too
far away from the ordinary world in which he moved. The first
vecherinka was given in 1925. The teachers after that tried to give
one or two more, but no one attended, so the practice was discon-
tinued. In 1930, however, the *Chitalishte* (Reading Room Association) started them again, with the result that in the following years
four or five were held during a winter.

Another innovation which played an important part in Dragalevtsy
courtship was the Sunday afternoon promenade, which had displaced
the traditional Sunday *horo*. The promenade course extended from
Renaissance Square up a rocky street which bends to the left for a
quarter of a mile. Here the young people in their Sunday best turned
about and retraced their steps to the Square. One reason for the
popularity of the promenade was its modernity; another was the
absence of a church ban against it during Lent in contrast to the traditional interruption of *hora* during that seven-week period.

Even in the promenade there was no pairing off except in the
case of some engaged couple. Indeed, walking in a twosome was
tantamount to announcing an engagement. So village boys in twos,

threes, and fours passed village girls locked arm in arm; appropriate (and inappropriate) comments were made as they passed. Up and down they went, greeting each other again and again, joking, blushing, laughing heartily, each wondering at the impression made upon some favorite member of the opposite sex.

These modern ways contrasted sharply with the laconic statements of those villagers who had married many years ago.

"When we grew older we began to know each other more intimately and went together for two or three years."

"We were neighbors before marriage. We met every holiday at the *horo* and in the evenings at the fountain. Our wedding festivities lasted three days."

"My wife and I knew one another as children. Outsiders urged both of us to marry, so I stole her. She would not agree to marry me until after I had stolen her."

Often the relatives of the couple involved kept saying that it would be a good thing to have the two persons married, and thus brought about a match they considered advantageous.

In Dragalevtsy human nature asserted itself in universal forms; for example, a village Lothario boasted:

"I had had thirty-five girls, and had gone 'hand-in-hand' with one for two years. But I fell in love with my wife because she was modest and had not talked to boys."

I might add here that the parents of the girl objected to the match, but only because she was taller than her suitor.

Two-fifths of the Dragalevtsy-born men, in their search for a wife, preferred the novelty that other villages afforded. More often than not a Bulgarian youth would all of a sudden get a fixed idea in his mind, "I've got to get a wife." The search was then under way. In such a state of mind the young man was not apt to wander far. The villages in their order of popularity were Boyana, Simeonovo, and Bistritsa. Only two other villages had more than four representatives among the married women. These likewise were not far away. It was significant that no man born in Dragalevtsy and currently living there had a wife born in Sofia. This meant that if a Sofia-born girl should marry a Dragalevtsy boy, she would make him get a job in Sofia and would not return with him to village life.

When a husband and wife born in different villages told their stories I once more began to believe in the improbable. These are typical accounts:

"I went to Kumaritsa to carry my sister's things since her husband was working at the railroad station. We stopped at a house where a niece was living with her uncle. When she heard that people from another village were at her house, she returned and found that she liked me and I liked her. We were both seventeen. Half a year later we married, during which time I came to see her only once. That means we had seen each other twice before we married."

"I met my wife when she was with her father selling onions near the Sofia *Obshtina*. This was on a Friday; the next day I went to get her from her village the other side of Sofia; the following day we were married in Dragalevtsy. The father agreed to this for I seemed to be her destiny."

The choice of a mate was not just an individual decision in Dragalevtsy, for the pressure on the part of relatives was steady and occasionally severe. At times the young people rebelled at this guidance but generally acquiesced, largely because they were so economically dependent upon their families. There were no professional matchmakers. In their stead some interested relative would take a hand at getting a daughter married off by seeing that a fitting young man was made conscious of the young woman's qualifications. This was often done so skillfully that the young man thought he had discovered the girl himself. In the 1930's the choice had to seem to originate with the young people, and there were few cases of families forcing their children into a marriage.

There were times when girls did marry against their will, but this was not because of parental command. These cases occurred when the bride was stolen without her consent. The actual stealing usually took place in the evening or late afternoon when the young man, assisted by companions, carried the girl from the fountain or the *horo* to his home. The girl's father was supposed immediately to hurry to the boy's home to ask if his daughter was willing to stay. The girl

"Zhenska rabota, woman's work" (whitewashing). *See page 53.*

"The school is largely responsible for the change." *See page 72.*

". . . a wedding was a village affair . . ." *See page 85.*

usually answered "Yes," since she had very little choice in the matter, even though she might be in love with someone else. One sixteen-year-old girl whom I knew had gone to Sofia to live until she was seventeen, when she married a young butcher there. Her family feared that if she had stayed in the village she would have been stolen by a local boy and been unable to marry the one upon whom she had set her heart. The stealing of the bride was a very common practice in the past, became incorporated in the marriage ritual, and was being revived for economic reasons during the period I studied Dragalevtsy. A stolen bride did not have to be married from her house with all the customary expensive ceremonies. She was married from the groom's house much more simply. Whether the bride agreed to a prearranged stealing or was the victim of a young man's sudden impulse, once she was taken to his home she dared not spurn his offer and return to her people. If she did, she would be in disgrace, with little possibility of a subsequent marriage.

Some of the stolen brides described their experiences in simple, matter-of-fact terms:

"In 1930 a group of us girls from Bistritsa had gone to the Monastery to card wool, and stayed there for a week. Some of the young bachelors from Dragalevtsy came up to see us two or three times and were with us for a long period on Sunday. My husband saw me working, liked me, and decided to capture me. He, with seven friends, waited outside the Monastery from eight o'clock to midnight knowing that I would have to go outside before going to bed. I came out with a *baba* [old woman] whom the boys frightened away with their guns; then I was taken down to Dragalevtsy. When we got to his home his mother and sisters met me in the yard with bread and salt ['so she wouldn't enter the house with empty hands,' interpolated the mother-in-law listening to the account]. The next day girls from Bistritsa went home and told my brothers that I had been stolen; they came here at eight o'clock that evening. I kissed their hands, gave them something to eat, and then they asked me if I wanted to stay or go back with them. I decided to stay, so they returned home."

The villagers described another traditional way of obtaining a bride, but I found that few young couples observed it. It involved a formal visit from some member of the boy's family, who brought the girl a hearthcake. If she and her parents accepted the proposal, the cake was eaten; then there was music and a general celebration. If the girl accepted but the parents did not agree, the guests went back home and sometime later on the girl ran away with the boy. Sometimes the girl knew the boy was sending a committee to ask for her hand; quite often she did not know. At times the young man himself made the request of the girl's father:

"We had known each other from childhood. He left bread and money for me to accept or reject, but my father turned him away, partly because I wanted to marry someone else in Simeonovo. He came, however, with three men, stole me, and wouldn't let me go."

A shy suitor acted differently:

"I was afraid to ask for her hand for fear she would refuse, so I got some older people to ask her married brothers, who agreed. Her parents were both dead and her brothers had been very strict with her, not allowing her to go to any *sedenki*."

This last incident illustrated the popular idea that village young people are loath to discuss love and marriage with each other and do so by means of third parties. Such traditional going around Robin Hood's barn was being subjected to heavy strain by the young generation and, in fact, had always had its exceptions. "Stealing the bride" when both parties were in agreement is more correctly termed elopement; if the girl did not consent and the boy did not have the permission of her parents, then it was a case of actual stealing. Examples of elopements are:

"We were both from this village and had met at the fountain. We associated for two or three years, and one day while back on leave from the army I stole her with her agreement and then returned to the army. She stayed with my mother until I was again on leave a month and a half later, at which time we married."

"She was from Simeonovo and I met her one day as she was carrying nuts to the Friday market. Her father was a very unsympathetic man and did not approve of the match, so she ran away with me to Dragalevtsy, where we married and settled down in my father's home."

The girls of Dragalevtsy had no way of proposing to a boy. The girl waited and, if nobody proposed to her, she remained unmarried.

Sometimes unmarried young people had sexual intercourse. If the boy did not want to marry the girl, then she told her parents; the boy was brought before the *Obshtina* and, if the charge was proved, was made to marry the girl. As one peasant said in matchless understatement: "In such cases they do not have a happy life."

One such case occurred during my sojourn in the village and was an exciting topic of conversation. A girl with an unsavory reputation, in the hope of gaining a certain young man as a husband, accused him of having had intimate relations with her; the parents, too, insisted upon his marrying their daughter. He refused and the matter was taken up before the village court, where several of his friends swore that they likewise had had intimate relations with the same girl. Whether the friends swore truthfully or falsely was still a matter of doubt in the minds of many villagers, but the young man was freed from all responsibility in the matter.

Chastity ranked high in the scale of village social values. Even though some couples had illicit relationships before they married, they were running a grave social risk. Public indignation was especially great in the case of illegitimacy. A girl giving birth to an illegitimate child was forced to leave the village. On this subject I had the following conversation with one of the more respected villagers:

"Where does the girl go if she is driven out of the village?"

"She goes to Sofia because she's a bad girl."

"Do the villagers try to find out who the father was and punish him for his part?"

"The father? Why should they? The girl is to blame, not the man."

"Are many illegitimate children born in the near-by villages?"

"In my time [the last thirty-five years] there have been two in Bistritsa, one in Dragalevtsy, and none in Simeonovo."

There was no particular stigma attached to being a widow or a widower, but the village mores decreed that, when remarrying, widows had to choose widowers, and vice versa. The explanation for this went back to the villagers' belief of the afterlife. They thought of

Heaven in concrete terms and believed that husbands and wives would be reunited there. Things would work out quite well mathematically if a widow and widower remarried each other, since in Heaven each mate would go to the first spouse, thus avoiding the unheavenly complication of a second mate left alone for eternity. For a second wife, they listened to the recommendations of neighbors far more than they did when marrying the first time. This was borne out by the testimony of a woman I found picking berries from a bush that overhung a garden wall. While speaking to me she kept a watchful eye turned toward the near-by house in fear that someone would tell her to leave the berries alone. "How did you happen to marry Nikola?" I asked her. Like the other women she seemed to welcome a chance to talk about herself.

"For three years I was a widow in Simeonovo before somebody recommended me to my present husband, at that time a widower living here in Dragalevtsy. One day he came over to Simeonovo, looked me up, and asked me to marry him. I accepted right away although I had never heard of him before. Winter was coming on and I didn't have any money to buy food for myself and my little boy. I went immediately home with him and lived with him as his wife for two months before we were married."

Her second husband was one of the poorest men in the village, and her life was decidedly unhappy; yet to the village way of thinking, she was better off than as a widow.

Most of these second marriages turned out successfully provided the question of stepchildren could be satisfactorily settled. Sometimes fathers sent away their own children to a relative and gladly took in those of the second wife. Quite often the children of both the husband and wife were brought up together as one family. A second wife was generally anxious to have children by her second husband in order to ensure her place in his affections, especially if she had children by her first husband who ate up the food and wore the clothes provided by their stepfather.

Widows and widowers were permitted by public opinion to live together as though they were married for awhile before the actual ceremony took place. This above all else emphasized the fact that second marriages were entered into because of convenience and necessity. But such tolerance was not shown to the previously unmarried.

In Dragalevtsy children married according to age, the oldest first. If a younger child wanted to marry before his brother, he had to buy permission, but in no case was a son or daughter supposed to have the customary wedding celebration before an older sister married, the only chance being an elopement followed by a very simple ceremony.

Most girls and men in Dragalevtsy married between the twentieth and the twenty-fifth year. At the time of the last census (1934) there were only one married man and eighteen married women under twenty. Men had begun to marry later than they had ten years before, although there seemed to be no such well-defined trend for the women.

Since marriage was the normal channel for sex expression, an enamored couple thought readily of a wedding. When they reached an understanding, they considered themselves engaged and sought parental approval. Of the thirty representative families that I studied, eighteen, or more than half, were engaged one week. Only two couples were engaged for longer than two weeks.

The engagement did not grant the couple any privileges of intimacy; indeed, the boy was not allowed to visit with the girl until the wedding. His sisters and relatives went to call upon her, or, if she had been stolen and was in his home, his parents kept the girl away from him until the day of the wedding. Therefore, the engagement period did not give the young couple any chance of getting better acquainted; it simply gave the families an opportunity to prepare for the wedding a week later. Whenever a wedding was to take place, someone usually sent a message to me at the College, and if possible I attended. As a foreigner I was attracted to those customs that were bizarre; so to offset this I persuaded three peasants of different ages and from different families to give me separately a complete description of the typical wedding. This showed me which points they thought most important and served as a check to my observations.

A wedding was a village affair, the parents of the girl inviting all of those who had previously invited them as well as those whose invitations they would like to receive. This meant the laying in of large quantities of wine and *rakiya,* the hiring of musicians from Sofia, and the baking of many pies and loaves of bread. Of course, the women of the neighborhood shared in the excitement by helping both the parents of the bride and of the groom.

Before the church service all of the young people who could find a wagon went to the bride's house, and after certain formalities took her possessions to the home of the groom. The bony horses raced around the curves in a cloud of dust while the boys cracked whips and shot guns. The procession to the church went first to the home of the godparents, a point of special honor, then to the home of the groom, and finally to that of the bride. As in America, there was room for great variety in wedding procedures, according to the amount of money the families could afford to spend.

Another important aspect of a village wedding was the custom of presenting important guests with some sort of garment. The groom's family gave a shirt, a belt, or a handkerchief to each of its close relatives, but the bride had to have something ready for the relatives of both families. When she was eight or nine years old she began preparing these numerous presents, doing them all by hand. In return she received a small sum of money from each person she honored. At the first weddings I attended I failed, through ignorance of the custom, to live up to my part of the bargain, but that seemed to make no difference in the way the people felt toward me. They never came to remind me of the oversight, because with natural courtesy they did not want to make me, a guest, feel uncomfortable or embarrassed. One evening when I was visiting one of the families I knew best, I asked a twenty-year-old girl to show me her hope chest containing the presents that she intended to give away as well as those garments that she planned to keep for her own use. This is what the chest contained:

25 pairs of socks knitted by the girl
55 long white shirts of homespun cloth (half to be given away)
35 homespun belts to be given to unmarried men
15 face towels
15 headkerchiefs worn by married women
20 *sukmani,* or black jumper dresses (most to be kept by the girl)

This girl was by no means from a rich household.

The church ceremony always took place on Sunday if neither the bride nor groom had been married before. On Saturday the groom, bearing up fairly well under the good-natured jibes of the officials and his friends, went to the *Obshtina* for a license. A little after sunset the intimate friends of the bride and groom carried water from three different fountains to the bride. After the first two trips she poured the water brought to her onto the ground, but when the company returned from the third fountain she kept the water to heat later on for washing her hair. I shall never forget accompanying a group of young people on such an occasion. The bride was from a distant village, had come to Dragalevtsy to help harvest grain, and had been stolen by one of the young men. She, of course, was taken straight to his home, whereupon the boy's father started on the thirty-mile journey to visit the girl's parents to get her hope chest and wedding finery. The girl herself had no chance to go home for a farewell visit, nor did she have a single friend with her for the wedding. She was a sad little figure that Saturday evening as she received the water from these kind but strange young people. We were all excited because the boy's father had not yet returned from the girl's home. As everyone expected a favorable reply, wedding preparations went on without any delay; but there was always the possibility, however slight, that these preparations might be in vain.

When the father did return with the consent of the girl's family, the wedding followed the usual procedure. Sunday was the big day, with the *horo* set for the morning. I left my room at the tavern about nine o'clock, after breakfasting on sliced bread, white cheese, and linden-leaf tea provided for me by Bai Penko. The *horo* had not yet begun, so I talked with the groom's father for more than an hour on the sunny porch. The bride was being dressed in a room on the first floor; women bustled in and out carrying garments, water, combs and brushes, and ribbons. Upstairs the groom was being shaved and spruced to the accompaniment of considerable horseplay. There was a noticeable difference of atmosphere in the two quarters: great solemnity and a certain sadness pervaded the lower room; hilarity, aided by considerable drinking, rang out from above. Several women who

were busily preparing the big meal to be served after the church ceremony every now and then rushed out with something for me to taste,
with the groom's father insisting that I sample some of the choice
wine or brandy purchased just for the wedding.

The dance I had come to see did not begin until afternoon. It
lacked the enthusiasm which I had learned to anticipate, but was
nevertheless colorful: the girls and women wore their most beautiful
costumes; the men were neatly dressed, some in army uniforms; the
leader of the *horo* carried the Bulgarian flag of white, green, and
red, taking care that it did not catch in the overhanging branches.
(In time of war the colors are reversed with the red bar on top.) This
dance really was the prelude to the gay procession which headed for
the church about two-thirty. First came the musicians with their
battered instruments; then the principals of the wedding, followed by
the guests. The flag was there, as well as Bulgarian tricolor sashes
over the shoulders of the men.

Ordinarily the bride was a gay figure in the procession, her
somber black overdress brightened with huge silver belt buckles and
cherished strings of thin gold coins handed down for generations
from mother to daughter. Hair and face shining with cleanliness,
she moved in her wedding procession, happy, although considerably
confused by her prominent position. But this particular bride had
no ornaments—(Had her parents refused to send them?)—except
a flower over her ear and the usual short, coarse white veil on her
head. She did have on real leather shoes, instead of the customary
pigskin sandals, but that was the only elaboration of her costume. It
was hard to get her to smile for her picture; but when her new brother
and sister each took an arm to encourage her, the broad, rather dull
face suddenly lit up and a pair of beautiful dark eyes looked shyly at
my camera.

All the village turned out to see the procession pass. Swarms of
children came racing down the principal streets at the sound of the
music. Once we had entered the churchyard I learned that they were
there to scramble for the candy and coins which were thrown in the
air along with rice to symbolize sweetness, wealth, and productivity.
But this came at the end of the ceremony, and the children stood

closely packed in the church as the wedding party entered to face the altar before a table in the center of the church.

The bride and groom had no more than taken their stand when a middle-aged woman hurried to place dough baked in the form of a male phallic symbol deep in the sash worn by the bride and another piece to represent the female organs around the waist of the groom. This was done half surreptitiously while the priest was busy about something else.

As the ceremony began I realized as never before the important part played by godparents in the ritualistic and spiritual life of the village. They stood behind the bride and groom, who were attended by the groom's brother as *dever,* or best man. The young couple shifted from foot to foot, each holding a bunch of flowers in one hand and a large burning taper in the other. The priest read from the Bible in his beautiful rich tones about the wedding at Cana of Galilee, and then asked God's blessing upon the couple.

At this point the priest stepped out of his role and said to me: "Would you like to take a picture now?" Then when I was set for a time-exposure, he said to the crowd: "Everybody, quiet!" My act done, he told the godparents to assist in the changing of the rings from bride to groom, as well as the fragile, bright crowns previously placed upon the heads of the couple. In addition, the priest, as part of the ritual, passed around the chalice so the young couple, the best man, and the godparents could sip the wine. These same people then followed the priest in a walk around the table on which a cross and the Holy Scriptures rested. Three times around they went, stopping four times during each circuit to symbolize north, east, south, and west. At each of these twelve stops the party bowed over the table and its sacred relics. It was during this walk that the godmother tossed the rice, candy, and coins in the air for the children.

Such a brief account fails to include much of the liturgy which was an important part of the Orthodox Church's ceremony, but the peasant accounts of a wedding skimmed over this as being either unimportant or else a topic about which they were uninformed. In fact, most of the men accompanying the bridal party to the church remained outside during the ceremony. The parents of the groom

had no important part to play, and, of course, the parents of the
bride did not attend because of the distance.

The musicians began to play as soon as they saw the people
coming from the church, and the procession formed again and went
back to the groom's home over a different route, for it was considered
unlucky to retrace the route. Back at the house a *horo* began with the
liveliness I had always associated with the wedding dances. While
many of the guests danced, others with special invitations went into
the house to eat what had been so laboriously prepared over open
hearths and sheet metal stoves. About dark the young couple were
led to their room and left alone with the best man on guard by the
door. An old custom, now falling into disuse, required the groom
after intercourse to present the undergarment of the bride to the best
man as a proof of her virginity. In the old days this was passed from
guest to guest in a flour sieve so that all could be personally assured
of the fact. But in the case of this young couple that custom was
not observed. Word did get around that the groom was satisfied
with his bride; if he had not been, then she could have been sent
home in disgrace and the wedding called off—that is, provided he
had not been guilty of previous incontinence with her. The groom's
parents in their joy passed "sweet brandy" around for all the guests
to drink.

Early in the morning the bride came out for the rest of the ceremonies. She was taken to the chopping block underneath the nut
tree to demonstrate her ability to wield the axe. The godmother then
took her bridal veil, wound it on a stick, and touched some of the
other village girls in the belief that they would soon get married.
In place of the veil the godmother tied a kerchief, brown in this case,
over the girl's head to show that the wearer was married. The bride
was then sent to the fountain for water of which all had to drink. The
musicians were aroused from their befuddled sleep and told to strike
up some lively music; the blaring horns and the beating drum woke
the whole neighborhood, and then the whole village, as another procession began. This time all were headed for a wedding breakfast at
Bai Penko's tavern, where they sat outside, just beneath my window.
The first thing I noticed was the brown kerchief which, with the cheap

gold ring on her finger, symbolized what a tremendous change had taken place in the life of the bride. A week before she had been a girl gathering wheat in the company of other girls; now that kerchief separated her from these former friends and meant that she was a daughter-in-law in a strange home, in a strange village, married to a strange man. But for this she had been born; there was no reason or precedent to complain, no matter how disturbed her emotions might be.

CHAPTER VI

MARRIAGE

THE BULGARIAN groom settled down naturally into the role of the married man as the embarrassment of the first few days of good-natured joshing wore away. He took less and less interest in the Sunday afternoon promenade, preferring to sit in front of the tavern with the other married men where he liked to be complimented on the woman he had chosen in the same way that he would appreciate compliments on a cow just bought. However, as marriage progressed he began to respect his wife as a person rather than as a possession.

It was when the first child arrived, in a year or so, that the husband suddenly felt a sense of tremendous importance. He was no longer just a married man; he was a father. Though the beginning of married life had little effect upon his behavior, the fact of parenthood changed even his facial expression, his earnestness in his work, and his whole attitude toward the future. I sensed this often in the requests that people made for photographs. Few young men came to ask for pictures of their brides; but many wanted pictures of their infants, especially of the sons. In the case of the first child they would hold him up squarely in front of the camera so that he would fill up the whole picture if possible. But as children continued to arrive year after year, the fathers often asked, "Could we get our new oxen into the picture too?"

Most of the men accepted marriage as they did the weather: inevitable, sometimes balmy and sometimes disagreeable, but utterly essential. They did not go out of their way particularly to adjust themselves to marriage, and spoke little of marriage. They patiently waited for parenthood, which was revolutionary in its effect upon them.

With women it was quite different, since marriage for them called for major adjustments. Not only did the wife have to become accustomed to the demands and habits of her husband, but she also had to fit into the routine of her husband's parental home. In some cases she had to subordinate herself to other daughters-in-law in the household. Should she and her husband live in a separate dwelling near the husband's childhood homestead, she still was so subject to the scrutiny of the in-laws that she found it expedient to conform to their ways of doing things.

The woman, much more than the man, had to give up the companionship of her former friends to move in the group of the married women of the neighborhood. In these groups she was initiated into much of the folklore about anatomy, conception, childbirth, and child care. The frank discussion by various women of their personal experiences was enough to make any squeamish girl terrified at the very thought of becoming a mother. Continued discussion, however, made the experience eventually seem less of an ordeal; in fact, it was often a source of comfort and encouragement when her time arrived.

These neighborhood gossiping groups did much more than shock the girl into some of the realities of married life; they also informed her of the personal peculiarities of her in-laws and neighbors; they let her know what she should and should not do. And if she was one of the first of her circle of friends to marry, she could look forward to the day when one or two of them would become brides in the vicinity and could join her in the company of these older married women.

The role of these women's groups in the village was interesting and far more important than the surface informality would indicate. Recreation for the older women was generally tied up with work. Distinctions, however, should be made between the women's work groups, such as those for spinning and carding, and women's gossiping groups, in spite of the fact that the membership was the same in both groups and that gossiping was the chief recreation in both instances. In the work groups, the women were invited formally by the hostess, were fed, and were expected to stay most of the day, definitely to work. Gossiping groups, however, were much more informal, since people

came together without an invitation. If it was a workday, a few
women of the neighborhood gathered in one of the yards to spin, sew,
or knit. If it was a holiday, they simply talked. The village women
spoke of it as getting together "to laugh, to be merry." The women
gathered in twos, threes, or more, almost entirely on a neighborhood
basis. If relatives were in the neighborhood, they were included, but
because they were neighbors, not relatives. Seldom did relatives from
other sections of the village attend. Among some women it was the
practice to go only when invited, however informally. As one woman
said:

"We take our work along. If there is anything to eat, we eat.
Age makes no difference. It is seldom that an unmarried girl par-
ticipates in a group with married women, because the married women
talk about things which a girl should not be permitted to hear. A
girl would be allowed to stay with the women only if the discussion
is not of a kind bad for her." She went on to add that the young and
old people customarily did not mix in conversation. "The old have
little to say which interests the young, so then they begin to give
advice and the young people run away."

I met five women varying in age from thirty-three to sixty-six talking one Sunday on the street corner. Some of the women had taken
off their shoes and were standing in the brook beside the road. This
group had a decided neighborhood basis. When I asked how these
five women happened to get together, this was the explanation:

"Slavina came to ask Geny about a sick neighbor across the street.
Maria saw them talking and came over to hear what the news was.
Stenna, who lives up the street, also came, and after her the other
Maria."

They had been talking there for almost an hour before I came
and were still talking an hour after I left, as I saw on my return
to the College. Since it was Sunday they were doing no handwork,
but said that often during the week they gathered to help one another
spin, hoe corn, and harvest. One said to me, "We live together."
Even in the wintertime they went around to visit, to inquire if the
friends had enough wood to see them through the winter, if the cow
was still sick, how much the taxes had been. Of all the women Geny

did the most talking. The women found it difficult to say which one helped the others most, because "this depends so much upon one's special knowledge of cooking, caring for the sick, and sewing." Each woman was expert in a different line, but all were willing to help in any way.

The distinction between age groups broke down when the group was hard at work, as the work was then more important than the flow of gossip. In general, the gossiping groups got together more frequently in the summertime and on Sundays. Women found their chief recreation with women, and men with men, though the men said they needed the stimulation of tavern society.

This willingness of the men to spend money for recreation and to limit their wives to the questionable joys of gossip illustrated the common saying, "Bulgaria is a man's country." A Dragalevtsy peasant saw nothing strange in the sight of a man riding a donkey while his wife trudged along behind carrying their purchases home from market. Or if a man returned alone from market, having ridden all the way in his wagon, his wife, tired from a day in the field, went out to carry in his things, saying, "He's weary and needs my help." She was always careful to make no queries about the day's activities, although she might be bursting with curiosity to know what had happened at market. She went about her work and waited until he was comfortably fed and settled, knowing full well that then she would have a complete report. Usually her husband made himself out to be the hero of each little episode, but "men are like that," she would say.

The well trained wife always deferred to her husband. If ever I asked a question in the presence of both, the woman turned her eyes to see what response her husband made. If he made a gesture as though to say, "You go ahead and answer," then she began to talk, becoming silent whenever her husband wished to interject any comments.

What was even more conclusive proof that Bulgaria was a man's country, and certainly that Dragalevtsy was a man's village, was the obedience of women to their husband's command. I asked thirty wives in the course of my family interviews:

"Suppose you wanted to go to market some Friday and your husband thought you ought not to go, what would you do?"

Not a single wife would dare go to market under these circumstances. Two or three said, "I wouldn't even start for the door."

"But suppose you wanted to make some small purchases in the city and your husband disapproved, what would you do?" Only two daring ones out of the thirty said they would make these purchases if they had money.

It paid the women to "behave," because the husband did have the right to beat a disrespectful wife. I never happened upon a wife-beating, but the fact that a few husbands told me with pride, "I never beat my wife," showed me that they considered themselves exceptional.

A wife who received rough treatment, especially if her husband had been drinking, could go to her father's home. She could not stay there very long after her mate had become sober, because her father and the village in general made her feel that her place was with her husband no matter how disagreeable he might be. Usually she waited until her husband came with a meek promise of good behavior to ask her to come back.

In those formal ways a village wife showed respect to her husband. She did not, most of the time, find them burdensome because she knew nothing else. All of her experiences from childhood to marriage had conditioned her to a subordinate role. Should any woman have tried to rebel against her lot other women would have been her most vigorous critics. They, more than the men, aided in the perpetuation of the existing order.

The woman, however, had a far more important place than the social amenities would indicate. Men frankly admitted that they could not make a living without their wives. This feeling of dependence overshadowed the traditional masculine superiority to the extent that a partnership resulted. The man, to be sure, was the senior partner, but he knew that he was a member of a team in which co-operation was essential.

This deeper sense of partnership was best shown by the practice husbands had of consulting their wives on every matter of importance as well as on minor matters. Out of twenty-six representative cases,

"The musicians [here a *gayda* or bagpipe player] began to play as soon as they saw the people coming from the church." *See page 90.*

"A village bride . . . wearing cherished strings of thin gold coins handed down . . . from mother to daughter." *See page 88.*

"Bulgaria is a man's country."
See page 95.

"The neighborhood gossiping groups did much more than shock the girl into some of the realities of married life . . ." *See page 93.*

nineteen husbands always consulted their wives before doing anything such as selling a calf, hiring a servant, or building a small stable; four husbands consulted sometimes, and only three were so strong-willed and dominating that they never asked their wives' opinions. Many husbands said that their wives knew more than they did about the management of the farm, though these same wives modestly asserted that they knew very little. One man said: "That's why we are married: to ask each other." Quite a few husbands, having learned that it paid in the long run to consult the women, betrayed this by saying, "We have to ask," or "We have to listen to women."

Consulting, however, was not always the same as catering to the wives' wishes. I asked twenty-six husbands: "Suppose you had set your heart on buying something but your wife objected, what would you do?" Twelve said they would make the purchase anyway, three hedged a little in their answers, but eleven would buy nothing contrary to the wishes of their wives. This last group of eleven showed that to many men the judgment or wishes of the women meant far more than one would expect in "a man's country."

Much of a woman's hold upon her husband came about quite unconsciously on the part of either. The village wife was artless and ignorant of the wiles of a sophisticated society, but she knew that as long as she was efficient, decorous, and dutiful she could count upon continued support from her husband. She also knew that she was not in competition with adventuresses or with women, jaded and disappointed, frantically seeking excitement to enliven their days. Instead, the Dragalevtsy woman felt secure. With her there was a solemn finality about marriage to which her husband and others in the village subscribed.

She expected no courteous gestures or terms of endearment from her husband. Her name sufficed. Only three couples out of twenty-seven used affectionate names for each other, these taking such forms as *bulka* (bride), *baba* (old woman), and the like, but never *dear, darling,* or *sweetheart*. One of the three men who used such names saved them for times when his wife did not listen, and then he used several to get her attention. The occidental practice of kissing was little used by the married couples, though the younger generation was beginning to imitate "the people of the world" in this respect. As the psychological aspect of the sexual relationship between husband and wife varied with each couple, no generalization could be made except to point out that sex seemed to be a concomitant of marriage rather than the basis of marriage. Mates were picked by young men more for their potentialities as hard-working farm hands than for their sexual attractiveness. Quite often before marriage a sort of affection had grown up between the couple; more often affection came after marriage and increased as the partnership proved successful and the feeling of mutual dependence deepened.

Most of these couples freely, sometimes jokingly, admitted that they quarreled more or less, even when they were in many respects fortunately adjusted to each other. Nevertheless, in only one-third of the cases did this quarreling lead to a permanent cause of conflict.

The disciplining of children by the husband frequently aroused the wife to indignation, but perhaps not to such a depth as did his late arrival from the tavern in an intoxicated condition. Few Bulgarian men drank to get drunk. Intoxication, when it came, was often the result of overenthusiastic observance of drinking customs. For instance, when men drank in the saloon all of them ordered drink and food not only for themselves but for the whole table, everybody paying for what he had ordered before leaving; the people always toasted health, long life, or happiness when they raised a glass of wine, beer, or whisky, at home, in the tavern, or in the field; at feasts *rakiya* was served before the people began to eat; during the meal they drank wine. A drunken man was sent out of the tavern at closing time, and it was up to him to get himself home, even though he fell down several times en route. If he was having too great a difficulty, some companions might lead him. If they were not around, the policeman or night watchman might act as guide. At his approach, the children hid and the wife became afraid. The villagers said: "Even an insane man runs away from the drunken." Sometimes in order to sober up the drunken man, people put a little urine or horse manure (substances rich with ammonia) in his mouth. The chief complaint the women made against drinking was economic, the spending of money "for nothing," as they said.

Husbands and wives also disagreed frequently over the importance of a certain task, since the husband was likely to order the wife to work in the field when she felt it necessary to complete some task at the house. Money was often a source of conflict. Since all the villagers were members of the same church they rarely argued about religion, the few discussions which did arise being about the desirability or undesirability of church attendance. One of the most significant results of this study of village families was to show how little disagreement there was concerning in-laws, since husband and wife usually stood together as a unit against these outsiders, whether they belonged to her family, his family, or had married their son or daughter.

In spite of these quarrels about discipline, drink, and jobs to be done, most couples considered their marital venture highly successful. I believe that an important reason for the success of marriage in Dragalevtsy was the recognition on the part of husband and wife that even love was not an answer to all of life's problems. They took each day's pleasures and disappointments as they came, rejoicing or sorrowing in quiet unison.

Many times as I listened to the husband or wife gravely narrating with satisfaction and pride the calm and uneventful story of their marriage partnership, details of the room in which we were sitting would strike me with such force that I had to recall myself with an effort to the conversation. We always sat in the best room; sometimes it was the only room. It was always the room where the family lived. The chief furniture was a bed, perhaps two or even three beds. And here two or three couples and their children spent their days and nights. I would try to imagine married life under such circumstances.

Life of any kind became not merely a matter of privacy, but really a problem of where to carry on the necessary daily activities without getting in another's way. And yet, in most of these crowded households the marriage bond had grown strong. If there was no actual happiness, I often saw a friendly contentment and a mutual regard, particularly as the couple grew older and could look back upon years of joint achievement.

Should quarrels become frequent the inhabitants of Dragalevtsy did not use divorce as a means of breaking up such a marriage relationship, unpleasant though it was. This was due partly to the influence of the church, the only institution at that time which could grant a divorce; but public opinion was an even stronger sanction against it. The oldest villagers could remember no case of actual divorce in Dragalevtsy. The village as a whole was considerably stirred up for more than a year while I was there by the relationship which existed between the village tailor and his wife, who were mentioned in an earlier chapter. When I raised the subject of divorce at one of the tavern sessions, one of the old men suggested gravely, but with what I soon learned was some suppressed amusement, that I interview Zdravka, the tailor's wife. "She is one of these modern women, you know; she has her own money and job. In fact, you have probably already met her for she is one of the servants at your school."

This looked like a gold mine in my own backyard, but I was somewhat hesitant about questioning Zdravka directly. I went to the Bulgarian teacher who had so often helped me in the more delicate questioning of village women. We learned that for over a year Zdravka had talked divorce and even claimed that she had consulted a Sofia lawyer about the matter. For weeks at a time she would stay away from her husband, leaving him in such an equivocal position that out of sheer embarrassment he used to hate to go to the tavern for an evening drink; then she would decide to spend the summer with him and help him make the garments which he sold. After two or three such separations and reconciliations Zdravka and her husband were together again. They lived in a neat little whitewashed house, quite new. There were screens in the windows— ("Zdravka learned that at the College," her husband said proudly)— and there were flowers around the door. Why she wanted to leave him no one knew exactly, least of all Zdravka. What it boiled down to was the strangely familiar cry, "I want to be independent." But even Zdravka, with all her surprising initiative and contacts with the intelligentsia, when it came to the point dared not run counter to the old village sanctions against divorce.

More often it was the husband who left the home. When he did and in rare cases interested himself in another woman, the villagers did all in their power to make him return. If he refused at first, they made him feel the indignation of public opinion, treating him as an outcast and sometimes going to the length of beating him. If he remained in the village, he had no choice but to go back to his wife. During the time he was away his wife also was put to shame, getting little sympathy from the general public. She knew, furthermore, that in case of a divorce both parties would be held guilty by the villagers, so she was willing to take her husband back and get along with him as best she could. A divorced man was considered to have loose morals; a divorced woman would have been thought thoroughly bad. There was thus a situation in which everyone was expected to marry, with no sanctioned way out once the marriage contract had been entered upon. Though such an attitude meant that unfortunate marriages had to drag on interminably, it also had the effect of forcing couples to adjust themselves to each other.

Dragalevtsy seemed a curiosity indeed: a village in which marriage was little questioned, where there was practically no marital unfaithfulness, and no divorce. What were the reasons for the family stability? For one thing, life was still lived according to ancient customs. People only recently had begun to wonder about the age-old patterns which they had been following so faithfully. Some writers would call them the "dead hand of the past," others "the cake of custom." Whatever their name, they were conducive to a common understanding of the place of marriage. All the people expected the same things from life and from the home.

Then, too, earning their living by farming was a joint enterprise. People got used to putting their shoulders to the wheel as a family group. In addition to what they all did together, women were supposed to do certain things, men other things, and children still other things. As long as every person did his part there was no friction, but quiet efficiency. Furthermore, the presence of a number of relatives made for greater stability. In the case of apparent misunderstanding between a husband and wife, the proper relative intervened to suggest a way out. Most of the husband's relatives were in the same locality with him and could keep an eye on his behavior.

One was not only tied closely to the husband's blood kin *(rodstvo)* but had to enter upon a formal relationship with one's in-laws. Families related by marriage felt close to each other, the intensity of the feeling depending upon the frequency with which the families met and the way the young couples got along. Ordinarily, however, the family of the bride was considered by the husband's parents to be as close, at times even closer, than blood relatives. For instance, if there was any sort of celebration to which guests were invited, the family of the bride was the first to be asked. One reliable informant estimated that ninety out of one hundred people in Dragalevtsy felt the force of *svatovstvo*, or this relationship springing up through intermarriage. The young people, who are usually so prone to make a break with the past, maintained it in all its vigor. Here was the way one young man explained the *svatovstvo*:

"If my sister married some man in Simeonovo, even though I had never seen him before, his brother and sister would be my *svati*, and if I met them we would feel like cousins. I would never curse them or quarrel with them and would call their father *'dedo'* and their mother *'baba,'* the same names I use for my own grandparents. My parents and the parents of my new brother-in-law would likewise be *svati* and would treat one another reverently." Two brothers could not marry two sisters from another family, though there was no blood relationship, because the second couple were *svati* after the first couple married, and *svati* could not marry. Two brothers could marry two first cousins, but not two sisters. This feeling of closeness in families related by marriage did not stop with the husband and the wife, nor with the single in-law gained by each family. It included, as well, the in-law's parents and brothers and sisters with whom just dealings and proper behavior had always to prevail.

More than anything else, however, the shared activities of husband and wife developed an understanding which lasted through thick and thin. Some of these shared activities were the trip to market, the

Christmas Eve feast, Easter festivities, and the ceremonies on St. George's Day.

Roughly two-thirds of adult Dragalevtsy was in Sofia on an average Friday. On Thursday evenings the village was already bubbling with excitement. The wagons had already been loaded. All that was necessary in the dim light on Friday morning was the yoking of the sleepy oxen. Soon cart after cart would creak heavily down from the village, overtaking those peasants who cheerfully made the long trip by foot. By the time sleepy city-dwellers were breakfasting, the village was well on its way to the outside world.

Once in Sofia there were four possible destinations for the peasant wagon: the cattle market, the mill, the big curb market, or the *Bezisten Pazar* (another smaller market).

The cattle market was located across the city, back of the railroad station, near the municipal cemetery. This market was owned and managed by the municipality. Every peasant before passing into the enclosure with a beast had to pay the tax of ten leva. The sun had already grown warm by the time the Dragalevtsy peasant and his wife passed through side streets to this square, packed with bargaining, shouting men and noisy animals. Usually the women sat outside the square in their wagons loaded with pumpkins and peppers in season, though once in a while a woman accompanied her husband through the bargaining and sale of the animal. The bright blue uniforms of the police were very much in evidence in this dusty confusion, where hard bargains sometimes led to fist fights. At the east end, gypsies raced their not too spirited horses up and down to prove to would-be purchasers the absence of defects. At the northeast side, the red-eyed water buffaloes and their dirty little black calves moved restlessly because of biting flies. To the northwest, along the iron rail the oxen ruminated.

Through the tumult and dust wandered the sellers of *boza* (fermented millet drink) and the vendors of round *gevretsi* (small rings of bread); here a man was eating a melon near a sucking calf. I was always interested in those performing *pazarluk,* which was the method of clinching a bargain. The buyer and the seller of an animal would stand shaking hands as the seller demanded an unreasonably high price, to which the buyer retorted with a ridiculously low price. As the two amounts approached each other the handshaking grew warmer and more rapid until finally the buyer and seller agreed on a sensible figure, at which time a third party added his hand to those of the other two. The third peasant, the witness of the sale, often enjoyed shouting as much as the principals. The bargain concluded, the men went to arrange a bill of sale, after which the newly purchased animal was led across the plain to its new home.

At this market in 1937 a sound young bull cost between twenty-five and thirty-five dollars; a fresh buffalo cow, between fifty and sixty dollars; ordinary cows brought slightly less, between thirty-five and forty-five dollars. Horses ranged from twelve to sixty dollars, while the humble donkey varied in value from twelve to eighteen dollars.

Not far away from the big cattle market, in the high-walled enclosure, was the sheep bazaar. There shepherds lolled in the shade with their flocks and waited for purchasers, often long in coming. This too was a municipal bazaar, and the peasants paid a small fee for the privilege of carrying on business there. Ordinarily a pair of sheep cost $3.60.

Near the Bridge of Lions spanning the narrow canal around Sofia was the mill which the people of Dragalevtsy had chosen to patronize. If they were tired out after their trip into the city, the villagers lay down on sacks of grain until their turns came. When at last they aroused themselves they were coated with a thin layer of flour dust which filled the air around the electrically operated machinery. In the mill courtyard the unyoked oxen rested beside the wagons, and chatting groups of women sat in the scanty shade.

From the Bridge of Lions there jutted off a narrow street lined with people displaying homegrown and homemade wares. This was the beginning of the general market which extended with innumerable side-street ramifications for several long blocks. This market did not really get into full swing until nine o'clock, owing to the drowsiness of Sofia housewives.

The real life of this market resided not so much in the great variety of products on sale as in the peasants: their dress, their immeasurable patience, and their childlike curiosity at strange things such as a tourist's knickers or the cheap gay contents of the toy-sellers' pushcarts.

Each woman had something to sell: a few eggs, some blueberries picked up on the mountain, two or three chickens, a bag of peppers, strong-smelling buffalo butter, a bunch of carnations, white beans for which Dragalevtsy was especially known throughout this region, or a few walnuts. The woman's merchandise, piled on the sidewalk before her, was her excuse for coming to town.

It was around the next destination, the *Bezisten Pazar,* that fondest memories clung, because this was the spot near the Sofia flower bazaar where young people from surrounding villages went upon completing their morning duties in town. It was here that young men from one village met girls from other villages. During the afternoon, brightly dressed, giggling young couples promenaded in the sunshine while the older people, especially the men, gathered in the *"Dulgata Mehana,"* the tavern to which Dragalevtsy peasants were especially loyal. They lunched and drank, rested, and swapped their stories here. Nor was it without pride that they told how the late Fiodor Chaliapin, the celebrated opera singer, in 1934 spent a very merry evening in this same *"Dulgata Mehana."*

This weekly trip to town on Friday did surprisingly little to introduce changes to the village. Even while in the capital city, the peasants still lived in a peasant world. In the animal bazaar, for instance, there was little social conversation and little opportunity for a villager to widen his knowledge of urban life. Too often in this place he learned to distrust the city-dwellers through frequent dealings with the keen-witted, professional cattle merchant. In the mill he was still in a peasant world even though noisy machines foreign to his village ran at lightning speed. It was true that in the general market all types of Sofia citizenry passed in review, but the peasants' chief contact here was with the servant girls accompanying the housewives on the Friday shopping expedition. Even after finishing their little business in the general market, the village men and women found most enjoyment in being with other peasants. Few people of Dragalevtsy ventured on the city's main streets; even if they should have happened into a movie house, it would have been one on some

back street.   I do know that the inarticulate peasant woman who
sat for hours crouched on the sidewalk wondered at the strange styles
of women's clothing, and that the village man, in his wandering,
coveted some glittering object in a shopwindow for his child.   In the
late afternoon as they went home, and during the days that followed,
man and wife talked about this trip to market.   For them it had been
a shared adventure.

Other activities which the family members shared besides the
tasks of home and field and the trip to market were the holidays.   The
traditional holidays were religious, while the ones most recently introduced were patriotic.

January sixth was *Malka Koleda,* or Little Christmas.   Many
Bulgarian villagers would tell you that Christ was really born on the
day before Christmas, but his birth was not made known until the
following day.   For that reason, great emphasis was laid upon the
celebration of Little Christmas, or Christmas Eve, with the meal on
Christmas Eve as the most important part of the season's festivities.

Each time I spent Christmas in a Bulgarian village home I was
deeply impressed with the simplicity and beauty of its symbolism.   I
was a foreigner and a Protestant nonbeliever.   Bai Milush and his
family received me as though I were one of their own large family.
Carefully and patiently they explained to me each bit of ceremony and
tradition and symbolism.   Often a ceremony was repeated so I could
photograph it.   There was not a single appurtenance of the Western
Christmas in the household; even the date was different, but the
Christmas spirit meant more there than anywhere else I had ever been.

To commemorate Christ's birth in a manger, straw was laid on
the floor and covered with a blanket which served as the tablecloth
for the evening's repast.   The whole family gathered around this
blanket after an incense urn had been carried as a good luck symbol
from the iconostas to each room of the house and to all of the animal
stalls.   Because the meal was late in starting, three of the smallest
children had gone to sleep, one in a crib and the other two on a
wooden bed.   In order to get the meal under way without further
formalities, the women passed hot, fiery *rakiya* (plum brandy) to each
person and stood patiently until the single glass had been emptied

before filling it for the next in turn; wine followed *rakiya* as the single glass continued to perform its simple function. There was a china cup, to be sure, but it was used by those preferring water.

Then the real ceremony began. The loaves of bread, crudely adorned on top with symbols standing for plows, sheep, the house, and sheaves of wheat, were passed to the head of the household, who broke the loaves with great solemnity. The loaves contained many notched pegs, the number of notches standing for objects on the farm; somewhere in the loaf was also hidden a coin, far more coveted than the notched pieces of wood. I, as the guest, broke open my bread first, only to find a three-notched peg, and was laughingly told that I would have to tend the sheep during the year and would not be as lucky as my neighbor who got the two-notched peg representing the cow. Still luckier was the elder brother who found the one-notched peg representing the house. A shrill shout of joy told at once that Mitko, the eleven-year-old boy, had found the coin and would be the luckiest of all.

The excitement subsided as all began to eat heartily of the special food which the women had been preparing all afternoon. Every home followed the same traditional menu, which featured the meatless main dish of pumpkin pie or *banitsa,* soggy in spite of long baking in hot ashes. The family, in between bites of *banitsa,* spooned with great gusto into the compote of stewed prunes to which pounded garlic and nuts had been added. Everyone had to partake of this for, as the villagers assured me with a twinkle in their eye, "it makes hair grow under the arms."

The other traditional dish was *surmi,* a combination of onions, peppers, raisins, and rice rolled up and stewed in brine-soaked cabbage leaves. The compote and *surmi* were eaten from communal bowls.

The meal was concluded by the serving of withered apples, stored just for this occasion, and nuts cracked in the mouth of a neighbor who soon discovered the guest's unwillingness to risk his teeth for a kernel. As the men got out their cigarettes a girl rose to pass, in lieu of a match, a live coal, held with tongs, from the sheet metal stove.

On important occasions like this, the animals were not forgotten. A piece of the specially prepared bread was dipped into the compote and given to each animal, though the chickens tussled over a large chunk thrown to them. Sometime during the night straw was reverently taken from beneath the blanket and tied in little tufts onto all of the fruit trees "in order to ensure a good crop of fruit the following season."

The feast was concluded around midnight. All of the family retired with the exception of Trayko, the young man with a sacred duty to perform: He had to watch the yule log *(budnik)* and see that it burned continuously until the rising of the sun. This log had been chosen with care up on the mountainside and brought down to the house on a crude sled. As the flames crept up its gnarled sides Trayko let his imagination run riot until he heard the sounds of husky voices cursing the dogs out in the yard. He knew that a group of friends who had been out caroling were stopping to have a word with him. The visitors were carrying lanterns and staves, which they waved recklessly because of the mixture of drinks and food given them at every house in which they had sung. They got a late start this particular Christmas Eve because they had had to go to Sofia to sing over the radio. Trayko was particularly anxious to hear about this experience. Before leaving, the carolers sang for the benefit of the now wide-awake family, but found difficulty in consuming all the food and drink offered to them. Trayko's mother insisted upon putting on the staff of each boy doughnut-shaped pieces of bread, prepared for this purpose.

On Christmas Day the rising sun did little to warm the wind-swept village. A few of the most pious men and women were returning from the early morning service, but most of the villagers were sleeping late. When at length the people got up they began to indulge in quantities of pork meat, for every home had killed a pig for the grand occasion. Those who had kept the long six-week church fast found the taste of meat most pleasing. In the afternoon the people gathered in the main square to dance, to visit, to watch the antics of tipsy men. Around midafternoon a lively band struck up a *horo* tune and the dance got under way. The chief social gatherings throughout the village at Christmas time took place at the homes of those named Hristo or Hristina (Christo or Christina), since these individuals were celebrating their name days with appropriate hospitality.

Bulgarian children did not hang up their stockings on Christmas Eve but, if their parents were being influenced by modern ideas, did find a present or two at the foot of their bed when they woke up in the morning. They immediately ran to kiss the hands of their father and mother. They called Santa Claus *"Dedo Koleda,"* which meant "Grandfather Christmas." He did not wear a bright red, white-furred costume but had on a brown homespun outfit that corresponded more nearly to the peasant's manner of dress.

On these ceremonial occasions the father and mother presided with quiet dignity over the celebrations. They were accorded every respect by their children. As the Christmases passed, the couple's feeling of partnership deepened. Each year left its accumulation of memories, about which husband and wife said little, but about which they could feel sure the other was thinking.

Christmas and the holidays that followed were only a prelude to *Velikden*—literally, the Great Day—the day of Christ's resurrection. On the eighth Sunday before Easter, or *Mesni Zagovezni* (meat fast), all those who kept the long Easter fast stopped eating meat. The following Sunday was *Sirni Zagovezni* (cheese fast) after which those fasting gave up all milk products. This Sunday itself was a day of great feasting on all sorts of cheese products. On both Sundays fires were lit; on *Mesni Zagovezni* there was a great fire at night in the village square, and on *Sirni Zagovezni* almost every household lighted a fire in the yard around which the youngsters waved burning straw stuck in the cleft end of a stick and chanted an ancient couplet

> Orata, Kopata!
> Dai mi, chicho, momata

whose significance had vanished with the ages.

On this Sunday, and the three days preceding, all quarrels among the villagers were settled, everyone visiting his neighbors and relatives to beg pardon for real or fancied offenses. The quiet that reigned over the village on the evening of *Sirni Zagovezni* was little short of wonderful. At the break of day the children had risen to kiss their parents' hands and ask pardon for past misbehavior, and all day long there had been a wandering in and out of homes by men to meet some other men with whom they had been at odds, and by a handshake to ask pardon.

I came into the tavern late in the afternoon of that day. It was snowing heavily and the warmth from the stove felt good. Near me sat a man rubbing his chilled hands. After we had exchanged formal greetings, I asked him where he was going, the usual village question.

"I'm going back to my village, eleven miles farther on."

"Where have you been?"

"I've been over to Durvanitsa [two miles away] to visit my parents and beg their forgiveness."

"Have you had any trouble with your parents during the past year that would make you take such a long walk in such bad weather?"

Patient with me, a foreigner, he said, "No, I've had no troubles with my parents. I've been to visit them. That is the custom."

A little later he went out into the snow to resume his eleven-mile tramp back home. His heart was at ease, for he had fulfilled the age-old custom of *Sirni Nedelya* (Cheese Sunday).

The Saturday following Cheese Sunday was *Todorovden* (the day of St. Theodore, patron saint of horses). Then the children stopped fasting, for their young bodies could not stand seven weeks of a milkless diet. Early in the morning they, together with some of the old people, took communion in the village church. Many of the young men visited the village of Gorna Banya, which had its *Subor* on *Todorovden*. There was a great deal of horseback riding and racing up and down the muddy village streets, in honor of St. Theodore and "to protect the horses from worms."

Eight days before Easter was the Saturday called *Lazarovden* (St. Lazarus's Day). *Lazarki* groups, consisting of six girls each, went from house to house to sing and dance, according to the villagers in honor of the resurrection of Lazarus. They were given coins and eggs by the peasants who believed that these girls would bring them good luck in the months to come.

On Thursday, Friday, and Saturday of Passion Week, all the people fasted and refrained from work. Even a stranger felt a certain awe at the grave anticipation filling the village. On Saturday evening all the village gathered in the church for the midnight service. The long liturgy led the silent, densely packed worshipers into a mood of growing suspense, emphasizing in word and music the tragedy of the tomb. But at midnight, reputedly the time when Christ's tomb burst open, a startling transformation took place. The glorious Easter hymn "Christ Is Risen" thundered forth to the clanging of the church bell. At first it was stately and restrained, but as the magic of its message spread, a joyousness exalted the worshipers. All rushed to light the tapers which they had held unlit throughout the service. They had been waiting for this moment for the holy fire sent down each Easter from heaven. Carefully they watched the taper while exchanging the happy greetings—"Christ is risen," "Risen indeed"— and passing red Easter eggs from palm to palm in lieu of a handshake. The church had come into its own. As the crowd dispersed, each villager protected the sacred fire from the breezes in an effort to reach home with the taper still alight, whereupon it would be blown out and put aside for special use later on.

At home the people broke their long fast by eating the hard-boiled eggs and the *kozunatsi,* or very yellow Easter cakes. Then a feast followed. For forty days afterwards the spell of the occasion was often recalled as pious villagers greeted each other with those sacred words, "Christ is risen," and received the answer, "Risen indeed."

Another holiday of importance to every family was May 6, or St. George's Day. The head of the house, no matter how poor he might be, contrived to have a lamb killed for the festivities. When the meat was roasted to a delicious flavor the family gathered, often in a sunny meadow with other relatives, to feast. The husband and wife planned carefully for this day, and together saw to it that everyone enjoyed himself. Though the husband might later go to the tavern to be with other men, he and his wife had experienced again an event for which both prepared and which both enjoyed.

The story of married life, of life in common, could be retold in many ways. Underneath it all was a realistic acknowledgment that marriage had its ups and downs. As long as one felt useful and needed, then it had its satisfactions too. Often people ask, "Are those peasants happy with such a family system?" There is no adequate answer. Happiness is a state of mind, and the meaning of happiness varies from culture to culture as well as from person to person. On the whole, Bulgarian husbands and wives were happy, for they were getting from marriage what they expected and were untroubled by alternatives. Furthermore, life to them was more than a frenzied search for happiness. It was rather the serious fulfillment of customary duties, the performing of daily tasks to keep one's people and one's animals alive, and the taking of sufficient time to cultivate the art, almost lost in our civilization, of forming personal relationships which stood the test of time. Under these circumstances happiness came as it only can, as a by-product of rich life experiences.

"To commemorate Christ's birth . . ." *See page 106.*

"The loaves of bread, crudely adorned on top . . ." *See page 107.*

"... the carolers sang. Trayko's mother puts on the staff ... doughnut-shaped pieces of bread prepared for this purpose ..." *See page 108.*

"*Lazarki* groups ... went from house to house to sing and dance in honor of the resurrection of Lazarus ..." *See page 110.*

CHAPTER VII

PARENTS AND CHILDREN

A RE children gods or kings that older people should tremble over them?" was the way one village woman reacted to what she considered the newfangled ideas of child rearing taught by the village doctor. Another woman said to me, "Why should so much be made of children when there is no sense of their living in such a heavy life?"

These attitudes reflected themselves in the statistics of infant mortality, which were given in Chapter II but deserve repetition. Back in 1926 one out of every five babies born alive died during its first year; this figure had fallen to one out of every eight in 1941, but was still much higher than the United States rate of one out of twenty-two. But the birth rate too has been falling. When I first went to Bulgaria in 1929 I found village after village where 45 babies were born annually for every thousand people. This number has fallen to around 30 for Dragalevtsy and 21 for Bulgaria as a whole. The United States rate was about 23 in 1946.

Childhood was a period to live through, not especially to enjoy. Bulgarian peasants, if they ever had given thought to it, would probably have agreed with the results of some of the American studies which suggested that childhood was not necessarily the happiest time of life. In Dragalevtsy it was, in fact, the period of greatest uncertainty and insecurity. The Dragalevtsy child early learned the basic principle of action: if you want to stay out of trouble, keep out of the grown-ups' way. The child's greatest errors were those of commission rather than omission.

"Children are the wealth of the poor. They are for God and for the peasants and so why should we worry about special care for them?" said one woman who realized that the townspeople had smaller families in spite of greater comforts. Her statement also showed how her people had reconciled themselves to comparative poverty: abundance of children in contrast to the abundance of goods. When I asked her if they gave the children any special food, she answered: "No, certainly not. They eat the same food as the older people. If they want to eat, we let them eat. If they do not want to eat, who is to be blamed?" Children's mealtimes were a matter of convenience. They asked for food when they were hungry, receiving a crust of bread if the adult was not too busy.

The mother-in-law usually took care of the children, especially while they were babies, because she was considered more capable and experienced than the young mother. There were cases in the village where a comparatively young mother-in-law took such complete care of her son's children that the mother of the children did not know what it meant to have children and to care for them.

When people went to work in the fields and there was no woman to remain with them in the home, the children were left by themselves on the streets.

"Doesn't the Village Council do anything to aid these children?" I asked.

"Oh, the *Obshtina* takes care of some children, but what can it do when it is not from the same blood? It is only to shut the eyes and the mouths of the peasants for the very high taxes they pay to the *Obshtina*."

The children were not well dressed. Their clothes were often dirty and ragged. One tired mother of several complained: "Can a child keep anything on his back clean and not torn? Now you put on his back something clean and new, and when he returns from playing in the street it is all wet, dirty, and often torn. So children do not deserve to have good and new clothes." Often their clothes were made out of garments discarded by adults, though they did receive new garments at Christmas.

But even though the peasants did not "tremble over" their children, they valued them highly. When they first came they were tokens of a successful marriage. The husband and wife had both borne fruit and so had conformed to the expected life cycle. As the children grew older, however, they became important as economic assets. They could do hard work; they could run countless errands. Later, they were the heirs to the father's fields and the chief support of the parents in their declining years.

One of the first women I interviewed about family life told me: "I had a little boy but he died when forty days old. Now I cannot help crying every St. George's Day [May 6] and every St. Dimiter's Day [November 8] when my husband goes out to hire a boy to care for our sheep. If my son had lived, he could have taken care of the sheep for us."

Later on in the course of a conversation with a garrulous *baba* I asked her if she did not think her seven children too many for one woman to have. She snorted, pointed out of the window to her sons unloading wood they had gathered in the forest, and said: "If I hadn't had lots of children, who would go to get our wood?"

Sons were greater economic assets than girls but even so would have normally received more attention in this man-centered society. As parents often had to go to some expense to get their daughters married off, they were always jubilant at the arrival of a son. The good-natured priest was occasionally the butt of a number of sly jests because he had three daughters and no son. One man in particular, Stefan, who had been in the same predicament, had recently acquired a son, who was now the apple of his eye. He was fond of his daughters, but made no secret of his particular pride in his boy. I thoroughly enjoyed a conversation between Stefan and the priest in which Stefan fully explained how to be sure the next one was a boy. I have known of fathers who refused to look at the newly arrived infant upon learning that it was a girl. Of course, they eventually acquiesced and simply hoped for better luck next time. Where parents had no sons, village curiosity reached a peak when a new child was expected, and an occasional wager was laid on the possibility of its being a boy. But favoritism was the exception rather than the rule. When you asked a Dragalevtsy parent which child he liked best he responded: "I like them all equally; they are just like the fingers on one's hand." He often added the proverb, "The fingers on one's hand feel pain equally, do they not?"

Whenever a child suffered from a physical or mental handicap Dragalevtsy parents, like most parents around the world, were more solicitous than they would have been if the child were normal. A peasant named Vladimir once invited me to his home for what I thought was to be a chat about life in general. We walked through the sturdy gate, slushed through the mud in the yard, and lowered our heads as we entered the house's one large room. The children scurried out of our way while Yurdanka, his wife, offered us each a low three-legged stool. Not far from the stove in the center of the room I saw in the dim light what appeared to be a teen-aged girl, drooling and entirely oblivious to our presence. Vladimir, Yurdanka, and I talked about many things while their younger children sat on the bed and listened intently. Then the father brought up the matter of their feeble-minded daughter:

"Tova e nashe neshtastie" (This is our misfortune), he said. And then he told me her story. Some illness, probably meningitis, had arrested her mental development at an early age. Doctors had given them no hope and they wondered if I, a foreigner, knew of something they could do. Their faces showed the suffering that had touched their lives: the comments of misunderstanding, superstitious neighbors, and the constant attention they had to pay to the child's physical needs. Truly she was their misfortune. I knew that the treatment of the mentally deficient and mentally ill in Bulgaria was still in that tragic stage where the unfortunates were confined and given almost no scientific treatment. The parents wanted more than that. It was with a heavy heart that I left them, for their misfortune was not only that of economic loss, but of seeing a wasted life sharing the one living room of the tiny house.

The child, whether grown or small, approached the father through the mother. Though not universally the case, most Dragalevtsy children told their mother what they wanted and then asked her to relay this request to the father. The mother did so quite willingly, for she felt much closer to the children than the father. In this way the distance between father and children was traditionally maintained, increasing filial respect.

There were accepted ways for children to show their respect to the parents. The traditional patterns all centered around the father: standing up when he entered the room; waiting for him to eat first;

kissing his hand and toasting him before drinking *rakiya* at ceremonial dinners. The newer patterns, such as little children giving a goodnight kiss, which had penetrated a few of the homes, centered around the mother.

For instance, in a family where three married sons dwelt in the same room with their parents and three unmarried brothers, one of the married sons said: "Our little children sometimes kiss the hands of the grown-ups before going to bed, and we married sons always kiss our parents' hands before drinking *rakiya* at home. We never quarrel with our father; if we are dissatisfied, we do not dare raise our voices." The married sons are thirty-six, twenty-seven, and twenty-five years old.

But sometimes the tables were turned. There was another case of a sixty-eight year old father who had entrusted the management of the estate to his thirty-four year old son. He had to consult his son before spending any money or doing anything around the place. The household still respected him in many ways though not leaving him much authority. He took comfort in at least one thing: "I am always the one to begin the meal, and all wait for me to begin before they start to eat."

One home which I studied made a great deal out of forms and ceremonies and was one of the best regulated and happiest homes I found. The children were doing excellently at school, and I came upon them studying their lessons even in the pasture while tending the sheep, a most extraordinary thing. The mother had been orphaned at an early age, appreciated a mother's role, and took her task seriously; the father likewise considered his parenthood as a real obligation and was ambitious for his children. When the children got up in the morning they put on their shoes, ran to the street fountain to wash, returned to say their prayers and then to kiss the hands of the elders, the youngest son kissing the hands of his older brothers (aged thirteen and twelve). Every day the mother reminded them: "Today you will be good."

When daughters married, they never returned to live at home except under the most unusual circumstances. If the father was without a housekeeper, he might ask his married daughter, accompanied by her husband, to come and live with him. Most married daughters liked to visit in their parental homes on Sundays and other holidays, with their children and their husbands. While the frequency of visitation naturally varied with the daughters' sociability, it was significant that the daughters of wealthy peasants returned more often for visits than the daughters of poor peasants. There might have been an economic as well as a filial motive involved in this visitation. Married daughters still living in Dragalevtsy frequently called on their mothers, and helped them through difficult times. In more than half of the homes the married daughter-mother bond was kept intact, a source of comfort to both parties.

Married sons living with their parents were far more considerate of them than sons who had separated and lived in houses of their own. While in the paternal home they were subject to the authority of the old people, especially to that of the father. Sons living separately had no reason to obey the father if, as was usual in such cases, the property had already been divided. Though he might go to his father for advice, he was just as apt to seek the advice of tavern cronies. Of course, there were many variations of this situation. One thirty-eight year old son, married but not living in the paternal home, consulted his father about everything of importance—buying land, selling animals, building a house.

In another case, where the youngest son and his family lived in the paternal home with the widowed mother, the son got along extremely well with the mother. For instance, when she slapped him resoundingly because he had gone to the drink-shop, he simply smiled and said: "All right, you have the right to do that." He consulted his mother about many things, saw to it that she did not do heavy work and that she had an honorable place in the household.

In one household the twenty-six year old son spent little time at home because of his job as the *Obshtina* courier. He and his father experienced considerable conflict because he did not hand over his earnings to the old man but spent them on his own needs. At the same time he was living and eating free of charge in his father's house, much to the satisfaction of his mother who championed him before her husband. Naturally the son was dissatisfied with staying at home, for, in the words of his father, "he does not like the village work and wants something lighter. He wants to go to Sofia." The son obeyed his father most of the time as regards work assigned, but paid less attention to what his mother said. He went with any girl he liked, though his father, who in his youth married a girl of whom his parents had disapproved, insisted that if the son did the same, he would turn the son's wife out into the street.

This case was quite typical of most village young men. They performed, though unwillingly at times, whatever tasks their father ordered them to do, but paid little attention to the mother, since "she is a woman and doesn't understand man's work." A smaller number listened to the advice of their parents in the choice of girl friends, but most looked upon that as a personal matter in which parents should not interfere. One father who made a matter-of-fact adjustment to the situation said, "I can't keep a candle for my son in the streets," meaning that he could not go before him to light up his path.

When young men kicked against the traces, the older people did not become particularly disturbed. At times they were annoyed, but there was a general feeling that once the boy got married he would settle down to the conventional routine. This tolerant viewpoint was supported by even the staid middle-aged men, who liked to give the impression that they had been wild and troublesome in their youth. This complacency would have been less widespread if the parents had realized how greatly conditions had changed in one generation.

Unmarried daughters caused little trouble to their parents. They were ordinarily obedient to both father and mother, but, like the sons, quarrelled most often with their mothers, for they were with them more and felt that the mother loved them more than the father. Daughters in three-fourths of Dragalevtsy's homes went with any boys they chose, though some parents were firm in stating that the young man must be suitable before they gave their consent to marriage. It was highly doubtful whether this threat had much effect on the young. One father, apparently devoted to his twenty-year-old daughter, whipped her for going with young men of whom he disapproved and quarreled much with his son of eighteen.

If a daughter failed to marry, she spent the rest of her life in her father's home and received sympathy only as long as her mother was alive. Her father and married brothers thought of her as a servant in the home and treated her accordingly. Fortunately there was rarely more than one old maid at a time in Dragalevtsy.

The treatment of younger children, of course, varied greatly with the home. Children in Dragalevtsy were accustomed to being yelled at from their first toddling days by displeased older people. As we have already seen, there was no question about boys being preferred to girls in most homes, especially if there was only one boy among several girls. In such homes it was the boy who received the presents when the father returned from town, and who was picked up first; it was the boy whom the parents held when they asked to be photographed.

Whipping, which was usually done by the father, was such an effective check on misbehavior that parents often needed only to threaten it. Another method of punishment was to withhold bread from the child for two or three hours, but, as one father said, "This doesn't always work, especially if the child begins to cry."

Some parents, when they were unable to make ends meet, sent a girl off to Sofia to work as a domestic. One family revealed that five years previously a twelve-year-old daughter had been sent to be a servant in Sofia; she would never return to the village to live, nor did she ever come to visit. In this case the parents could not support an extra person, so chose the simplest way out. The fact that many Bulgarian families in cities sought female servants from twelve to eighteen years of age made such a practice possible. Indeed, on St. Dimiter's Day (November 8) and St. George's Day (May 6) there used to be a "servant bazaar" in Sofia. Village girls went to a certain place and stood in a row where housewives could look them over like heifers and choose a maid. Changes in servants, including shepherds, were ordinarily made only at these two times during the year.

Should parents find a job for a teen-aged boy, the father might require the boy to accept the job. Most boys wanted work; only a few resented working at all. If a father had more sons than he needed on the farm, he sometimes chose a trade for or with the boy. Such boys usually became cobblers, tailors, or tanners. In all cases where the sons remained to work in the village, they were expected to turn over to the father a part or all of their earnings. This practice once more emphasized the economic importance of children.

As far as I could discover, none of the villagers resented my questions into their personal affairs. More than once, after the routine interviewing was over, a man unburdened himself of some hurt or grievance that revealed more than any questionnaire could. It was through such outpourings that I realized how land could dominate or warp completely otherwise normal family relationships of father and sons or brother and brother.

Lonely old Bai Dimiter held especial interest for me since his wife had earlier told about incidents in his past which helped me to understand better why he began to drink so much that his girls felt ashamed of being called his daughters; to see how he bore his loss of economic and social position in the village owing to bad business methods coupled with a disabling accident. The key to the whole situation was the fact that his own father had tricked him in his early married days. After the son had paid off a heavy debt owed by his father, the father refused to deed him meadows in return but frankly confessed: "I fooled you in order to get money." To make the deception harder to bear, Dimiter inherited no land from his father, all of it going to another son with whom the father had been on better terms. Naturally, Dimiter had a falling out with his brother, and took the matter to the courts where, after long litigation, he failed to obtain any part of the inheritance.

The books I had read about Bulgaria in the old days pointed out the role the older brother formerly played when the father died. One village home was actually operated on the old principle of subordination of the younger brother to the older. Hristo, the older brother, was smaller than the younger brother, standing huge and stooped in the low-ceilinged room in such a way that the kerosene lamp cast a grotesque, mountainous shadow behind him. I knew, of course, about these men, as I knew about most village men, from the talk of tavern groups and other willing informants. I knew that they were ashamed of their family name which meant "the son of a donkey," and I knew that Hristo had served in the first World War and had been taken as a prisoner to France, which gave him a definite claim to distinction in the village. He talked easily and willingly of the war but just as willingly turned to discuss the arrangement whereby his brother and he, with their large families, lived in the same room in comparative harmony. In the first place, Sando, the younger, submitted to Hristo's authority, but Hristo, in turn, did not make or execute any plans without consulting his brother. Hristo had the task of managing the farm and doing the field work, marketing the products, and laying in the meager supplies; Sando worked as a teamster and as a day laborer if necessary to earn extra funds for the common treasury kept by Hristo. Some idea of the trust that the younger brother had in the older came from the knowledge that the wages of each long day's work, the pay for every laborious haul, went to the older brother. He spent it as it was needed together with the profits from the farm; he gave the money to the younger brother for clothing his children, for buying his wife new *tsarvuli* (pigskin sandals); he also took for his own use whatever he deemed necessary, though never abusing his prerogative. This was the only such relationship which I came across, simply because brothers did not live together as much as they used to, even in Dragalevtsy, ordinarily so tenacious of the older forms of life.

The lot of an unmarried brother in the paternal home managed by an elder brother was likewise one of subordination. I visited one home which bore the unmistakable signs of belonging to a dairyman: milky buckets littered the inside; cows hopelessly switched at flies coming from the ever-present manure piles all over the yard. In the course of the conversation I learned that there was little difficulty between the brothers concerning work: the younger together with the wife of the older got up long before daybreak to milk and prepare the milk for Sofia; later on the older brother got up at the same time as his widowed mother to breakfast and started on his daily trek to Sofia and back. Whenever the younger man had extra money he gave it to the older, with the understanding that he could ask for what he needed. There was one source of trouble in the brotherly relationship arising out of the attempt on the part of the older to dictate whom the younger should marry. The inconsistency in this demand cropped out when the older brother's wife and mother admitted that the older brother had married against the wishes of his parents, and had brought his wife home to a round of constant toil and insufficient sleep. It was not surprising that the younger brother insisted on the right to choose his own friends, probably with the determination that upon marriage he would not live with his older brother, no matter how desperate the financial conditions might be.

Married sons living with their father and under his domination usually relied upon one another for mutual sympathy and understanding, at times acting as a unit in dealing with the older people. Between brothers who lived apart the relationship was often cordial, especially if they had been able to clear the greatest, most dangerous hurdle of all, the division of the inheritance. The younger continued to call the older *bate,* "my big brother," and went often to him for counsel, for loans, for aid in the fields, gladly repaying in kind. They saw much of each other in a social way, since they associated with men of the same age; their familial problems were often the same. The bond existed, not crystallizing into a situation where one submitted to the authority of the other, but rather into one in which the brothers felt equal. This type of relationship was growing with the trend toward smaller households.

The relationship between sisters never had to take the definite form which the brother-brother relationship assumed, for there was no situation possible from the village point of view in which a married sister could command a younger married sister. In the first place, married sisters always lived apart, and distance lent enchantment. In the second place, their husbands, and not they, were primarily disturbed if there was any irregularity in the division of their estate; therefore, any ill-feeling developing over a lawsuit was reflected rather than actual. When the parents died, unmarried sisters found refuge in a married sister's home if there was no married brother; normally, however, the unmarried sister went to live with a brother, since he was still living on the father's farm in which she had a right to share. Sisters who lived in the same village saw much of each other when they got together to card and spin wool on weekdays; and they visited together on Sundays.

Although this insight into the relations between parents and their children, both adult and immature, has taken us beyond the period of childhood, it does show us why the children had to learn obedience and respect and why the village would soon show its dissatisfaction with anyone who flouted the established rules. Children also learned to defer to an older brother or sister, and assumed responsibility for those who were younger. In the main, a child's life was centered about the home and about those activities which he shared with members of his immediate family or the relatives in the neighborhood who were young enough to be his playmates.

Children became acquainted with their relatives in other villages on the annual *Subor* or "At Home Day" which each village observed. Dragalevtsy families had four village *Subori* which they could attend; on Pantaley Den (August 9) they could go to Boyana; on Spasov Den (the Monday of the eighth week after Easter) they could go to Durvenitsa; on Petkov Den (October 27) they could visit Bistritsa; and on Archangel Day (November 21) they could visit Simeonovo.

I once attended this Simeonovo *Subor* with the Dragalevtsy families. I was told gravely by the old women that on this day everyone must be especially good, for the Archangel Michael was the one who received the souls of the dead into heaven. On the day preceding, the Simeonovo women had gathered to make many loaves of bread from flour previously donated to the church by its loyal supporters. Early on the morning of the *Subor* the church sexton with some helpers killed four sheep for the big meat stews; later he gave terse commands regarding the flavoring of the stews: bean and mutton, cabbage and mutton, and rice and mutton—a somewhat monotonous menu, but one hallowed by tradition.

We started our four-mile walk at an early hour. The air was crisp and so clear that the great Balkan range, miles across the plain, stood out sharply in its rose and blue. By midmorning a large number of people, including the children, had come into the churchyard. Most of them entered the church and attended part of the service; the women carried bread and boiled corn to be blessed by the priest, who received a portion. At noon, the church service was concluded and the priest blessed the meal prepared under the auspices of the church. Then it was that a few hundred people—guests, villagers, and total strangers—partook of the common meal. This dinner was typical. There was wine in abundance, for, as a member of the financial committee told me, wine induced a generous spirit in the hearts of those making their annual pledges to the church. After the meal and the pledges, the crowd dispersed. Visitors went home with family groups for further eating and drinking. The village square became a kaleidoscope of colors when peasant boys and girls began to dance the stately *horo* to the music of the pipes and drums.

With the coming of evening the guests left the village. Simeonovo moved again through a period of quiet and almost unbroken monotony until Archangel Day next year. Of course Christmas and Easter brought celebrations, but not the dash and gaiety that the presence of several hundred outsiders invariably created.

In spite of these set occasions for visiting, a surprising number of Dragalevtsy people stayed put, at least as far as going to other villages was concerned. *(See Appendix V.)* They had business in Sofia, and could justify going there. But almost half of the *stopani* never went to another village, even though there were four villages within five miles of Dragalevtsy. The same held true for their wives, the *domakini*. But those that did take such trips usually let their children go along, at least on some of the visits. These proved to be gala events in the lives of the youngsters.

In addition to the commemoration of Christmas and Easter and the celebration of St. George's Day, described in the last chapter, there were other holidays during the year which interested the children as much if not more than they did the adults. On the few summer holidays the villagers avoided any strenuous field work; since most of the special days came in the winter it was simple enough "to remember the holiday and take it easy." If the people found it necessary to do some important job on a holiday, they had a precedent set by no less a personage than St. Peter himself. On his own name day (July 12) he saw that the grain needed harvesting, so he took a piece of hearth cake in one hand and a sickle in the other and went to work reaping his wheat "so that the ripe grains wouldn't fall to the ground."

This was the peasant version of the Sabbath being made for man, not man for the Sabbath.

One holiday which children particularly enjoyed was New Year's Day, which, like Christmas, came two weeks later than our own because of the Old Style Calendar still in use by the church. Boys and girls were up at break of day to tap every passer-by with a gaily decorated branch of a cornel cherry tree. As they tapped they chanted:

> Fresh, fresh New Year
> Happiness to the end.
> Let mother and father be healthy
> Like the past year!
>
> Striking with a cornel-twig higher than the cap;
> Wishing you a houseful of corn,
> Yellow as the gold,
> To ripen early, early in
> The fields during the summer.
>
> Let wedding guests again pass by
> With full wine casks
> To present us with white kerchiefs
> And embroidered belts.
>
> Fresh, fresh New Year,
> Let us get sister married! . . .

With this chant they wished good health. In return they expected a coin or something to eat. This tapping continued until nightfall. Most members of the family looked sleepy during the day because they had stayed up late the night before to gamble. Their success or failure on New Year's Eve was supposed to foretell what luck the new year had in store.

Early in the morning the older boys and girls told fortunes by gathering around a copper kettle in which each one had placed some identifying article, such as a ring or knife. The group sang a song, connected with some occupation, while one token was drawn from the pot. If a boy's token was drawn, the occupation described would be his; if a girl's token was drawn, then she would marry a man engaged in that occupation. After this they all danced the *horo*.

Epiphany or Bogoyavlenie on January 19 commemorated the baptism of Christ. The Dragalevtsy boys and girls knew how the day was celebrated in other villages near the rivers or the sea. There the altar cross was thrown into the icy water. Naked youths dove in and struggled violently for it. The winner, carrying the cross, then collected money from the crowd. More important even than the money was the feeling that he would be fortunate during the coming year. But Epiphany did not pass unnoticed in Dragalevtsy, even though the river was nothing more than a racing mountain brook. The priest brought the cross out to sell at auction. The buyer, of course, returned it to the priest, but with his purchase received the assurance of God's blessing in the days to come. One year, a hiker happened to be passing through on his way up to the top of Vitosha. He saw the crowd gathered around the priest, bought the cross, went to the tavern for a free drink, returned the cross to the priest, and went on his way up the mountain. Peasants marveled for some time afterwards over the dispatch he showed in the whole affair.

Formerly on this day, children were christened with cold instead of lukewarm water, and all brides of that year were bathed in the river. When I asked why such custom was no longer practiced, Bai Angel, the village registrar, shrugged: "Oh, then the people were stronger and could stand such treatment."

On the previous day the children had all awaited the priest's arrival to sprinkle holy water in every room of the house. As we have already seen, many families collected bottles of the water that had been especially blessed for Epiphany, in the belief that it would cure various illnesses later on.

Bulgarian boys and girls never celebrated their birthdays. Instead, they made much of their name days. Each child bore the name of some saint, with a special day on the church calendar. Each Ivan (John) celebrated on the day following Epiphany, January 20; each Grigor (Gregory) on February 7; each Iliya (Elijah) on August 2. And so it ran throughout the year. Those with names not appearing on the calendar generally chose the day of "The Forty Holy Martyrs." Whereas Americans would expect to receive gifts on their birthdays, Bulgarians, especially those who were married, expected to entertain and provide food and drink for their friends on their name days. Children had to grow into the many practices surrounding holidays just as they had to grow into understanding of how to become a good farmer. It took some time to learn, for example, that on September 11, the Day of the Beheading of St. John the Baptist, one should have nothing to do with objects colored red. That color symbolized blood and guilt. On the first of March, however, red was very much in evidence. In the cities the young people exchange *martenitsi*, equivalent to our Valentines. This day was popularly called *Baba Marta* or "Old Woman March," because the weather during March was changeable and whimsical.

Although the villagers themselves paid little attention to the patriotic holidays which had been started within the past few decades, children welcomed them, for they meant a variation in the school routine. Schoolteachers would never think of letting a patriotic holiday go by without some special exercises. Among such holidays were those commemorating the liberation of Bulgaria, the King's birthday, the King's name day, the King's ascension to the throne. A special holiday for students was also becoming firmly rooted. It was the one honoring the missionary brothers, St. Cyril and St. Methodius, who were the patron saints of learning.

These holidays, both religious and patriotic, were often the occasion for relatives to come to the village. The buses, mysteriously held together in places by baling wire, chugged up the hill to the square to disgorge their load of people and grotesque bundles. Children crowded around to greet the newcomers and merrily skipped beside them as they walked toward the house. However, one-third of the homes had *no* visitors from outside the village during the year. Many of the visitors were originally from Dragalevtsy. A record of one year's migrants, twenty-one in all, showed that six had married outsiders and settled elsewhere; four had gone as soldiers, four as students, two as laborers, and the rest as cabmen, watchmen, and a coffeehouse proprietor.

All these holidays meant much to the children: exciting food, observance of age-old customs, and the arrival of guests. A few holidays were of special importance to godparents and godchildren. On

"Studying their lessons in the pasture while tending the sheep . . ."
See page 117.

Dragalevtsy families on their way to a *Subor* in Simeonovo.
See page 124.

"Boys and girls were up at break of day to tap every passer-by with a gaily decorated branch of a cornel cherry tree." *See page 126.*

Epiphany the godparent went to the home of his godchild, poured water on him or, in a rare case, pushed him into the river for the sake of his health during the coming year. On Cheese Sunday, however, the godchild went to his godparent's home with a gift and begged forgiveness for all sins committed during the year. On certain other holidays and special occasions the godchild was also supposed to pay his respects.

Some features of this bond between godparent and godchild were strange to one unfamiliar with the Orthodox Church. Behavior in the presence of godparents was highly formalized and correct. A person would not lie to his godparent; nor was he supposed ever to swear in his godparent's presence. These customs emphasized the mystical spiritual union which was supposed to exist between godparent and godchild.

Because the office of the godparent was hereditary, the same family provided godparents for the members of another family for generations. Consequently a feeling of strong relationship had come about. A godparent was considered one of the closest of relatives. "The godfather is closer than an uncle, and the godmother is closer than an aunt," the peasants used to say. Children of the two families could not marry even though madly in love, because, in the sight of the village, they were related. The taboo against marriage into the family of the mother's godparents further complicated matters. A woman, upon marriage, adopted the godparent of her husband, who assumed the same responsibility to the children of that couple as he did to the father. If a godparent was called upon to officiate at a wedding or a christening and was unable to attend, he could send one of his children to perform in his stead.

We have already seen the part that the godparents *(kumove)* played in the wedding ceremony. The rite of christening revealed even more of the relationship between godparent and his spiritual ward. He went with a friend or relative to the infant's home, some two or three Sundays after its birth, and took it to the church. He had previously discussed the child's name with the parents and usually followed their wishes, but had the right to give the child any name he thought proper. In the case of the first son he was apt to follow the custom of giving him the "little name" of his paternal grandfather.

After the morning church service a small group of interested people would gather around the priest up near the front of the church. The priest, dressed in his richly decorated robes and with his long auburn hair uncovered, made an impressive figure. The sexton and a woman or two scurried around getting lukewarm water ready in a basin. The air of the room was heavy with the combined smell of incense, used in the church service, and melting tallow, as the tapers in the front candelabra sputtered toward exhaustion. Before they flickered out an attendant doused them in water and threw the stubs into a tin receptacle near the bowl of sand, in which worshipers had placed candles in memory of the dead.

After the layers of swaddling clothes had been removed from the infant the priest quieted the small group by saying: "Let us begin." While the godparent held the baby he listened to the solemn obligation which he was assuming, an obligation made more impressive by the use of scriptural passages and a charge by the priest. Levity quickly replaced any serious thoughts as the godfather jocularly affirmed three times that he "resigned" from the devil, and spat across the baby resoundingly onto the floor to signify that he would keep everything unholy from the child.

The high light of the church ceremony was the immersion of the tiny baby three times in warm water mixed with olive oil. As Father Sava had had ample experience with the three little girls of his own, he deftly balanced the child in palm and forearm while laving it three times in the name of the Father, the Son, and the Holy Ghost. Then the woman assisting the godfather, usually his wife, dressed the baby in an entirely new outfit. While this was taking place the priest was washing and drying his hands with a bar of soap and towel which the godparents provided and which they expected him to keep as a part of his fee.

The infant's mother had remained at home because her purification ceremony at the church could not take place until forty days after the child's birth. Of course, she was expected to help prepare the christening feast which followed the church ceremonies. The christening party invariably arrived at the home in a gay mood and stood around laughing as the godfather turned the child over to the mother with these words: "I took the child away a Jew and now I return him to you a Christian."

There was usually an awkward wait of half an hour or more until the meal was ready and the priest had come to give the blessing so the feasting could begin. The christening dinner was one of the most significant of all family events for both adults and children. A child could not attend school without a baptismal certificate, nor could he later join the army, get a passport, or do anything of real importance without this church record. For a child from an Orthodox home to be unchristened was worse than having him unnamed; he did not exist legally. The national government, however, honored the equivalent of these baptismal certificates given by religious minority groups for their members, and also considered valid their marriages and divorces, be they Moslems, Jews, or Protestants. This religious freedom and tolerance had been a source of pride to many a Bulgarian in the past.

There were times in Dragalevtsy, though rare indeed, when the two families involved felt it best to break off the godparent relationship. If a woman, for instance, had three or four miscarriages, the godparents, who officiated at the wedding, might say: "You're not having very good luck with your children. We've been talking it over, and believe that things would work out better for you if you had different godparents." The husband and wife could then invite another couple to be godparents.

There were a few instances where babies did not have godparents at birth. Former godparents for the family might have died, moved away, or been unwilling to serve. In such a case the baby, no matter what the weather happened to be, was left on a street corner near the church just prior to the Sunday morning service. Naturally, the cries of the child attracted the curiosity of some passer-by. At the moment that he went over to look at the baby some elderly woman rushed out of hiding to say: "Congratulations, sir. You have the honor of serving as godparent to this child." So off he was marched to the church, be he foreigner, gypsy, drunk, or on important government business, to participate as godfather in the christening. Should he move to some distant place, he was still expected to keep in touch with his unexpected charge and, if possible, return in due course of time to take part in the godchild's wedding. This strange custom illustrated that where there is a *must*, such as *having* to have a godparent, there was a traditional method for correcting any irregularity.

Another *must* for the children, at least from the government point of view, was school attendance. The child began his formal education at seven years of age. In the "good old days" much ceremony attended this event. The peasants called the teacher *"Kandilo,"* a candle, the one to light the path for the child entrusted to him. As education became more common, the old ceremonies died out. All that remained of that old ceremonial respect was the handful of flowers the children sometimes gathered in the fields for a favorite teacher.

In Turkish times, only boys attended school. Educational activity in Dragalevtsy, however, took a new lease on life with the completion of the excellent building in 1931, made financially possible by the help of the Ministry of Education and the Ministry of the Interior. The school consisted of four primary grades and three classes which were termed the "pro-gymnasium." Boys and girls were supposed to complete the pro-gymnasium, though they could drop out as soon as they reached their fifteenth year. The director was in charge of all of the school's activity, under the supervision of the school inspectors.

The diagram on the following page illustrates the educational hierarchy of the country.

Few decisions were left to the local school authorities, whose duties had become largely administrative, in the sense of observing the regulations handed down from above. As the school director said, "Everything is controlled from the *Inspection,* though the teachers have much freedom in the classroom." Even this freedom was supervised. At the conclusion of each class the teacher had to go to the office and list the work taken up that hour, the questions asked, and assignments made. The inspector made surprise inspections of the health situation, the records of the director, and, if he chose, of the lesson notebooks of the school children. The purpose of this inspection was to check up and control, not to supervise constructively.

The school was supported financially by the Dragalevtsy *Obshtina,* though the salaries of the eight teachers were paid by the national

MINISTER OF EDUCATION

Division of Elementary Schools

Division of Secondary Schools

Division of Higher Schools

Office of Regional Inspection

Office of District Inspection

City

Large village (director)

Small village (head teacher)

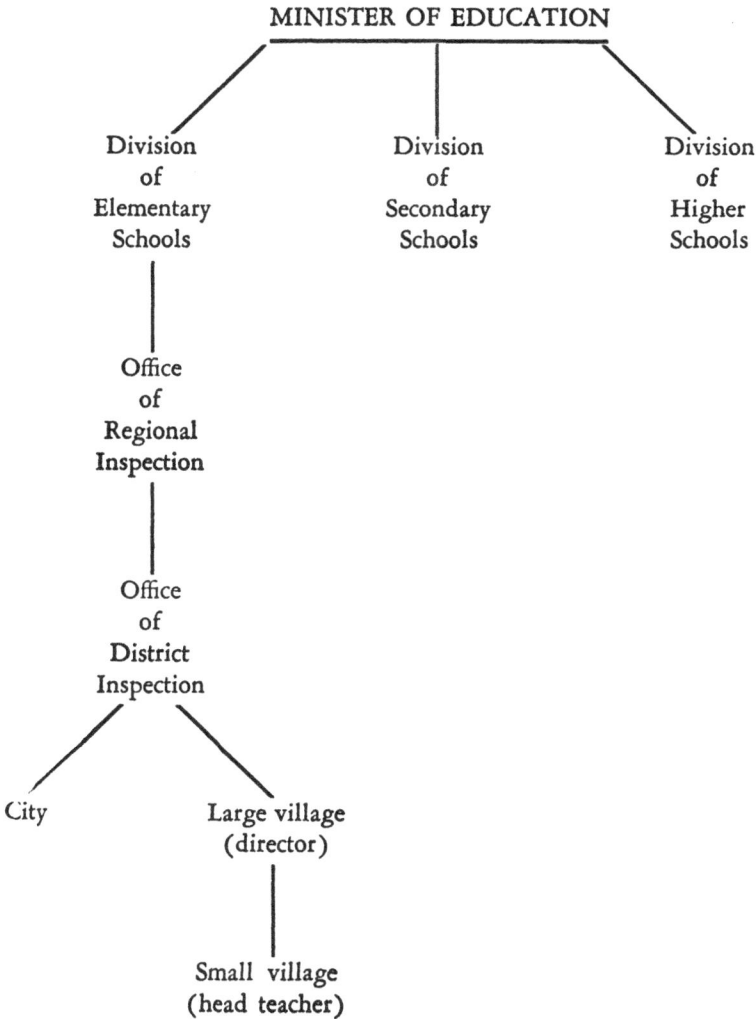

The Educational Hierarchy of Bulgaria as It Affected a Village Schoolteacher, 1937

government through the Ministry of Education. Parents had no fee to pay, unless the child continued his education in a gymnasium in Sofia.

There was, the director said, a noticeable relationship between the type of home and success in school work. Uneducated parents did not provide good conditions for study, since the pupils had no tables on which to write, no quiet, and lived in unhygienic surroundings. The more intelligent parents did their best to remedy such defective conditions. Most of the children had a great desire to study, but unfortunately many parents killed this enthusiasm. They either sent their children to tend the cattle, or, if the student gave lessons as an excuse for not doing some task, the parent said, "You don't need all that stuff from books."

At times the teachers gave some of the poor but bright students garments, shoes, and caps. The students receiving the mark six (excellent) were taken free of charge on a trip to a theater in Sofia, were given a free bath at the public bathhouse, and a large bowl of soup in a Sofia restaurant. As the director said, "Prizes help a great deal to stimulate study, and those who do not attain them are very disappointed." Five or six times a year the teachers took the older pupils to Sofia to visit the zoological gardens, the museums, a monastery, and sometimes a movie theater.

A glance at the list of courses on page 135 shows how the subjects were distributed through the first seven years of school. The tendency had been to follow the conventional courses of Western Europe, without any real adaptation to the needs of the villagers.

The textbooks, uniform for the whole Sofia district, were chosen by the Ministry of Education. While most students bought their own paperback textbooks, the school had approximately $245 in its budget for a textbook loan library to aid the poor students. The teachers assigned written work at intervals; for instance, the teacher in history and geography would give homework every five or six lessons, the teacher in arithmetic every day. All students recited daily because of the small number in the class, but written tests and examinations were not employed to the extent they are in American schools. Near the end of the semester one written lesson was required in each

CURRICULUM OF BULGARIAN ELEMENTARY SCHOOL
(1937)

Hours per week

SUBJECTS	PRIMARY (Grades)				PRO-GYMNASIUM (Classes)		
	I	II	III	IV	I	II	III
1. Religion	1	1	1	1	1	1	1
2. Bulgarian Language, Reading	9	9	7	7	7	6	5
3. Storytelling	3	3	—	—	—	—	—
4. French, German, or English	—	—	—	—	—	—	2
5. Arithmetic	4	4	4	4	3	3	3
6. Practical Geometry	—	—	1	1	—	—	—
Geometric Drawing	—	—	—	—	1	2	2
7. Civics,	—	—	4	4	—	—	—
General, Bulgarian History	—	—	—	—	2	2	3
8. General, Bulgarian Geography and Civics	—	—	—	—	3	4	3
9. Natural Science, National Economy and Peasant Hygiene	—	—	3	3	—	—	—
Natural History, Physics, Chem., and Hygiene	—	—	—	—	3	4	3
10. Drawing and Handwork	2	2	3	3	4	4	4
11. Penmanship	—	—	—	—	1	—	—
12. Singing	1	1	1	1	2	2	1
13. Gymnastics	2	2	2	2	2	2	1
Total hours per week per class:	22	22	26	26	29	30	28

subject, the date to be fixed by the teacher. Sometimes this was the only written test the class had during the course of that semester. At the end of the year there was a formal examination to help the teachers in judging the progress of the pupil.

It was the duty of the director to visit classes for purposes of supervision. She gave suggestions and occasionally taught a class to illustrate teaching techniques to less experienced teachers.

Judging only from the deportment marks, which were perfect for all students, there was little or no trouble with discipline. The truth of the matter was, however, that in Bulgaria a student's deportment mark was written on his diploma, thus following him throughout life. Therefore teachers found it more of a trial to lower a student's conduct mark than to fail him scholastically. All discipline cases were sent to the director, who reprimanded the student or sent the child home to his parents. The law did not permit corporal punishment, although many parents would have been glad to give the director the right. The final step, to which the director seldom resorted, was to require the student to attend school in a neighboring village.

There was little friction between the parents and the local school authorities, probably because the schools were a branch of the government and one seldom protested loudly against the government. If some trouble arose, parents complained to the school director, who passed the complaint on to the mayor.

There was nothing in Dragalevtsy, or in any other Bulgarian village, comparable to our Parent-Teacher Association. The very old peasants still regarded the government school as an outside and, therefore, slightly suspicious innovation—valuable for "the people of the world" perhaps, but yet to be proved indispensable for the village. Most of them agreed that the school widened the already existing difference in attitude between young and old. I once heard a good-humored disagreement between a mother and her twenty-five-year-old son. The woman had been explaining to me that she went to church to pray to God to help with the fields, to send rain and sunshine.

"But mother," interrupted the son impatiently, "the rain doesn't come from God."

"From where does it come then?"

The son sighed as though he were exhausted by endless repetition of a lesson to a stubborn child.

"From vapors up above, as the books tell us."

The old woman grinned undaunted.

"Well, God gives the vapors."

In spite of the suspicion toward anything new, the peasants were, on the whole, favorable toward education. While they slyly pointed out instances of unemployment among the intelligentsia, they were shrewd enough to see the economic advantages of formal schooling. Many villagers told me of a Dragalevtsy man who got a gymnasium (secondary school) education, found no work in Sofia, and came back to farm his land. The fact that he could survey his fields, keep his accounts, and do various other things more quickly and efficiently than his unschooled neighbors, had made him a living example of the benefits of education, as far as the Dragalevtsy farmers were concerned.

I had often heard both Bulgarians and foreigners say that children in Bulgarian villages did not know how to play. Though such a statement accurately describes the past, it was certainly becoming less true because of the growing influence of the school. Nevertheless, with the exception of certain games played in the pastures, children's group games were new to the village.

The older people said that fifty years ago there were almost no games; even these few were played only by men and boys while the women and girls always carried their knitting needles or distaffs with them. "The women sang while they worked and that was their game. The lonely shepherd boy had his *kaval* [flute]." Most of the old people had absolutely no recollection of games they played when young, which probably accounted for their unfriendly attitude toward children's games. One laconic old *baba* snapped: "The children throw stones at one another for a game."

There was much difference of opinion among the adults as to just what the children did in their playtime and with whom they played. A young man told me that children played together even if the families were unfriendly, but an older woman insisted that parents completely controlled their children's choice of playmates. The simplest way of getting at the truth was to talk to the children themselves. The children were used to seeing me and were uniformly friendly, often running to meet me as I came up the lane from the meadows. I had photographed many of them and knew their parents, so it was easy to get them to talk.

One solemn little group of five girls told me they were playing, which I took to mean that they were at leisure for the moment, for they were simply sitting on the ground by the stream trickling down the village street.

"What do you play?"

"Oh, we play 'woman's work' and talk about the cattle, school, and such things."

"Don't you ever play with dolls?" I ventured, for only one of the group was as old as thirteen. Five pairs of black eyes looked at me seriously.

"Some of us have never had dolls, and now we are much too old."

Shocked exclamations greeted my last question, when I asked if they ever quarreled.

"Never, for we are neighbors, and share our bread, and play together every day."

Borislav, Ivan, and Boris (one thirteen-year-old and two eleven-year-olds) were an entertaining triumvirate. The father of Borislav was a streetcar conductor in Sofia and often took his son to the city. On one of these trips, the boy had seen Sofia children rolling hoops. When Borislav got back to the village, he showed his cronies how to make and play with hoops. The boys said they shared food as well as toys, and helped one another with work. Ivan had to work a great deal, which curtailed their games considerably. When I asked this group if there was any fighting, the boys grinned.

"We fight with the other boys because they make fun of us when we don't know our lessons."

"What about fighting among you three?" I persisted.

"Well," said Borislav frankly, "we have to beat Ivan once in a while because when we fight for fun to see who is strongest and Ivan wins, he boasts, and then we have to fight him seriously." (Boris told me later in private that he didn't like Ivan very much, but "I take him as a friend so as not to be without any one.")

While I was sitting on the curbing near the fountain with the three boys, a tiny, six-year-old girl wandered up. I asked her if she ever played with boys. The thin little braids bobbed vigorously up and down for the Bulgarian "no," as she gave the universal reason, "My mother doesn't let me."

All the children to whom I talked agreed that it was more fun for boys and girls to play separately. (Seven-year-old Mara did play with Peter, but only, she assured me earnestly, because she had no one else in the neighborhood.) It was also better to play with relatives because "one doesn't quarrel so much." The boys in general liked to play in the schoolyard "because one meets one's friends from outside the neighborhood there." One brown-skinned imp in ragged hand-me-downs said that "Lots of us play near the school because our parents cannot see us and call us to work." Both boys and girls said that the teachers showed them many games which they still played in the summer.

The children of Dragalevtsy seldom acted out stories or dramas which they had seen portrayed in books or in a *vecherinka* (entertainment). The boys did almost no tree-climbing because there were few trees in the village large enough. All the climbing that was done was "for work," to get nuts or fruit. Games with balls or marbles were brought to the village by students going daily into Sofia to one of the higher schools. The group games of a formal nature requiring ten or fifteen children were learned in the village school and were usually played in the schoolyard. Some of the most popular children's games were the following:

Na svinkya (Playing swine). Several boys hit a wooden ball into holes with the use of clubs knotted at the end. There was a boy guarding each hole and one in the center. The idea was to get the ball into the hole. This was a peasant form of golf and was one of the oldest games played by Bulgarian villagers. It was the special favorite of boys who were keeping the animals in the pastures.

Sus kukla (With a doll). Some people estimated that one out of every six little girls had a doll, while others maintained that the number was nearer three out of six. There were no statistics on this subject, but playing with dolls was uncommon enough to make it a source of great joy to children who did so. Some of the dolls were very crude and ugly, though many parents were buying western dolls in the market to bring home.

Na Tsiganeta (Playing gypsies). Since every boy caring for animals carried a stick, it was natural that a game using this stick originated. The game called for the contestants to bounce their stick from one end to the other in rapid succession, much as one would "skip" a rock on the surface of water. The stick might jump five or six times before falling motionless. The least skillful contestant received a beating from the others.

Na machuklin (In New England called "Peggy"). Consisted chiefly of tapping the end of a small stick so that it would rise into the air to be hit again before it fell to the ground.

Na Kokumish. This was a form of tag played by children sitting around in a circle.

Na gonenitsa (Form of running tag). The one to be "it" *(gogan)* was chosen by "counting out" with the use of the following poem, which corresponded to "eeny, meeny, miney, mo":

> *Ala bala nitsa,*
> *Turska panitsa,*
> *E, gidi Dancho,* .
> *Nash kapitancho.*

> Ala bala nitsa,
> A Turkish plate,
> Hey, you Dancho,
> Our leader.

The children when counting out spit on their fingers. The *gogan* would run and try to touch the others.

Na zhmish (Hide and seek). The one who was "it" said the following poem while the others hid:

> *Dve vrabcheta*
> *Se skaraka*
> *Na Popovota vrata.*
> *Pop izleza i im kazva*
> *Ish, pish, tish, stesh, mish.*

> Two sparrows
> Quarreled
> At the Priest's gate.
> The Priest came out and told them
> Ish, pish, tish, stesh, mish.

After he said this he went to hunt the others. Wherever he found anyone he spit in the place where he was. The others tried to run to the homebase and spit there before he did.

Kosharki (Sheep folds). This was a game which had been played extensively a generation ago, but its use was dying out in the village. The children would build miniature sheep folds, houses, and fences out of rocks. This game corresponded after a fashion to our building with blocks.

The outstanding characteristic of all these games was that they required little equipment and few participants. At home, the play groups were inevitably restricted to the family and nearest neighbors, often relatives. At school, children could choose relatives and other children in the same grade. Play groups in the fields were formed on the basis of family ownership of land and common pasture. These latter groups often gathered in the village and went to the fields together, the youngsters carrying loaves of bread, baked peppers, and fresh tomatoes. Even in play, the family was important, for every type of play group almost automatically included relatives. As was previously pointed out, there was less quarreling among the children who were related. I often heard: "You shouldn't hit him; he's your relative."

The new types of play were still limited. The radio, comic papers, and movies were almost unknown to the village child, just as they were to the average adult. Only twenty-five newspapers reached the village daily, and these had few comic strips. Magazines and books were a rarity. Sofia bookshops had some exquisite children's books, but I never saw one in the village. Sometimes when I came into a village home on a winter evening, I would see an unforgettable picture. Near the fire the father sat quietly, elbows on knees, the mother was spinning near the one dim electric bulb, and in the center, crouched at the low table, a boy, nine or ten years old, was laboriously reading some fragment of a periodical to his parents. Their pride and pleasure was unspoken but obvious.

There was one radio in the village, and the children were of course conscious of it as it blared incessantly in Renaissance Square, but it was not a part of their life, any more than the movies or trains. Only 45 per cent of the total population, including babies, had ever attended a movie, and less than 40 per cent had ever been on a train.

With Sofia, a city of over a quarter million people, only five miles away, the ability of the villagers to resist, however passively, the influence of the "people of the world" was astonishing. It was a remoteness, not to be measured in miles, but in generations.

Such pleasant customs as keeping pets were almost nonexistent. The tiny puppies with which the children sometimes rolled were bred for strictly utilitarian purposes, to guard the sheep, and were taught to be unfriendly to man.

The very young and the very old in the village spent much time together. When I was taken to pay my respects to the oldest man in the village, a venerable figure of over a century, we found him sitting in a sunny corner of the yard under a gnarled pine tree. Tumbling around him were half a dozen tiny children, somewhat hampered in their movements by their clumsy, heavy clothing but very proud to show off their ancient relative.

The older children derived a quiet amusement from their position as spectators at the village ceremonies. There were always little boys making merry along the path of a wedding procession or tramping along wide-eyed beside a funeral. At *Subori* and *hora* mischievous little boys were ubiquitous. The little girls stayed solemnly by their mothers; only their eyes wandered, alternately solemn and amused. The village child had no routine planned for him, either for his physical or his psychological needs. There was no emphasis upon self-expression for the child, only upon conformity to the routine of the family.

Yet there was warmth and affection for the children. When a child died, the tempo of the household perceptibly slackened. "It is God's will. It is Kismet [Fate]," the family said, but the father grew more taciturn and the mother wept silently as she spun in the evenings. And when a funeral procession reached the cemetery, the new mourners often found there other mothers who had lost their children. These wailed again for the long-departed and begged the spirit of the newly dead to carry messages to their babies.

And when a family grew rich according to village standards, it was on the children that gifts were lavished, perhaps a wish-fulfillment by the elders inherited from their own drab childhood.

The irrepressible fun of childhood could break through even the hard crust of conformity to village life. The older villagers might suspect and even condemn the amusements of the "people of the world," as they did the trouser-clad women skiers who streamed through the square on winter week ends. The youngsters were different. As I was leaving the tavern one February afternoon I saw a pigskin-sandaled urchin, seven or eight years old, attempting to go down the hill on a crude pair of homemade skis. The snow was thin and he stuck fast in the mud. He took off his skis, put them on his back, and started up the steep slope to try again, and again.

"Hey, there, what have you got?" I called. The answer was a sly smile and a revealing comment: "Skis, like the 'people of the world.'"

CHAPTER VIII

FAMILISM, A CHANGING WAY OF LIFE

THE DAY at last arrived when I could anticipate the peasants' answers to most of the questions that I asked them. When I inquired what they would do if they had five hundred dollars to spend, I could list in advance the items they would name. The older people, especially, thought and acted largely in terms of the Dragalevtsy of the "good old days," when life was lived in a *familistic* way because the family played the major role in the community. When I understood the characteristics of familism, as a result of observing and reading about peasant life in other parts of the world, the many interesting but isolated facts I had noticed in Dragalevtsy began to make sense and to form a pattern. In a familistic society, whether it is in the Balkans or China, life is largely customary and traditional. Individualism is discouraged because of the crises that the unusual person creates in the daily routine. People prefer a dead uniformity, or a leveling of the best toward the mediocre. The family plays the leading part in this task of molding an individual into the accepted pattern. From childhood to old age the kinship group brings pressure to bear upon any nonconformist, since the family as a whole loses prestige in the community if a member gets out of hand. The family, too, is the chief training ground for the young, and parents cannot blithely transfer any responsibility of this sort to an outside agency such as the school or the church. Village opinion holds the parents accountable.

Furthermore, economic life is centered about the family. Since family members grow or make for themselves most of the things they need, they depend only to a minor degree upon stores, factories, and other commercial agencies. The family is the productive, distributive, and consumptive unit. This is one reason why village families can weather so many wars and so many depressions: they can satisfy most of their immediate wants at home.

"The family is the productive, distributive, and consumptive unit . . ."
See page 144.

". . . religion . . . has become rigidly institutionalized." (The altar of the church). *See page 145.*

"... they threshed the wheat of fifty-five farms ..." *See page 151.*

"The people ... customarily associated liquor with holidays and leisure times." *See page 155.*

Visitors suddenly confronted with the familistic way of life for the first time are often shocked at the low level of living which they observe: animals sharing the same dwelling; monotonous diet and low health standards; waste of time and energy with inefficient tools and methods. Before the peasant is condemned as unambitious, indolent, or stupid, there are a few things the outsider must bear in mind. In agricultural villages throughout the world the land base has been shrinking while the population has been expanding. This has meant decreased economic opportunity. Farms which were once adequate are now divided up strip by strip and handed over to many descendants, with the results that the term "eking out a living" has come to have real meaning for the peasant. The outsider often forgets that the rise in the level of living in the cities through the techniques of mass production and mass distribution has been relatively recent and phenomenally rapid. The villager is not really so far behind the times if one compares his life with that of many cities a few decades ago, or with the blighted areas of these same cities today. But one cannot deny that quite a few peasants seem to take pride in resisting social change; they are slow to experiment with new methods, and they assume that what was good enough for their fathers is good enough for them. This resistance is based, to a great degree, upon the realization that accepting too much from outside will seriously affect the social organization of their community. Urban society is not nearly so close-knit and can allow for contradictions and inconsistencies on a much broader scale than can the village, where life is still intimate and face-to-face. Dragalevtsy people, for example, in 1937 were conscious of the far-reaching changes brought about by the abandonment of sheep raising in favor of dairying. Sometime ago, a number of the peasants actively resisted this economic trend. In the opinion of many, these conservatives were stupid; at the same time they were bright enough to figure out that changes would result in the economy to which they were accustomed. Because they were accustomed to it, they wanted to preserve it.

In a familistic society religion has usually become rigidly institutionalized and is closely allied with the family. All family events call for the blessing of the religious intermediary; there are usually household shrines; there is considerable emphasis upon observing the forms of the religion; and usually the prevailing religion has a monopoly in its field. Where there once existed two or three competing religions, the peasants now have a syncretistic set of beliefs that almost all of the people accept.

- The population in a familistic society tends to be stable. The folk legends and religious beliefs stress the importance of remaining at home. Permanence becomes a virtue, for travel outside introduces too much novelty. Separation places a strain upon the family relationships, which must be kept at full vigor in the interest of community self-preservation.

Recreation is personalized instead of being commercialized. Peasants, as far as possible, spend their leisure hours in the company of others, to say nothing of the many hours women spend working with each other within a family or neighborhood circle. Just as the villagers have ceremonial ways of doing many things, they also have formal ways, or proverbs, of saying many things. This we saw earlier in the description of the *Sedenki*. Proverbs reinforce those beliefs that help maintain the familistic society, and serve as convenient means of self-expression. At the same time they are standards of behavior.

Because recreation and economic life are personal, the familistic society has little need for much reading and writing. The priest, the middlemen, the taxgatherers, and a few others who early associated themselves with the village economy needed to "figure," but the rest of the people had little concern with that.

In most family-dominated societies, life is man-centered. In some areas this arrangement is related to religious beliefs; in others, it is related to the economic organization of the family in which somebody has to give orders necessary to the carrying out of the daily activities. A recognized head, conscious of his own importance, acts authoritatively in directing his family group.

The local government is traditionally managed by elders, who represent families rather than political parties or individuals. The village elders make their decisions from the standpoint of what is good for the village as a whole in the light of precedents rather than from a narrow legalism. The religious writings or sacred legends are conveniently cited to justify the actions they take. Such governmental activity exists primarily to meet crisis situations and to keep the established ways of life moving smoothly. The giving of relief, the provision of education, healing of the sick, insurance of cattle and crops are all left to the family rather than to the government.

It is quite possible for several societies to use the familistic approach, in the sense that the family is the dominant institution, and still differ as to the relative importance of many community values. Most of them would probably respect the heritage from the past, but even here there would be variations. As far as Dragalevtsy was concerned, the chief values or virtues were land ownership, hard work, frugality, premarital chastity, observance of some of the more important religious rites, and being a good neighbor. In connection with the last, the villagers said, "God help those with bad neighbors" and "Without good neighbors life couldn't go on."

The Dragalevtsy people, although their underlying organization and philosophy was primarily familistic, had adjusted themselves to a number of modern ways. Some ways persisted because they fitted in with the established customs, and others because they were kept in vogue by force or by the authority of the mayor.

Commerce, as represented by about ten merchant groups, had become established in the village because it was conducted essentially as a family enterprise. From time to time a local man sold some of his land and started in business for himself. He always employed members of his family rather than outsiders, because he trusted his own. If he needed extra help and had an unmarried son, the normal thing was to urge matrimony. He carried over into his business the same idea of division of labor which prevailed at home and in the field. The men ordered the goods, settled the accounts, sold the liquor in the taverns. The women acted as cooks or clerks. Some of the wives who helped keep the store could not read, write, add, or subtract and had to give whole measurements or else depend upon the customer to hand them the right amount for fractions. A husband explained when I discussed the matter with him, "It is better to lose money through error than through dishonesty." Both men and women co-operated in keeping the place clean. Here the man made a concession which he would seldom have made in the home.

These merchant groups, with the exception of two or three of the most prosperous, led a precarious, short-lived existence. During the three years in which I knew the village, three successive proprietors managed a business undertaking in one building alone. Bai Penko's tavern, the largest of all, was founded thirty years ago by his father; another tavern which was founded fifty years ago had been owned by the present proprietor for ten years; one grocery store was started in 1935, and another was taken over by its present managers in 1936.

The largest grocery store had stock, which I carefully inventoried, approximating $200 in value. It included many articles which would have been found in an American country store a generation ago. *(See Appendix III.)*

The degree to which the old familistic way of doing things pervaded the local businesses was shown by the nature of the groups that conducted these businesses. In the case of one grocery store two men were in partnership. One partner took care of the cardplaying, which he promoted in a small space at the end of the store, and his wife took care of the grocery section. The second partner, in addition to helping with the cardplaying and the grocery work, mixed bread for the bakery downstairs, and sent his wife up to work in the store when she was not busy in the bakery. The stock of goods in this particular store was very small, and so was the clientele. The proprietor of a second grocery store was usually away from his place of business, leaving his wife in charge. She was quite dissatisfied with the present arrangement, saying, "I have to get up at two or three in the morning to do the housework before coming to the store. I go to bed at night between eleven and eleven-thirty. Life is full of hard work, but life is more sure now because we have food and money." This couple, incidentally, was one of the few childless couples in the village.

Bai Penko, too, made use of members of his family. He himself was the general manager and worked several hours a day in the tavern; his wife was in charge of the kitchen; the older daughter took care of the six or seven upstairs rooms which were rented to the veterinarian and summer guests when not occupied by members of the family. The older son, Pano, was in charge of serving drink and food, and of all accounts connected with this service.   His younger brother was in charge of the small grocery store next door, though he often turned the store over to his mother while he served drinks at rush hours in the tavern.   The younger daughter helped with both housework and the grocery store, while the eighteen-year-old grand-daughter did the heavy, disagreeable work.   Both sons married shortly before I left Dragalevtsy and their wives spent several hours each day working under the direction of Bai Penko's wife.   Because of this large family circle Bai Penko hired two men only on holidays, one as an extra waiter and the other to roast meat freshly killed for the occasion.

Familistic, or at least personal, reasons determined why families traded with one particular merchant.   Reasons such as these were most frequently cited:

"We are close friends."

"We are slightly related."

"He loans me money when I need it."

"We were members of the same political party."

"I had a quarrel with the proprietor of another grocery store, so changed to this one."

Only occasionally did the people say:

"He sells pure and fine goods."

"His prices are cheaper."

Just the same, there did seem to be considerable shopping around on the part of the villagers.   They favored those places where they could get credit.   But here again family connections helped decide whether or not a man could get credit from a given merchant.   Credit was extended with discrimination.   A poor risk, when credit was re-fused, frequently transferred his trade to a different store.   The older proprietors were often called upon to give advice, and thus enjoyed an advantage over the younger businessmen trying to establish them-selves.   One of these young men said to me: "Because of my age, nobody comes to me for advice.   That is why my trade is small."

Commerce also made its way into Dragalevtsy through a few commission merchants who regularly visited the peasants to buy eggs, poultry, and livestock.   Occasionally they speculated in land.

In Dragalevtsy, therefore, familism had yielded some ground to commerce. People did make occasional purchases in the village and in Sofia. They talked more and thought more about money. They even valued it more highly than a generation ago, but the basis of their economic life remained self-subsistent, with an emphasis upon goods, not cash.

Co-operatives had also come to Dragalevtsy. In a very real sense village life itself was a co-operative enterprise, although it did not possess the specific characteristics of an economic co-operative. The large joint family, which has been widely prevalent throughout the world, also had many elements of the co-operative which have been maintained, at least in the sentiments of the people, even though the family group has become individualized and smaller.

Self-subsistent peasant farmers are accustomed to working together when something needs to be done. Theirs is, after all, a co-operative way of life. They also know that their own hard work and their own planning are responsible for whatever success they achieve. They are suspicious of outsiders who seek to organize them, and are fearful that any tie-up with the business interests outside the village means loss rather than gain. They are not accustomed to using money to make more money, although they know well enough what it means to pay interest on borrowed money.

Agricultural co-operatives often gain adherents more quickly when there is a feeling of distinction or distrust between city and the country people. This is because co-operatives have been identified in such places with the agrarianism which unites the peasants. The profit motive of capitalism is linked, in the minds of many villagers, with the urban businessman, in spite of the fact that the villager who owns his land is also a capitalist. Perhaps it is this idea which Americans find hardest to grasp in their evaluation of peasant Europe. Land is not something to be bought and unfeelingly sold for money. It is rather a means of livelihood, an extension of oneself and one's family.

As the merchant groups in the villages are few and insecure, the co-operatives do not have the opposition of vested interests which they face in a more highly developed economy. I realized from the beginning that co-operatives had made much less headway in Dragalevtsy than in many other Bulgarian communities. The secretary of the General Union of Bulgarian Agricultural Cooperatives explained: "The farmers live near the city and prefer to market their goods themselves rather than through the medium of co-operatives. They find that they get higher prices in the Sofia bazaar than they would receive from co-operatives."

Nevertheless, the three co-operatives represented in Dragalevtsy gave me some insight into the reasons for success and failure of those which did get off to a start. The co-operative which had made most progress in Dragalevtsy was a purely local affair which arose to meet a definite need. In some respects it was more like a corporation than a co-operative, but it was a "combining together" to get something done.

One of the richer families in the village used to spend twenty-five days threshing its grain with horses. As a result, the family began to think of using a machine to do the work. The idea incubated until Trayko Danev decided to take the initial plunge and persuaded his relatives to plunge with him. Two other men joined them in the purchase of a threshing machine in 1930. Their purpose was to thresh their own wheat and, if possible, thresh the wheat of others for a fair return. The first years of the ring's existence, when the price of wheat was high, were the best years. Between 1935 and 1937 the prices were so low that the group just managed to cover its expenses. However, because of their 400,000 leva ($4,878 at 1937 exchange rate) investment, the men did not think of giving up the ring.

The structure of this group was simple. Annually, a president, a treasurer, and a manager were elected to control the operations of the ring. The manager, who had technical training, received a salary. Two workers and a machinist were employed from outside and were paid a percentage of the wheat threshed. In 1935 they threshed the wheat of fifty-five farms, including that of the original ten partners. A written agreement existed among all members, who paid in wheat, which was sold for a sum to be divided among the members.

The familistic background of this group was interesting. The originators were all members or cousins of the Danev family except two rich landowners living in the center of the village, who were close friends of the Danevi. After four of the original partners died, their sons or sons-in-law succeeded to the control of their shares. The five Danevi outnumbered the others, forming a unit around which clustered three other members. There was some friction whenever meetings were held, but the minority was easily suppressed by the majority.

Most of the group considered membership an honor, symbolizing wealth and importance. Generally the village approved its existence, as shown by the increasing number of families who sought its services at threshing time.

Twenty-one Dragalevtsy men also belonged to the Animal Husbandry-Dairy Cooperative, with headquarters in Sofia. This group had a twofold aim: (1) to enable members to get animal feed on credit and more cheaply; (2) to develop a milk distributing center. Though Dragalevtsy members did not have regular meetings in the village, most of them attended the annual meeting held in Sofia at which the reports of the officers of the co-operative were read. Before this annual meeting the Dragalevtsy men got together in the village and agreed on common action at the Sofia meeting. Dragalevtsy had one representative on the Executive Committee and one on the Control Committee. These men kept the villagers informed as to the condition of the co-operative. Two or three Dragalevtsy people had resigned, recently saying that "there were hidden matters." Most of the men who still belonged said that their membership entitled them to cheaper feed for their animals. I asked ten of the members why they belonged to the co-operative:

"I get cheaper feed through the co-operative."

"I joined in order to work collectively; to have a central depot for milk."

"The co-operative gives credit for food at a lower price."

The agricultural crisis through which Bulgaria had been passing reflected itself in the life of this co-operative. With the hard times, peasants said they did not have enough ready cash for their dues, and so dropped out. However, one could not consider this a true village organization because its physical basis was Sofia, and there was no formal organization operating in Dragalevtsy as a local.

In 1934 the Association for the Insurance of Horses and Cows was organized in the village with the help of the veterinary doctor stationed there at that time. He was acting under the guidance of the Bulgarian National Cooperative Bank. The idea back of the association was to make it possible for peasants to obtain additional credit, since no credit could be extended by the bank on uninsured animals. Insured animals were considered better collateral than land and were allowed a greater percentage of money in proportion to value. When the organization was first founded, the fifteen or sixteen charter members entered because they were in favor of insurance. The seventeen members who joined later did so because they needed to insure their animals to get a loan, regardless of their attitude toward insurance.

In the normal life of this organization almost no difficulties were encountered. The members used the schoolhouse for the annual meeting, which was open to all outsiders. There was an executive council, a control committee, and a committee for the evaluation of animals. A president was elected every year and a treasurer every three years. Some of the committee members were changed each year. If a farmer wished to join the association, the proper committee appraised his animals and insurance was assessed at the rate of 4 per cent of the total value of the animal.

The conservatism of the peasants prevented any rapid growth of such an organization. As one peasant, not a member, explained: "I haven't joined because I feel that here we have good air, good food, and good water for our animals, and therefore they aren't as subject to diseases as are the animals nearer Sofia. God is kind."

A few years ago a private insurance association was organized which ended unfortunately for the investors. This failure was cited by some people as an additional reason why they should not join the present association, though it was backed by the Co-operative Bank.

In order to get a better idea of the relationships among the members and between the members and the officers of the Insurance Association, I interviewed fifteen of the thirty people registered and found that:

1. Friendship played little part in determining who should become members.

2. The reasons for joining were varied:

    a. "I have six cows. Need help in case a cow dies."

    b. "I wanted to get money from the bank."

    c. "The veterinary doctor enrolled me when he organized the association."

3. All members were satisfied with the officers who represented them.

4. The relations with the Co-operative Bank in Sofia had been cordial. Once a year the bank sent out a commission to see that everything in the village was in order; a commission also came out in case of the death of an animal.

The Insurance Association illustrated the way many village organizations arose in Bulgarian villages. The idea of the organization originated in Sofia, was put into effect by a State employee, and members were recruited from those who thought that their interests would be served by belonging. A glance at the list of members, ranging in age from twenty-four to sixty, showed that they were among the most enterprising in the village. The organization would doubtless have been only half as large had it not been for the ruling of the bank which required insurance on any animals put up as collateral. Since the association did not attempt to teach the peasants how to feed or stable the animals, it was missing a real opportunity for further service.

The traditional economy of Dragalevtsy had therefore been subjected not only to the incursion of commerce with its emphasis upon money, but also to the formation of co-operatives to meet some specific needs of a group of interested persons. In addition there was a concerted effort throughout Bulgaria by the national government to raise the peasants' plane of living. Some of this activity found expression in Dragalevtsy, largely through the initiative of the county agent or *agronom* who was concerned with the improvement of agriculture and livestock. Since he had to care for almost a score of other villages, his visits to Dragalevtsy were few and far between, so the peasants were quite correct in saying that little was being done for the improvement of agriculture in the village. While the county *agronom* gave lectures at intervals during the year and consulted with some farmers regarding their work, he could not initiate and carry through a thorough program without the help of a local *agronom.*

As far as livestock was concerned, there were two boars and one village bull for breeding purposes. The law required that each *Obshtina* take charge of its own breeding animals. There was supposed to be a local breeding association, but the mayor was the only member. A fund was being collected for a village barn. Meanwhile, the animals were boarded out to various peasants who received a fixed sum. Improvement of livestock was more easily managed through the control of male animals, which were inspected each spring. Those of bad quality were castrated (the veterinary's fees for this work being the following: pig, 10 leva; donkey, 20 leva; horse, 40 leva). If the animal died, the State paid for the loss. I happened to visit the village at the time the veterinary doctor was making his inspection of horses. Before he could begin his thorough examination, the representative of the *Obshtina* looked over the bills of sale to be sure each man had his own horses. This bill of sale cost 3 per cent of the amount exchanged. If the horses had been foaled at the home of the present owners, the men presented certificates of ownership which they had previously obtained from the mayor for fifteen leva. If the doctor found that a horse was ill, a second examination was made two weeks later. If the animal was still sick, State officials bought the horse for a small sum and killed it. A fine ranging from two hundred to five hundred leva was charged if the horses were not brought for the examination. While a national program for home demonstration work had been prepared, Dragalevtsy so far had received few benefits.

Recreation, like economic life, had been subjected to efforts at organization. The people of Dragalevtsy customarily associated liquor with holidays and leisure time. In the earlier days there was little organized opposition to the use of alcohol, but by 1922 considerable public opinion had been aroused against the *kruchmi.* On January 1, 1922, all the taverns of the village were closed by order of the Village Council, which thought that the drink shops were a social evil. The village was very much stirred up, most of the men siding with the tavern keepers and the women with the Village Council. The tavern

keepers immediately petitioned the higher court in Sofia, which reversed the decision of the Village Council on the grounds that the
order had been issued illegally, without having a vote of all the
people.   On March 12 the taverns opened again.   A large sum of
money was due the tavern keepers in the way of damages, but they
did not try to collect for fear a referendum would be carried out and
the taverns abolished indefinitely.   Between January 1 and March 12
the men of Dragalevtsy had gone to Sofia and to other villages so
frequently to drink that they had lost much time from work, to the
distress of their families.   Since Dragalevtsy became a resort place, it
has had summer guests who demanded alcoholic beverages; this
clientele aids the tavern keepers, although many peasants are still in
favor of closing their places of business.

In 1935, largely at the suggestion of one of the schoolteachers,
a temperance society was organized among the young men.   The score
of members took their organization seriously, though many villagers
ridiculed it.   This organization gave a *vecherinka* at which a "drunk"
comedy was presented in order to discourage drinking.   The temperance pledge included not only drinking but smoking and was so difficult
to keep that a year later some of the members had fallen from grace.
The village registrar, who was active in the Village Council in 1922
when the taverns were closed, was not permitted in the temperance
association because he smoked.   His admission would have greatly
strengthened the work of the organization as far as alcoholic temperance was concerned.

The monthly dues were five leva, which were to be spent for
buying temperance literature and sometimes in helping the poor.   One
member was sent to the city of Stara Zagora for a conference of all
temperance associations in Bulgaria.   The priest could not be a member "because he has to drink in his work," that is, communion.   The
organization was almost extinct because the initial enthusiasm had
waned and some of the original members had dropped out.   In order
to justify their own actions those who quit talked against the remaining members and accused them of smoking and drinking on the side.
The society's value as an aid to temperance would have been hard to
estimate.   While it must have had some effect on the minds of the

young people connected with it, it had little reforming influence upon the older people. The government was trying to control the sale of liquor by limiting hours of sale and by excluding minors from taverns. For example, the taverns were closed during the time of Sunday morning service.

Here, then, we have three efforts on the part of villagers and authorities to promote abstinence or temperance. The first, in 1922, used the local governmental machinery but lacked the support of the men who were the only ones with the right to vote. The second was the voluntary association of strong-willed youths, who soon found that formal organizations had short lives in Dragalevtsy. The other method consisted of the mayor's arbitrary edicts, which he had power to make people obey. From time to time he overlooked infringements of his rules, being more interested in avoiding excessive drunkenness on the part of well-known sots than in decreasing the tavern keeper's revenues.

The chief objections raised to the use of liquor were economic rather than moral. Although recreation was not commercialized in our sense of the term, the tavern keepers did make an adequate income from catering to patrons with free time on their hands.

The only formally organized recreational group in the village was the *Yunak* organization. It began its career in the village in 1932. The local group was one of hundreds scattered throughout the whole of Bulgaria for the purpose of organizing the youth for sport and physical education. The activity of this organization was intense in the beginning. Since then, however, interest died down to the point that the young men gathered only two or three times a year for exercise in the schoolyard where there were rings and a horizontal bar, and once a year for election of officers. Many of the members felt that it was an honor to belong because it signified to the rest of the villagers that "you want to be healthy." The older people, however, thought that such an organization was unnecessary since, in their opinion, "if the young people did enough work in the fields and around the stables they would not need any organization for exercise." As is the case with many clubs of this sort, there were four or five people who really carried the load in an effort to keep the group alive. Because this organization was so utterly out of line with the familistic point

of view, its members got little encouragement from the older people
and had little lasting enthusiasm for its program.

The Reading Room Association *(Chitalishte)* was organized
locally on February 10, 1921, upon the initiative of men who had
been outside the village and had returned with the desire to raise the
cultural level. From its founding, however, it concerned itself more
with financial than with cultural problems. In the words of the constitution, the purposes of the organization were:

A. to influence the people of the village, especially the young to self-
improvement.

B. to cause to grow among the people a feeling for public unity in life
and for intelligent usage of the village domain.

C. to cultivate love towards the fatherland and towards the good and
morally edifying elements of the national literature.

The *Chitalishte* planned to achieve its purpose by opening a public
reading room free for all inhabitants and visitors and supplying the
room with suitable books. The *Chitalishte* group also planned to organize evening lectures and other public performances and entertainments "in order to create a patriotic feeling and appreciation of the
nation's past."

The first act of the newly organized society was to buy a large
sign inscribed with the name of the organization. After that the
officers spent money for chairs, lamps, benches, bookcases, stovepipes,
and tables, while individuals donated inkstands, water jugs, a box for
gathering money, and a picture of the Madonna. Unfortunately this
left practically no money for any form of reading matter. The expense of having a share in the construction of the *Obshtina* building
further drained the financial resources of the organization. It was
also a factor in keeping away prospective members who preferred to
wait until the building was paid for before they joined. In 1937
twenty-two people, most of them charter members, were looked upon
as active supporters of the work of the *Chitalishte*.

Most of the members were critical of the present officers, and
recognized that the organization's activities were at a standstill. When
members were asked to tell how they would improve matters if elected

to a position of importance they answered: "We should choose a new executive committee, put the library in order, lend out the books, have more evening entertainments. To do this we should get in touch with people in Sofia."

Part of the trouble arose from disagreement among the officers. In the words of one member, "An organization cannot get ahead with that sort of business." But even more of the trouble went back to the fact that the organizers had not convinced the villagers of the importance of the group. Meanwhile, most peasants looked upon it as an importation of interest only to the intelligentsia and their hangers-on.

The experiences of the *Chitalishte* and other organizations in Dragalevtsy revealed that the peasants were not organization-minded. Even if we included the governmental groups to be discussed in the next chapter, we would find that less than ten women in the village belonged to any formal group, and only 107 of the 510 men over twenty years of age had an organizational membership. Where people's homes were so conveniently located one would expect greater participation on the part of the men, at least. But almost four-fifths of them avoided any organizational affiliation, largely because they were not accustomed to using an organization to do what they thought needed to be done. One of the most frequent reasons for failure to join was this: "Why should I pay the fees charged when I would get nothing in return?"

In this world of competing *isms* Dragalevtsy represented in 1937 a modification of familism, the oldest and most widespread way of life we know, perpetuated by agricultural villages all over the world. But familism was slowly losing out. In some quarters of the world the commercialism of a capitalistic system was supplanting the older values with money values; in other quarters the collectivism of a communist society was shaking the economic foundations of the large family group.

As far as Dragalevtsy was concerned, commercialism was in its infancy. Back in 1937 communism might have seemed to the outsider to have a hold on this village as well as on others in Bulgaria because of the old affection the Bulgarian peasants had felt for the Russians since the days when the Tsar Alexander II of Russia helped free Bulgaria from Turkish control. Contemporary Russia also was making its appeal through Bulgarian communists who had taken the agrarian, or "rights-for-peasants," aspect of the modern Russian system and expounded it to the peasants as communism. Although it was doubtful whether the Dragalevtsy peasant had any clear idea of collectivism, it was certain that he would have been completely bewildered by the idea of giving up his cherished holdings to the state.

Dragalevtsy, therefore, was something of an anachronism, for the familistic system still had a firm grip on many of the adults. Their ideas had been set a generation ago by parents who subscribed unquestioningly to the familistic way of life. The young people, on the other hand, were receptive to other values and other standards and were ready to look more and more to the "people of the world" for guidance and leadership.

"Even the priest was a government employee . . ." *See page 163.*

"The mayor [with his family] was the spearhead in the attack on the old ways." *See page 163.*

"Trayko Danev . . . one of the richest peasants in the village." *See page 164.*

CHAPTER IX

THE NATIONAL STATE AS INTRUDER AND REFORMER

IN DRAGALEVTSY, as in agricultural villages throughout the world, the national state was building up a loyalty in competition with the unquestioned loyalty people used to give to their family group and their community. The spread of the government-sponsored school, though its scientific teachings were elementary, weakened the hold of the formalistic, institutionalized religion which went along with a familistic society. Because of the school there was increased conflict between the older and younger generations.

Not only in time of war but also in time of peace the national government had been calling its young men to leave their plows and their cattle to take up pick or rifle. The *trudovatsi* handled the picks, and those in military training the rifles.

After the first World War Bulgaria initiated an ambitious program of compulsory labor as a substitute for military training, formerly required. The original plan called for service from both young men and young women. Recruiting of women later ceased for they proved unsuited to the system. The young men of the country were enrolled in labor camps where they performed their *trudova* (compulsory labor). Each young *trudovak* was required to serve eight months, though for two thousand leva, or less than $25, he could buy himself off at the end of six months. Some young men paid a total ranging from 9,000 leva to 32,000 leva, according to their economic status, to be entirely exempted from service.

The *trudovatsi* built many highways and bridges, and worked without pay in government shops, factories, and lumber plants. Their achievements were significant although much of this potential man power was unused or misused because of the lack of sufficient engineers to give proper direction to the work.

The *trudova* system existed in principle until Bulgaria joined the Axis, though, she like all countries defeated in the first World War, passed through a period when compulsory labor was gradually replaced by compulsory military service. After the *coup d'état* of May, 1934, various groups of army officers controlled many of the country's policies; so it was not surprising to learn of the strengthening of the military forces of the nation. One sign of the government's changed policy was the fact that in 1935 not a single young man from Dragalevtsy went as a *trudovak*, but sixteen were called to do military service. Those eligible for service were called before a commission of army officers and examined; the successful ones passed on to receive military training, and the rest were returned home. Those who were rejected lost some standing in the eyes of the villagers, because it was thought that they had inherited some family weakness. The *family* rather than the individual was blamed.

There was undeniably a great influence exercised upon the village by the practice of taking young men, in their impressionable years, away from the village for an interval of several months. They lived in an army barracks or a *trudovak* camp with other young men from different parts of the country. For a time they ceased doing some things which the village thought essential, and they learned to do other things which older family members would perhaps have frowned upon. They went out from a family system where each member worked more or less as a part of the whole; they returned often very conscious of their own individuality, and had to pass through a process of reconditioning before the early customs, habits, and patterns of thought once more closed about them. There were some individuals who never again fell completely into line and who turned to Sofia for employment and a more congenial atmosphere.

Older men who returned to the village as retired noncommissioned officers enjoyed a certain prestige that lingered after brass buttons and clumping boots had been exchanged for the conventional village attire. On the wall of the office of the Village Clerk, the names of all local officials and public employees were posted. There was considerable information regarding each man, but the concluding and perhaps most important item was the statement of the person's service to the State, either as a soldier or a *trudovak*. All had served in one of these capacities, else they would not have been employed.

The young men were the only ones called to leave the village. As for the rest of the people, the national government went to them in the persons of its civil servants, who comprised most of the intelligentsia. Even the priest was a government employee, since the state supported the church. The doctor received most of her salary from public funds, since private practice in a village would have been financially unrewarding. In addition to these, the veterinarian, the schoolteachers, and an occasional lecturer from outside formed the advance guard of the national State. All of these public servants knew that they would be held accountable by their supervisors or inspectors, and identified themselves much more readily with the national bureaucracy than with the peasants whom they were supposed to help. Of these, the mayor was the spearhead in the attack on the old ways. One of his duties was to preside over the village court, where he stood for the law and order of the land.

One day as I was leaving the office of the mayor he asked me to stay and attend court. I sat in the corner of the room next to a bookcase jammed with documents. The mayor sat behind his desk, covered on such occasions by the white, green, and red Bulgarian flag, on which there was a stack of folders, one for each case to be heard. On the wall over his head were pictures of the King and Queen, a beautifully colored coat of arms of Bulgaria, and a patriotic calendar. Through the window I could see the small memorial garden in which forty-four fruit trees had been planted in memory of the forty-four local sons killed in the battles of Bulgaria's several wars. Two rifles for use when the policemen were on patrol stood in the gun rack not far from the desk. A bench lined another wall close to the small cast-iron stove. Near me there was a hat rack, and a spittoon less popular than the floor. A muddy, unshaven policeman stood at the door to bark people in and out.

The first man to come in was Iliya Trunin, a thirty-two year old villager in a *kozhuh* (sheepskin coat), who was being sued by Ivan Katsarov, a tavern keeper. Iliya, instead of going to the expense of running an electric line from the main electric cable, had arranged with Kátsarov to extend the line from Katsarov's tavern to Trunin's tavern for a sum of five hundred leva. Bai Ivan, in testifying before the court, said that on the Day of the Virgin he had let his friends talk him into favoring Iliya, although he knew he was helping a competitor. A year passed, however, without the sum being paid to Katsarov, so the case had been brought to court. The witnesses upheld the plaintiff's side and the mayor charged Iliya to make the payment.

A peasant man in ragged clothes, worn *tsarvuli* (pigskin moccasins), and uncut hair, brought action against a peasant proprietor, who had engaged the plaintiff's son to work for him for a small amount of money from May until the time school should begin. The defendant claimed that the boy was to serve until the eighth of November. The father maintained that the agreement had been until the beginning of school in September and not until the eighth of November. Unfortunately for the father, in writing out the official charge he had mistakenly said that the contract period ended on November 8. The mayor, seeing the situation, persuaded the peasant proprietor to release the boy for school against a partial refund of the wages on the part of the boy's father. This satisfied both parties.

After these two men went out, Trayko Danev, whom the reader knows by now as one of the richest peasants in the village, brought charge against a Sofia merchant for breach of contract in a financial transaction involving hay. Trayko apparently had justice on his side and was ready to prove his case by the use of two witnesses, one of whom was to testify regarding the agreement made and a second to testify regarding the partial fulfillment of the agreement. The first witness testified:

"As I recall the incident, I was at the table with this merchant and Trayko Danev and heard them make an agreement whereby Trayko said he would give 780 leva for hay. He went away and that is all I remember."

Trayko then asked for the testimony of the second witness whose name had been written on the brief as Nikola.

The Judge (Mayor): "Nikola, Nikola. But the last name is not written."

The Merchant (Defendant): "Your Honor, I object. This man has not indicated the last name of his second witness and God knows how many Nikolas there are in Bulgaria. Furthermore, the second witness was present in the courtroom while the first witness was testifying. Therefore, the second witness, according to law, cannot testify, no matter what his last name is."

Trayko: "I didn't tell him to come in here. It's not my fault."

Judge: "The defendant's objection sustained. We cannot accept the testimony of the second witness unless the defendant agrees."

Defendant: "I do not agree."

Judge: "In that case, the plaintiff loses, since he cannot use the second witness and cannot prove his charge."

Trayko: "I am just a villager but I don't want any crook stealing money from me. I'll take this to a higher court."

The defendant (who had just walked toward the door) returned and said:

"Your Honor, I want it put in the record that this man called me a crook so that when he takes this to a higher court, I'll show him that I, too, know how to act."

I could see that the Sofia merchant was well posted on legal procedure. Afterwards Trayko and his two witnesses went to Bai Penko's tavern for a round of drinks which seemed to do little to console Trayko's aggrieved feelings.

The next suit did not get very far because the plaintiff wanted the judge to have the defendant swear that he did not owe the plaintiff any money. The defendant answered:

"I will swear if the plaintiff will swear first that the sum mentioned in the statement of the case is accurate down to the very last lev."

The plaintiff was unwilling to do this because the mayor, in the short time he had been in the village, had made the peasants afraid to swear falsely, something which they commonly did before. The plaintiff, seeing that he was at a disadvantage, agreed to compromise.

Court adjourned with a brief formality and the mayor came over to discuss the afternoon's proceedings, with evident enjoyment of the flashes of humor.

Local administration of justice was not the only thing the mayor had changed. Upon his arrival in Dragalevtsy he had replaced the traditional Village Council, composed of peasants, with an Advisory Council, made up of other public officials. Later, when the national authorities wanted to restore the appearance of representative government they worked out a scheme for establishing a new Commune Council. They took care, however, to rid it of any candidates that they did not like.

On March 28, 1937, six councilors were elected for the Dragalevtsy commune: three from Dragalevtsy proper, two from Simeonovo, and one from the "quarter" near Sofia. In addition to these six, the following were ex officio members of the council: the mayor, the representative of merchants, the representative of the agricultural zadruga, the director of the school, the physician, and the veterinarian. To obtain its three members, the village of Dragalevtsy was divided into three districts, from each of which one representative was chosen. Any man over thirty and with an elementary school education who signed the following petition could nominate himself as a candidate for office.

> To the Judge of the Commune
> in the village of_____
> County _____

PETITION

With this I wish to declare:

1. that I wish to offer my candidacy for a village councilor in the elections which will take place on _____ 19__ for the purpose of electing members of the commune councils.
2. that I offer my candidacy in _____ elective district of _____ commune _____ county.
3. that I do not belong to any secret or open organization forbidden by the laws of the country.
4. that I do not have ideas against the government, that I am not in favor of communist, anarchist or violent methods for social and political struggles.
5. that if I am elected as a commune councilor I will not favor any class, society, groups, nor will I serve my personal interests, and in my work I shall be guided by the common interests of the commune of which I am a member, and

6. that I have been registered under No._____ in the election list of the commune.

    I wish to have my candidacy recognized as legal and confirmed.

    I enclose certificate No._____ from _____ 19__ year issued from _____ commune, which shows that:

    (a) I have the right to elections (commune elections)

    (b) that I am 30 years of age and have completed my military service (or the regular labor service)

    (c) that I have completed _____ (education)

    Village, City _____ year 19__

Respectfully:_____

The names of those wishing to run were posted publicly by the mayor; all the villagers had the opportunity to contest the fitness of any candidate; afterwards the mayor sent the names to Sofia with his own recommendations. The final decision was in the hands of the judge in Sofia. Thirteen Dragalevtsy men decided to stand for election. Three of these were rejected by the authorities. People from each district voted only for a candidate from their district. Mothers were the only women permitted to vote.

Before the election, with the permission of the mayor, the candidates were allowed to make speeches. After the election, as is frequently the case in countries elsewhere, some people were dissatisfied with the results and demanded a new election. However, everything seemed to go off in an orderly way and the voting was fairly done. This election, though, was the prelude to the national elections which were later held, resulting in the restoration, after a fashion, of the *Subranie,* or National Parliament.

Re-establishing a commune council seemed to be a very complicated affair to the average peasant, and afforded quite a contrast to his usual way of getting things done. In order to fulfill the law requiring ex officio members to represent the merchants and the agriculturists, two new organizations had to be started in the village before the time of the election. The merchants organized a Merchants' Association, had one or two meetings, elected a representative, and discussed general policies for the future. Although nothing definite had taken shape by the time I left the village, the merchants hoped to practice price-fixing, standardization of products, and the like. The representative appointed by the merchants was Ivan Katsarov, previously mentioned as a manager of one of the village taverns who appeared as a plaintiff in court. Furthermore, the farmers had to organize themselves into an association called a zadruga (which had no connection with the old form of joint family known by that name). Such organizations followed the Italian system of corporations under the Fascist regime and insured representation in government on the basis of occupation rather than political preference. These agricultural zadrugas worked well in theory around the council tables in Sofia, but met with resistance in the village. In the opinion of many leaders of co-operatives, the zadrugas ran counter to the strong co-operative movement which had already made such headway in Bulgaria. Their critics point out they not only struck at the very foundation of this movement, but also had the fault of being handed down from above instead of springing from natural needs in the village itself.

Should there have been a number of industrial laborers in the village they too would have had an ex officio member on the council. The presence of the other ex officio members on the council was easily understood. The doctors, the school director, and the mayor were expected by the national authorities to take an active part in deciding the policies of the village government. Such a council, in spite of the great furor connected with its formation, was still an advisory rather than a governing body.

In order to get a better understanding of the way government affected the life of the individual peasant, I sought answers to several questions.

How were the taxes paid? On February 25, July 25, and October 25, people were supposed to come to the *Obshtina* and pay taxes. Those who did not show up were summoned by the courier. If this summons went unheeded, the individuals were sent red notices reminding them that they had to pay within three or four days. If they failed to do this, the *Sekretar Birnik* made out a list of their possessions for a public sale which was held if the taxes remained unpaid. There had been several instances where goods were actually sold for failure to pay taxes, much to the shame of the people involved.

What happened if a man owed some money and didn't pay? If the sum owed was over 1,000 leva, the people had to go to Sofia to court. If it was under 1,000 leva, the people appealed to the village court (the mayor was judge, and the registrar was secretary). The creditor made an application for the sum due, and had either to give a certificate that the sum was due or, having no certificate, swear by a cross and the Bible that his claim was just.

What happened in case two men got into a fight and hurt each other? In case of a fight or a disturbance of the peace, the men were subject to fine up to 500 leva. However, the mayor smiled when he said: "I haven't given any fines for fighting yet, for I am a man with a Christian soul." Should the mayor feel less virtuous he would fine a drunk, together with the tavern keeper who let him get drunk. The fine would range from two to three hundred leva, leniency being shown to drunken men because they are "not responsible for their actions when drunk."

How did people transfer property? The transfer of animals was performed at the *Obshtina.* A bill of sale was made out and signed by the mayor. The transfer of land and houses had to be made through a notary public in Sofia since the banks in such cases usually needed to be consulted regarding indebtedness on the property.

How were public lands administered? Because the forest pertaining to the village was not large enough to justify a special forester, it was placed under the care of the *Okoliyski* (county) forester who was in charge of planting new trees. A forest policeman, regularly employed by the *Obshtina,* saw to it that the villagers cut no wood without the special permission of the local authorities. The land belonging to the *Obshtina* had decreased greatly during the past twenty years because of its sale as building sites. If the *Obshtina* decided to sell land valued at less than 200,000 leva, then the *Okoliyski* governor could give permission. For more than that, the Minister of Interior had to approve the transfer.

Who saw that roads were kept up and bridges repaired? If a bridge was broken, the fact was reported to the mayor, who sent a man to repair it. The State took care of all the roads outside the village, and the *Obshtina* of those inside.

What other things did the village government do for the people of the village? The *Obshtina* saw that pure water was piped to the different neighborhood fountains. In addition, the *Obshtina* had the only telephone in the village, which anyone might use upon the payment of two leva. It also had a fire pump, which, so far as could be learned, had never yet been put to work in an emergency.

The national government encouraged its village representatives to set up organizations to promote specific activities. One of these was the Red Cross, to which a score of adults, most of them of the intelligentsia or official group, had paid membership fees. The village doctor was one of the leading spirits in this association, though the mayor, having been connected with the Red Cross in Sofia, was also interested. Its activities did not get under way until after 1937, with the exception of the placing of a few posters and a drive for members. The more active Junior Red Cross, headed by the school director, stimulated the interest of children in first aid and good health practices.

A second organization was a local branch of the Union for the Protection of Children, organized by the mayor, who was also its president. Its chief activity was the serving of hot lunches to all school children who did not go home for lunch. This applied to rich and poor children alike, because the wealthier parents were often away from home and thus unable to provide a hot meal for their children. Sometimes as many as eighty of the children received their meals in the *trapezariya* (dining room). The adult members of this association or Union were also for the most part from the intelligentsia and the official groups. This hot-lunch movement had spread throughout Bulgaria into hundreds of schools. Many times it was financed outright by the government; oftentimes by private groups aided by government subsidy. This association, with the support of the *Obshtina,* distributed food to the poorest families of the village at Christmas time. For instance, the officers gave two pounds of sugar, two pounds of rice, and two pounds of meat to each of 120 families at the Christmas season. The pride and independence of the peasants was demonstrated by the fact that no families came to ask for these gifts, because no family wanted to admit it was poor enough to require them. However, those in charge of the distribution were well acquainted with the economic situation of the villagers and distributed the food accordingly. There was an annual meeting of the Dragalevtsy Union to hear the reports of the retiring officers and to hold the election of new officers. The basis for membership was payment of the annual fee. In other words, it was purely philanthropic, in that the members expected to get nothing in return. I was not surprised to find the names of but very few farmers on the membership list. Peasants did not yet understand organized philanthropy, though individually they might be unusually generous on occasion.

Another group in the village was known as the Association of the Decoration for Valor. In 1935 the mayor got together all of the men who had been decorated for bravery during time of war. A Sofia major talked to them and persuaded them to form a local association, after pointing out that no harm could come and that possibly some advantages might follow, such as price reductions at State baths, special rates for traveling on the railroad, and pension legislation through collective lobbying. At the time I studied the group three or four meetings had been held with unusual group harmony. There was an initiation fee of twelve leva, and an annual fee of twenty leva per member. The membership totaled twenty-eight, which showed Dragalevtsy's reputation for bravery in war. I obtained facts about the organization not only from the officers, but also from interviews with fifteen different members. The reasons given for joining were varied:

1. "To have pensions."

2. "We who have decorations are to get help from the State by working together better."

3. "The privileges of free baths, freedom from school tax, reductions on the railroad, free medicine."

4. "We were ordered to form the local association from Sofia."

5. "Said I would get an iron cross. I wrote down my name but I don't know why."

Some conflict had sprung up between the village veterans with decorations and those who received no decorations but still thought they should have been allowed to enter the association and obtain the same privileges as the others. Many association members felt the same because some friend was in this predicament. The situation became

more complicated when the members of the association began to receive public recognition on certain holidays while the other veterans
remained in the background.   Although this was an organization
planned in Sofia and organized in the village by a Sofia man, good
local men were elected as leaders and, judged by the number of meetings, the organization had been very active since its founding.   However, since the interest in the organization was dependent upon the
benefits the members expected to receive, the organization could be
expected to die a natural death if no such benefits materialized.   Then,
too, it definitely ran counter to village practice in that it gave promi-
nence to a few peasant men, setting them up over others whom public
opinion considered just as worthy.

The local doctor, like the mayor, was also concerned with changing the ways of the people.   She was sent to Dragalevtsy by the Department of Public Health, which had charge of selecting and locating
all physicians in the State service.   Because she was married, she received the higher salary of $41 a month, was allowed a private practice
in the afternoon, and could charge 30 leva for a night visit.   For
assisting at a birth, she got 500 leva ($6).   Since the people were
poor, she was able to collect little money from private practice.

The doctor did not keep her office hours regularly "since the
villagers don't understand office hours."   During the month of August,
for example, she was asked to visit only five or six houses, which
showed that most of the patients wanting her services came to her
office, where the treatment was free.   The patients suffered chiefly
from stomach trouble in the summer and from bronchial trouble in
the fall; in the latter case coming more often for consultation.   Because
of the expense involved, rarely did the patient ask for a second visit.
"The poor people who don't pay apologize; the richer people who
don't pay do not apologize," the doctor commented.

There were national laws which, if stringently applied, would
have done much to raise the level of sanitation and health throughout
the country.   Their application depended upon the initiative and
knowledge of the local health authorities.   In Dragalevtsy considerable
effort had been spent in seeing that the laws were kept.   The doctor
and the mayor, or the mayor's representative, visited the taverns and

sent samples of liquor and wine to Sofia to be examined. They also noticed what disposition was made of all sorts of waste and where manure was stacked. The doctor then wrote a report on the basis of which the mayor made a decree as to what changes were to be made. After thirty days the two made a second examination. The doctor usually found that the people did not really carry out these orders, and assessed a fine which the *Sekretar Birnik* had to collect. Such fines were imposed upon a baker who had been warned several times that his place was not clean enough. He did nothing to improve the situation, so he was fined five hundred leva to be paid within a month. If the fine had not been paid, he would have had to spend three days in prison for every one hundred leva due. A local confectioner was fined 22,000 leva ($266) for using saccharine, banned simply because the government had the monopoly of sugar.

Specimens of the village water supply, sent by the doctor, were examined at least once a month by the Institute of Public Health in Sofia. The doctor also had the right to analyze samples of all food-stuffs and household articles on sale, such as soap, cheese, sugar, pepper, and canned goods, but could hold the grocer responsible only for things which were unpackaged. Bread sold in the tavern and bakery was examined for an excessive percentage of water.

Vaccination against smallpox was scheduled three times in a village person's life: before he reached one year; when he reached seven, the age for going to school; and when he was twenty years of age. Typhoid inoculations were given only "if there are more than ten cases in the whole village." Diphtheria serum was given only in case of real need. Plans called for giving all school children the Pirquet reaction test for tuberculosis. In addition to the steps just mentioned, the doctor, through the *Obshtina*, organized a few health lectures during the winter and conducted a mothers' course. Young mothers especially were encouraged to visit the health station every week with their infants.

Assisting the doctor there was a midwife provided by the State, who aided not only in deliveries of infants but also worked with the children of school age and, in order to fill up her time, helped the doctor in her office work. She had had a gymnasium (secondary school) training and worked for two years in a lying-in hospital. The midwife, who had difficulty in winning the co-operation of the old *babi*, could not set a charge for her services but had to take only what the women gave. The State paid the midwife the equivalent of $16 each month. There was a health committee, composed of the doctor as chairman, the priest, the director of the local school and the mayor. The midwife attended unofficially. This committee met once a month to consider the problems of village hygiene and sanitation and tried to enlist public support for the doctor. The county doctor came twice a year without advance warning to visit the village doctor for the purpose of seeing if her reports were made out properly, if she exercised suitable control of the merchandise, and if she gave the school children proper supervision.

Another impact, of an educational sort, upon the traditional way of life was the *Naroden Universitet,* or People's University. This consisted of a series of lectures in the schoolhouse on such topics as these:

1. "Our National Awakeners: A Patriotic Talk"—by a local schoolteacher.

2. "Problems and Purposes of the Zadruga"—by the local president of this agricultural group.

3. "The Insurance of Cattle"—by a veterinarian from Sofia.

4. "Alcohol and Effects"—by a medical man from Sofia.

5. "What Village Homes and Food Should Be Like"—by a different medical man from Sofia.

6. "Concerning Faith"—by a priest from Sofia.

7. "Concerning Tuberculosis"—by the local doctor.

8. "The Cleaning of Seed"—by the district *agronom.*

9. "The Significance and Service of the Producers' Cooperatives" —by a former attorney and by the Superintendent of Cooperatives of the Bulgarian Agricultural Bank.

The mayor encouraged the peasants to attend in the hope that they would be inspired to improve their living conditions or become more loyal to the government.

Another educational group affected by the intrusion of the State was the school board. Formerly the peasants themselves controlled the board's membership, but it had become an ex officio body composed almost entirely of the intelligentsia. The peasants no longer had much to say about the employment of teachers, or what or how they taught. They and their children accepted what the national government, through its local representatives, provided for them. They took it or left it, but mostly took it.

The national government, along with its other activities, maintained a close connection with the national church. Before the liberation of Bulgaria, the practice arose of having three or five members act as a church board in each village. Even if there happened to be no church building, this group was elected to see about the construction of one. Such a board followed the familistic practice of expecting elders to manage local affairs. After the growth of the national state the board was continued, but subjected to outside control. In Dragalevtsy it consisted of five people: the priest (who was the president), a treasurer, and three other village men who acted as a control committee to audit the work of the old board which they succeeded at the end of its two-year term. In the past the biennial election was held on a Sunday morning immediately after church. But the government took care to see that only those men who had the right to vote *politically* were eligible to elect the church board from a list of candidates prepared by the priest. As the priest prepared his slate with the help of the older people in the village, his choices usually met with the approval of the majority of men.

A candidate had to be an Orthodox Christian by baptism, should never have been in a lawsuit, should not be a drunkard, thief, and the like, nor an atheist opposed to the church. The elections had to be approved by the Sofia Metropolitan, or the high church court, thus removing the authority still further from the village. An office of an elective nature such as this carried a great deal of honor with it. The duties of the office were not burdensome because the church possessed no lands to be administered. Traditionally the church board was supposed to aid in enforcement of Sabbath observance, but members were not particularly zealous in carrying out this obligation. The priest had been having trouble of late with one board member who had become such a tippler that the board's prestige was suffering. If some question needed to be decided, as was the case about five or six times a year, the priest asked the board members to assemble at the church, minutes were kept, and no outsiders attended. The government's influence was further felt during the period 1934-1937, when all political elections were suspended, and with these all church board elections too. No one was eligible to vote.

As the national school and church authorities had not been satisfied with the type of religious training that the children had been getting in the average peasant home, they had set up in each village an organization called "The Association for the Orthodox Christianization of Bulgarian Youth." In general, the work of the group consisted in teaching the school children the significance of the iconostas, church ceremonies, and other related matters. School hours were used, and attendance was compulsory. The school director, who had been asked by the Archbishop in Sofia to conduct the work of the association in co-operation with the priest, said that they had had about twenty-five meetings during the year. Parents and others who were interested attended these meetings. This was one activity which the peasants had accepted quite willingly because, as one woman said, "the children are kept off the streets when there is a group gathering, and thus do not learn so many bad things." This was the woman's way of berating parents for failing to take better care of their children. But fundamentally the acceptance was based upon the traditional recognition of the church's importance. In the past, whatever had bolstered up the established church had bolstered up the familistic system.

Such a barrage from the batteries of commerce, government, and education had left the familistic way of life in Dragalevtsy battered but not crumbling. The peasants were still amused at the intense activity of the intelligentsia; the few who were asked to confer with the authorities enjoyed reporting back to their families and friends just what they said and did. The people co-operated in the campaigns for this-and-that only when they knew that the mayor would send the policeman along if they did not co-operate. They attended lectures when ordered to do so, but they joined few of the organizations planned outside. Perhaps the best indication that this beehive of governmental activity was still on the surface was the failure of the peasants to seek advice from the intelligentsia who were supposedly there to help them. An exceptional peasant did; but the vast majority kept an eye upon what was going on without becoming involved in any newly initiated affairs.

Just the same, changes were in the making. Year after year, within given limits, people would be content to do what the authorities told them to do. This was because their family life, with its emphasis upon obedience and respect, had made them docile. If the commands proved too disruptive, however, or took away the things they counted most dear, their family and their land, they resisted.

But the peasants were little interested in fighting for political rights; these were individualistic and not in keeping with familism, which emphasized the welfare of the group rather than the rights of the individual. They did not yet want to have a hand in what went on in Sofia, in Berlin, or Washington. They still were village oriented. To be sure, war affected them, as did the price of grain, but in much the same fatalistic way that a heat wave or a cold snap would. They did not yet feel that they, and millions like them throughout Bulgaria, had the power to control many things affecting their daily life. Some of their fellow villagers in other parts of Bulgaria were alive to this fact, but Dragalevtsy was still politically illiterate.

The leaders in the village were aware of their lack of success. Some of them were disappointed in the peasants for not accepting at face value the words of wisdom they proffered so freely; others cautioned patience. They said, "We can't change things overnight. We will work with the children in the school. Our future lies with them." And they were right. But it was clear that the future they anticipated would be much more distant if the leaders continued to force upon the peasants a way of life imported from "the people of the outside world." Their quickest success lay in evaluating the familistic society that existed, in deciding what should be retained, and what changes should be made. The next step would be to discover by what means, already in use in the village, these changes could be effected. Then, above all, the leaders should have sought to persuade the peasants to help themselves. The governmental paternalism at work in Dragalevtsy created as many local problems as it solved.

The conflict was on, then, between the old and the new, between familism and the forces from the "people of the outside world." It was a stirring struggle when viewed in terms of people I had come to know and respect. It became a significant struggle when I remembered that Dragalevtsy was only one village out of hundreds of thousands where the conflict was even then being dramatically staged.

The new way of life that emerges may be more democratic or it may be the basis for additional authoritarian states. Democracy can be assured only if its representatives, who introduce the new, have an insight into the peasants' way of life, a sympathy that is so genuine that it can be quickly sensed by untutored folk, and a skill that can weave into the fabric of the past the strands of the present, in keeping with a sensible pattern for the future.

DEPARTURE—AUGUST, 1937

THE VILLAGE seemed unusually peaceful on that August day in 1937 when I made the rounds to tell my friends in Dragalevtsy goodbye. Many wanted to know how long the trip to America would take, others asked about my future plans. The majority said, *"do vizhdane"* ("till we meet again"), but several of the older people, who had patiently endured many hours of interviews in the previous months, sensed that their "time" would come before I set foot in Dragalevtsy again. They used the other form of leave-taking— *"sbogom"* ("God be with you"), and also asked God's blessing upon my trip. The mayor told me how much he had enjoyed having me study his village, the priest asked me not to forget my many friends, and Bai Penko took great delight in showing off his new grandson whom I had never seen.

The weather was hot. Few people moved through the Square and only occasionally did a wagon creak down the streets to the fields below the village. Even the flies, usually so troublesome, seemed languid. The dogs slept. Vitosha had lost its cap of snow. Storks grazed in the meadows, enjoying the frogs or snakes which they some-times caught. Three of the few planes recently added to the Bul-garian air force flew overhead with a roar that was ominous and quite foreign to a village where the ringing of Iliya's anvil, the grinding uphill of a dilapidated bus, or the squealing of pigs coming home from pasture were ordinarily the chief disturbers of serenity and quiet.

As the train pulled out of the Sofia station late the following afternoon I watched Vitosha slowly disappear from view. Ordinarily the sight of this mountain would have been merely an enjoyable esthetic experience, but now, with the realization of actual departure, Vitosha stood as a symbol of the way of life I was leaving behind, and I became aware of the degree to which I had identified myself with it and with its people. I knew that months of patient working with my Dragalevtsy data would be necessary before I would feel objective enough to describe, rather than champion, my Dragalevtsy friends. That is because once the "Balkan bug" has bitten an Ameri-can, neutrality is difficult to maintain; one either sides with this faction or that faction, this country or that country, and thus becomes a partner in perpetuating in "the outside world" those differences which periodically rend the Balkans asunder.

Even as I left Sofia I knew that my village study had proved personally rewarding. Most important of all I had learned the im portance of trying to view the world through the eyes of others before I passed judgment upon them. I knew that merely being different did not mean being inferior, and that physical appearance and material possessions were not the most important indices of contentment and security. I also knew that in the Balkans, the term *peasant* carried a connotation much more dignified than that usually ascribed to it. Bulgarian farmers were neither serfs nor dispossessed day laborers, but for the most part were proprietors of their land and home, and were respected by their families and associates. The sense of belonging to a large mass of kindred spirits, who shared the agrarian point of view, dressed in village clothes, and abided to a great degree by tradi-tion, gave each peasant a "consciousness of kind" which in our society has to find its substitutes in the Farmers' Union, the Farm Bureau, the National Grange, and a host of other organizations devoted to serving those who farm.   This self-identification with a mass of other peasants of course nourished conservatism and made the Dragalevtsy farmer of 1937 feel so secure that he had little incentive to rise above his present lot.

Another fact which became increasingly clear as I studied and reminisced about life in Dragalevtsy was the importance of the village community, not only in the economy and social structure of the country as a whole, but in the life scheme of each individual.   In a very real sense, as preceding chapters have indicated, the village was the peasant's social world.   And from his point of view, life was far from dull.   Although he never formalized his thoughts on the matter he was quite conscious of the play of outside forces because he simply watched what was happening to the church, the school, the business life, and government administration in his small community.

In Dragalevtsy, as well as in many other villages throughout the Balkans, the leaders of these various local institutions were in competition for power and prestige.   As an earlier chapter has shown, the family remained a basic institution, although it was experiencing changes year by year.   No longer were village matters formally decided by elders who represented the different kinship groups of the village, but instead, the national government in the person of local officials whom it appointed was making many decisions for the people. Religion, which had been traditionally allied with the family as the source of authority, likewise had been giving way to the State at the village level.   Furthermore, the word of the schoolteachers was of less importance than formerly because, as the population became literate, what seemed to be the skills of a few became the accomplishments of many.   There was no longer any magic to reading or any esoteric knowledge which the teacher alone could impart.   The increase in commercialization made the businessman an important figure to watch, for he seemed to deal, as the teacher did formerly, with terms and processes, such as the pricing system, the demands of the outside market, and the occurrence of depressions and boom periods, which the peasant did not comprehend.

As a matter of fact, these representatives of the different institutions might be considered actors in a drama which the peasant watched curiously and carefully.   He knew by heart the roles of the priest and the family heads; but he was less decided about the schoolteacher. The peasant was on the edge of his seat, though he attempted to hide his excitement, when a new governmental representative walked on the stage, reciting no memorized lines of his own but parroting off what the prompter whispered.   Nothing else could be expected from one acting under orders of the national government located outside the village.   The businessman, the fifth character, would be dressed for the occasion as a manager of a local co-operative or as a traveling buyer.   Both he and the governmental representative had a self-assurance which commanded respect, and both tended to disregard the other characters on the stage, probably because they understood that they symbolized something foreign to the village.

Strange as it may seem, the peasant of Dragalevtsy in 1937 watched this struggle for institutional leadership in the detached way a critic views a play and considered the outsiders on the stage only as a slight threat to his mode of life.   He also knew quickly when an actor was out of character.

As I approached America and again fell under the spell of the hurry and bustle that fills our days, with its emphasis upon novelty and having something just as good if not better than the neighbors, the importance of tradition in Dragalevtsy stood out in contrast.   From the peasant standpoint basic decisions were relatively simple because past precedents usually indicated only one course of action; fellow villagers steeped in the same tradition expected compliance, so that a person easily became contented with things as they were, subscribing to rationalization which made him satisfied with and even smug about the *status quo*.   Thus Dragalevtsy proved an interesting illustration of the paradox that a traditional society, while deadly from the standpoint of scientific, material, or intellectual progress, nevertheless accentuated those traits which made for contentment and for developing a perspective toward death and time which helped keep life going on an even keel.   There individual maladjustment was at a minimum, for each conforming individual had the backing of all other guardians of tradition.   In our western society the material prizes are much greater but the risks are greater too.   Truly, the individual stands alone against the world, the captain of his soul, capable of reaching heights of achievement of which no peasant would ever dream, but likely to grow disappointed in his failure to accomplish more. Widespread personal insecurity is the price we pay for the possibility of advancement. In Dragalevtsy of 1937 the peasants would gladly do without very rapid advancement or progress for the security inherent in their devotion to and perpetuation of the past. This was borne out by a letter from Father Sava, the priest, which came months after my return to America. He wanted some children's story books which he felt would aid him in quickly acquiring a reading knowledge of English. (If English-speaking visitors to Bulgaria should hear a black-robed village priest with a red beard talking about Little Red Riding Hood, Cinderella, or Goldilocks and the Three Bears, they will have come upon Father Sava!) He ended his letter by saying with seeming approval, "All is the same in Dragalevtsy. A few people have died, a few have been born since you left, but there has been little change." Time was apparently standing still in the village while the world was rushing into conflict.

CHAPTER X

PRELUDE TO COMMUNISM (1937-1944)

RETURNING to Bulgaria in the fall of 1945 meant returning to a defeated, occupied enemy country. Because I had followed the political events only from a distance, I was anxious to see how native Bulgarians, and particularly my Dragalevtsy friends, would interpret what had happened during the intervening years. Overshadowing all, of course, had been their active collaboration with the Germans.

Germany's entrance into Bulgaria proved a comparatively easy achievement. Basic to the plan was the conviction on the part of the Bulgarian people that Germany would actually win the war and give them a safe way of profiting at their neighbors' expense. Economic penetration had come first. Gradually Germany bought more and more of Bulgaria's goods and by 1939 was taking almost seventy-five per cent of all of the country's exports. Even before I left, Bulgarian friends were deploring the anti-Semitism of the Nazis, but when I asked them why Bulgaria seemed to be receptive to German propaganda they usually replied, "But Germany is our best customer. And one always humors one's best customer." Ideological penetration accompanied the economic. The German School in Sofia was managed by ardent Nazis. The greater part of the student body was composed of loyal Bulgarian boys, but any boy of German parentage (and there was a fairly large German colony in Sofia) had to belong to the Nazi Youth organization to remain in the school. Bulgarian army officers came back from trips to Berlin ardently pro-German. A few highly placed officials acquired an opulence that made people raise their eyebrows, until these same officials acted friendly toward the Germans; then people understood. A large contingent of Bulgarians made a trip to the 1936 Olympic games held in Berlin and returned with increased admiration for German efficiency. Inept British and French diplomacy made the German success even more outstanding.

But the Germans had fertile soil. Defeated in the second Balkan War and in the first World War, the Bulgarians were quick to grasp what seemed to be a sure thing. They had built up a chauvinism in their educational system that made the end of getting back what they considered former Bulgarian territory more important than the means chosen. As the smaller countries fell one by one, the Bulgarians began to squirm. Then came the debacle in the West illuminated only by the shining stand of Britain. The satellites, Hungary and Rumania, had fallen into line. While Hitler helped Bulgaria obtain South Dobrudja from a badly disrupted Rumania, Russia, Bulgaria's former champion, was still bound by a nonaggression pact with Germany. Over and over again the Germans showed moving pictures of their European conquests to groups of Bulgarians. Thus the idea of German invincibility took root and was in full bloom when the Nazi armies crossed the Danube to join the hundreds of German "tourists" already filling up the country's hotels and inns. Bulgaria had been duped, but this, like ignorance, afforded no justification, and certainly little comfort, in the days of Allied Victory.

The tragedy of Greece and Yugoslavia, to which Bulgaria was a party, made plain to all what the "New Order" actually meant, as if Poland and Norway were not evidence enough. Bulgaria took over the job of policing some of these occupied territories and officially annexed part of them to the Greater Bulgaria. Millions of leva went into the building of highways, railways, school buildings, and land reclamation projects in these new territories, and enthusiastic attempts were launched to make "good Bulgarians" out of all of the newly acquired citizenry.

Bulgarians traveled in great number through Skoplje and Ochrid of Eastern Macedonia in order to see these places which one-sided history and geography books frequently said should belong to Bulgaria. Then clouds, black for the Bulgarian nationalist, began to appear on the horizon: Stalingrad, El Alamein, Italy. As the Allied might grew, the Bulgarians became restless; as they became restless, the secret police became more active, and the handshake of their German ally proved to have the strength of steel, at least for a while.

Anglo-American bombings of Sofia and of strategic railway yards helped pave the way for eventual Russian occupation on the heels of German evacuation.   September, 1944, saw the arrival of the Red Army and the beginning of a new phase of Bulgaria's history, to be described in the following chapter.

All of these facts were running through my mind when, with a feeling of genuine excitement, I went to Dragalevtsy one mild November morning in 1945.   I had little idea of what my investigation would uncover.   The village had a tidiness I had not remembered, a tidiness noticeable despite the mud from the previous day's rain which, as I sought firm earth on which to step, slowed down my brisk gait to the easygoing tempo of former years.   A flood of memories came over me as I went through one street after another: in this house I had attended a funeral; there Yurdan with considerable merriment had told me about his second courtship and marriage; around this corner had lived the only "old maid" in Dragalevtsy; and the Obshtina, or Municipal Building, now completely done, had settled down to being a definite part of Renaissance Square.

Bai Milush, I knew, would tell me about the Germans, so I stopped at his big wooden gate, and one of his sons escorted me to the house.   Vicious dogs still protected the place and had to be kept at a safe distance, but these belied the warm greeting I received once I was within the house.   First, I heard the story of the three oldest sons who no longer lived with their father but, true to their intent, had built homes of their own not far away.   The other two married sons, who had been in the Army during much of my previous stay in Dragalevtsy, now lived with their wives and children in the old ancestral dwelling.   Then, I looked over the score of pictures which I had taken in earlier, happier years and which were mounted on the wall as part of the family's most important mementos.

"We were foolish to declare war on America," he declared, before I got around to asking anything about the Germans.   As he talked I knew that he was afraid Bulgaria had forfeited America's friendship. Like the old man that he was, he began to reminisce about the last World War and to recite how America had helped his defeated nation then.

"We would have starved," he said, "if America had not sent that ship of food to Varna on the Black Sea." Truly such an accomplishment by one ship would necessitate a cargo legendary in size, but nevertheless symbolized to Bai Milush and others of his generation the humanitarian America, the land of plenty, opportunity, and democracy. And then he told me of the work that Dominic Murphy, an American State Department representative in Bulgaria, had done in the wake of the last war to meet the relief needs of the people. And even Bai Milush knew that a street in Sofia bore Murphy's name transliterated into the Cyrillic alphabet.

Bai Milush's wife, his helpmate through the years, had survived the war too. She proffered food and drink and seemed relieved when I suggested that instead of eating then I would like to take a little of the cheese away with me to use in rounding out my meager hotel breakfasts in Sofia. Later, when I was photographing her outside, I realized that she was unsteady on her feet because she had taken too much *rakiya* as a medicine for a racking cough. *Rakiya* remained the cure-all for every ailment as well as the solace to every sorrow.

Wherever I turned, whether to look at the new houses Bai Milush had erected, or to talk with the peasants about the past few years, I was impressed by the prosperity that the war had brought. Since I had last seen Dragalevtsy, almost one hundred new houses had made their appearance, constituting a decided boom for a village which had boasted only three hundred earlier. Some of these houses had been built as villas by people from Sofia because the city law prohibited any new construction there. The various bombardments had caused so much destruction in the city that nothing but repairs were allowed. Nevertheless, the peasants of Dragalevtsy themselves were replacing old homes with new ones simply because they could afford it now.

I had already learned that during the war the peasants had been the favored element of the Bulgarian population; they had been paid good prices as incentives to increased production; earlier in the war they could use that money to buy articles which they had always wanted but had not been able to afford. For example, the number of radios in the village rose from three or four in 1937 to more than a hundred in 1944.

But peasant prosperity, especially in a village so close to Sofia, was also based on black-market activities. Even in 1945 economists estimated that about ninety-five per cent of all dairy products reached the urban consumer through the black market at prices fantastically high. The peasants, moreover, had learned new ways of circumventing government requisitioning during the war. Just after harvesting, while rye and wheat crops were still in the field, they would shake from one-fifth to one-fourth of the grain onto blankets and secretly hide this amount from the Germans. Then they would, as the law decreed, take the sheaves to the village to be threshed. A part of this threshed grain, varying in amount each year with the size of the harvest, had to be turned over to the authorities at prices fixed by the government, but the previously sequestered grain could be used at home or disposed of at black market prices.

One additional economic factor of importance was the rise in land values, which surpassed the general rise in prices. For instance, I had not been in the village long before I learned how valuable was the land on the right as one approached the village from Sofia. Within two years the land had gone up ten times, from 35 leva per square meter to 300-400 leva. No wonder then that peasants had been ridding themselves of their debts, selling a field or two if necessary to put them in the clear. Some of the poorer families had been deriving extra income from the earnings of about twenty teen-aged girls who went daily to Sofia to work in the knitting mill. This was a concession to industrialism which the Dragalevtsy peasants would not have made back in 1937, and it was already having some effect upon village life.

But perhaps one of the greatest economic changes was the reversal of the trend toward dairying mentioned in earlier chapters. Shortly after my departure from Dragalevtsy, a milk producers' co-operative had been established in the village, largely through government prompting and support, and collected all of the milk formerly taken to Sofia by the individual milkmen. The co-operative also ran a grocery store and sold large quantities of feed to the farmers. Owing to price policies of the co-operative and the government price-fixing agency, the peasants began to consider dairying unprofitable. They began to compare the cost of feed with their income from milk and realized that they were losing money. As the war progressed the government bought more and more forage for military animals, feed costs went up, and dairying profits went down. Once this fact became evident and was noised throughout the village there was almost a wholesale withdrawal from dairying. Whereas three or four years before 1,300-1,400 kilos of milk were sold daily, by 1945 only 40 kilos were sold. The 1945 situation was aggravated by the excessively dry season and the reduced yield per cow from 15 liters daily down to 4 or 5. In other words, the number of cows fell off by as much as 90 per cent owing to the low prices of milk and feed difficulties. The peasants liked to mention the fact that *boza,* a fermented millet-seed drink which tastes like sour, liquefied chicken feed, sold for 40 leva a kilo and milk for only 22 leva.

The loss in dairying, temporary though it may prove to be, meant a corresponding gain in sheep-raising, with 1945 estimates of sheep numbers varying from 12,000 to 15,000. Sheep had also become popular because of the wool they made available for garments in the days of clothing shortage during and following the war. A return to sheep had created interesting social problems connected with pasturing. The sheepmen wanted to go back to the days when sheep could graze freely on uncultivated land, but many of the peasants wanted to keep pasturelands for their own use rather than common use.

As I talked to the peasants and heard the concerns expressed by the parents and the aspirations voiced by the young, I began to realize that the family trends already under way in 1937 had progressed further than I would have anticipated. Parents, although very much interested, had less to say about the choice of mates for their sons and daughters. Some of them were quite skillful in making use of relatives to advise the young people in choices which the older members of the family group considered wise.

Brides were still stolen but, contrary to the case in former years, the girl could return home immediately if dissatisfied with the man desiring to become her husband. Shortly before I visited the village a young man had "captured" the girl of his choice and taken her to his father's home. When the girl's parents came to ask whether she chose to return or remain, the girl decided to go back to her parents. In 1937 this would have made her ineligible, in a sense, for further consideration as a wife. Now she simply explained that when the boy had asked her in advance if she would marry him she had thought that he was joking and told him "Yes," in what she considered to be a jesting manner. She was greatly surprised two weeks later to find that the boy had been serious. The whole affair turned out happily in the end because within another two weeks the young man had found a willing girl, had become engaged to her, and married her.

Another evidence that the family system was having to change to meet the stress of new times was the lack of social disapproval shown to widows and widowers who married persons previously unmarried. Heretofore, only widows and widowers could marry each other, and this was chiefly because of economic necessity. Although not yet common, it was a growing practice for a widower to take a fancy to a girl whom he later married. The age of marriage was becoming lower, dropping to 18 and 19 years for many of the couples. The engagement period still lasted only one or two weeks, a time sufficient to allow the girl to make her wedding preparations.

Accompanying these changes was a greater freedom among the young people both in relation to each other and in relation to their parents. The *sedenki* for young people followed practically the same patterns which I had previously observed but had not yet popularized the kissing games which featured *sedenki* in northern Bulgaria. Clandestine love-making was increasing as was the tendency on the part of the young people to pair off.

The changed relationship of sons to their fathers was shown by the failure of many of the sons to turn over their earnings to their parents as part of the common family treasury. Formerly more than half of the young men had followed this practice, but estimates in 1945 placed the number at approximately one out of ten.

Of especial interest was the pattern which younger couples were establishing after marriage. Whereas, ten years ago even the young wife would have given implicit obedience to her husband's orders, today many of the families were becoming equalitarian. The older women, however, still clung to the patriarchal pattern, though they were willing to grant that the changes introduced by the young people were a part of the times and might not be so bad after all. In talking to these older women I noted a touch of envy, which I would not have suspected ten years ago.

In contrast to these changes many phases of the family system remained the same. These included the attitude of intolerance towards a childless couple, the role of the mother-in-law in the caring for infants, the parents' preference for boys, the reserve between father and the children, the continued dwelling of many married sons with their fathers, and the importance attached to being an older brother or sister in the family. The godparent relationship and the attitude towards the *svatovstvo* (in-law relationships) were still of major importance.

The moral standards remained relatively rigid, with continuing intolerance toward illegitimacy. The one such case within the past ten years had caused a great amount of unfavorable comment. The mother resolved her predicament by leaving her child with relatives in the village and marrying in another place.

Many other traditional practices besides those related to the family still maintained their strong grip on the people. The Christmas Horo took place as always and the Sunday afternoon promenade had become more firmly established. The *babi* (older women) were called in whenever illness or childbirth occurred. The smaller families, of course, numbered fewer children these days, but the *babi* were kept just as busy since the state-employed midwife no longer worked for the Obshtina. The dead were buried much the same as formerly, although the priest forbade people to cry messages to the dead while the funeral procession paused at the crossroads on the way from the home to the church.

The people still made much of the mice and wolf holidays. One day after St. Dimiter's Day (November 9) the peasants continued to fast to keep the mice from coming in and eating up not only stored food but even clothes and other prized possessions. Bai Yurdan, the tailor, told me in all seriousness, "When I was in Sofia I didn't observe such holidays but now that I am back in the village I must."

When I pressed him for his reasons, fully expecting him to say that he was yielding to the pressure of his wife or public opinion, he gravely replied:

"You see in Sofia I did not own any of my own cloth but now I have a great deal downstairs which I must protect from the mice." I might mention in passing that Bai Yurdan had become a faithful member of the Communist party.

The wolf holidays were still observed for three days following the Day of the Archangel Michael, which comes on November 21. During these days the peasants were careful to do no work and refused to cook or boil anything. Such rigid observances, they believed, protected their sheep from wolves, which were still numerous upon the mountain.

One event of overshadowing importance in the changes which had occurred in Dragalevtsy since 1937 had been its incorporation in Greater Sofia in 1939. Even though their village was close to Sofia, Dragalevtsy people had always considered themselves quite apart, and looked upon Sofia ways as alien ways. However, Sofia politicians managed to bring the village under the sway of the city's municipality. Most villagers considered this an evil day in the history of their community and could cite a number of disadvantages which had occurred as a result. One of the village officials, whom I had known previously, complained particularly about the following points:

1. The city municipality had taken over the forests.

2. It had taken over the meadows which the peasants owned in common. For instance, the villagers no longer did the haying in the meadows which used to belong to the school because all of the revenue from the sale of this hay went to the Sofia School Fund. This meant that the three Dog Days, described in an earlier chapter, were once more days of idleness.

3. Formerly the Dragalevtsy Obshtina collected seven or eight million leva in taxes, but since incorporation with Sofia had only a budget of one million on which to operate. My informant failed to mention that much of this money came from the factory district down on the Sofia plain which had once, much to the dissatisfaction of the

people living in the district, been a part of the village Obshtina. This area had always been referred to by the villagers as the Mahala, or Quarter.

4. Repairs in the village, such as putting a wooden bridge back into commission after a heavy storm, could be made only after the Sofia authorities gave their approval. Thus, maintenance of roads and other services in the village were said to suffer.

5. No longer did the village have its own doctor, and it had even lost, so the villagers said, all the medical equipment including microscopes and blood-testing units which the village Obshtina had once owned. Instead, a doctor came at irregular intervals to render whatever medical services were required. This loss of medical equipment, even more than the loss of the physician's services, was a hard pill for some of the more active village leaders to swallow.

6. In place of the veterinarian, who formerly lived in the village, one came twice a week to examine animals and to see that the various veterinary regulations were observed.

But whether they liked it or not, the Dragalevtsy people were a part of Sofia, even to the extent of being included in the city's wartime rationing system. The old rural-urban differences persisted, reminding Americans of similar situations in the United States where the businessman's daylight saving time was anathema to the farmer.

As I tried to reconstruct the chief occurrences of the years intervening between my departure in 1937 and the end of the war, I inquired often as to the whereabouts of some members of the intelligentsia whom I had known well. I learned that the mayor, who had been so helpful during my earlier visit, had given up his post during the days of German collaboration. Apparently he had disagreed with the local committee as to procedures and amounts of grain to be requisitioned from the peasants. He had already been suffering from ill health and could no longer stand the pressure of troubles, arguments, and dissatisfactions which each day brought to his office. From Dragalevtsy my mayor friend had been transferred to the picturesque village of Panchevo, which I shall long remember because of the lunch I had there one summer's day many years ago.

A friend and I had been cycling on the road which followed the Iskar River and stopped at a Panchevo inn. The waiter brought us white peasant cheese, wrinkled brined olives, and freshly made bread to which warm ashes clung. Cold beer made a perfect drink.

The village priest, who had become such an integral part of village life and managed to keep harmonious relationships between the church and the state functionaries, was no longer in Dragalevtsy. Three years ago he had become involved in an administrative argument with his superior and was told to transfer to a much less desirable parish. Rather than make this shift he went to live in Sofia where, true to his training in finance and commerce, he had a share in a small business enterprise. He still wore his priestly garb, occasionally officiating in a Sofia church. Someone described him as "a minister without portfolio."

The directress of the school was the only member of the intelligentsia who had stuck to her post through thick and thin. She still took the same interest in the all-around development of the children, emphasizing in particular their hygienic training and their religious tuition. There had been considerable shifting in the membership of her teaching staff, but she still had five teachers who, like their predecessors, were more interested in Sofia week ends than village welfare.

The Sekretar Birnik, who had much to do with the collection of taxes and thus enjoyed a social standing out of line with his educational preparation, had also left Dragalevtsy and had been replaced by a local person.

It seemed strange to visit the now completed municipal building and to find the woman doctor no longer there and to notice the absence of her husband from the taverns where he had enjoyed playing cards. Since both were White Russians they knew that their lot under the Communists would be full of uncertainty. No one seemed to know just where they had gone.

Much had been happening to the village organizations as the intelligentsia faded from the scene or were replaced by others with different points of view. The Red Cross, in which the mayor had taken such an interest, had long ceased to have any importance. This was also true of the Union for Protection of Children, which had had as its chief function the provision of school lunches for the poor children. The Association for the Decoration for Valor was still tottering along, and its members hoped eventually to enroll three or four members who had participated in the recent war. The School Board had become a thing of the past as the control of the school passed into the hands of the Sofia School System. The Church Board, however, was maintaining its existence and was giving its support to a new organization called the Christian Union which had been founded during the Fascist regime as a religious welfare organization. Before the coming of the Russians this Christian Union had collected and distributed to the poor families at Christmas time and the New Year an amount varying from sixty to seventy thousand leva. In 1945 it boasted about seventy-five members and was flourishing.

For the most part, however, the village organizations died at birth or perished in early infancy, as an earlier chapter showed. The Dragalevtsy peasant had not yet become a joiner. He gained his social status by the position his family held rather than by the numbers and types of organizations to which he, as an individual, was elected.

Such, then, was the prelude to Communism. The coming of the National State to the village back in 1934 set a pattern by which each peasant household was later on closely geared in with a totalitarian wartime economy. The majority of traditions were holding firm among the middle-aged and old, while many of the younger people no longer disguised their interest in the fascinating ways of the West. The net effect of the war was to commercialize more fully the village's economic life and make the peasants more money-conscious. Their incorporation into the Sofia municipality as well as the Fascist nature of their state made them feel less responsible as individuals for governmental affairs and drew them farther away from the democratic Slavic tradition inherent in their old joint family system. Religion continued to be accepted as a matter of course, for no one questioned the propriety of having a priest officiate on ceremonial or patriotic occasions.

The peasants became more nationalistic, since they knew that their own fortunes were closely identified with the fortune of the Bulgarian (that is, Axis) armies. Their social world expanded, and their horizons broadened in a dim, vague way. As defeat stared them in the face, however, they watched their leaders try to extricate the nation from its inevitable doom. A beaten, humiliated people, they knew not where to turn, until Russia made that decision for them.

CHAPTER XI

COMMUNISM KNOCKS AT THE DOOR

C OMMUNISM came in the dead of the night. Dragalevtsy people awoke on September 6, 1944, the morning after Russia had declared war on Bulgaria, to find big posters proclaiming throughout the village such slogans as "Welcome to the Heroic Red Army" or "Long Live Stalin."

The peasants realized in retrospect how well organized everything must have been, for these signs showed that the local Communist sympathizers had been ready for this big event. One or two had fought in the mountains against the Germans as Bulgarian Partisans and had been schooled in the part they were to play when the Germans were finally driven out.

On September 16, 1944, at least eighty villagers from Dragalevtsy had gone to Sofia to welcome the Russians. Traditions live long in Dragalevtsy, and especially the tradition of brotherly Russia and its overwhelming contribution in emancipating Bulgaria from the Turks in 1878. So this demonstration of admiration for the Russians was genuine and spontaneous. Many parents took their children along so the youngsters could describe to their children and their children's children the excitement and greatness of this day. And the spectacle was one that was memorable, not like the arrival of the Nazis for whom there had been admiration mixed with fear, but rather the arrival of brother Slavs who would help Bulgaria grow great and strong. Thus the peasants had thought.

But news travels fast in Bulgaria and usually becomes altered in the traveling. Within five days, the people of Dragalevtsy heard so many rumors about the Russians that they soon had become afraid. They were especially nonplussed by the Russians' disregard for property. They heard about a man from another village who had been hauling corn in his oxcart. Russian soldiers told him to stop, get out, and give them the oxen, the cart, and the corn. He insisted that they must pay him, at which they laughed. Stubborn as only a *Shop* peasant can be, he sat rigidly in his cart to protect his own. From this point on versions differed: some said he was pulled out and beaten, others that he was shot and left dead by the roadside. And always the tale ended with, "The Germans always paid us, but the Russians never did."

But the Communists offered an explanation for the differences in the behavior of the two armies. The Russians invaded in battle order, which necessitated eating off the land on a catch-as-catch-can basis. The Germans, on the other hand, had sent large staffs ahead to make preparations for the coming of their troops. The net effect upon the peasant mentality was radically different, since property rights seemed violated by the Russians and respected by the Nazis.

Eventually a detachment of Russians had been established around Dragalevtsy. They frequented the taverns so constantly and with such enthusiasm that the peasants had a new saying: "There's nothing worse than drunken Russians." They began to judge the Russian nation by the off-time indulgences of its soldiers.

Although the "great disillusionment" regarding Russian soldiers had begun soon after their arrival, the people still hoped that all would go well politically. Most of the major political parties—the Agrarians, the Zveno, and the Democrats—joined with the Communists in September, 1944, to form a coalition, which they called the Fatherland Front. It was this government that conducted the purge, or the sentencing of about three thousand men and women by the people's courts on the grounds of collaboration with the enemy. About two thousand of these were executed. Some observers now feel, in the light of later developments, that the real basis of selecting victims for trial was not only their complicity with the Germans but also their danger as potential rallying points for a counterrevolution against the Fatherland Front. Two Dragalevtsy young men were tried and executed for collaboration with the Nazis. According to village reports, Communist sympathizers tried to exert pressure upon the new priest in the hope of preventing his officiating at any funeral ceremonies or memorial services for these men. According to the Communists, they were traitors. The priest still considered them children of God and officiated anyway, although they were not buried in the local cemetery.

By the New Year, 1945, many of the political leaders in the Fatherland Front discerned the handwriting on the wall. The Agrarians and the Democratic party especially recognized the Front for what it was—a Communist screen for actual control. All the while, the Communists—a minority party—had been growing stronger and were nurtured by the Red Army officers who really directed Bulgarian affairs. British and American army officers were represented in the Allied Control Commission which was under arbitrary Russian direction. American and British diplomatic representatives were somewhat more effectual, but only within a rather limited sphere of activity. With the cards stacked in their favor, the Communists controlled the key ministries, chief among them being the Ministry of Interior which had charge of the police and local administration. Therefore, early in 1945 there was a gradual loss of popular enthusiasm for the Fatherland Front, with the real defection coming in May. At that time the leading representatives of the Agrarian and Democratic parties, as well as a section of the Socialist party, withdrew from the Front to form an opposition. In Dragalevtsy, this move met with tremendous support, for there the Agrarian was the major party. The Zveno group, which had engineered the *coup d'état* of 1934 against the king, stayed with the Fatherland Front in which they held the premiership and other prominent positions.

A few former acquaintances of mine had joined the Communist party and were sincerely trying to win their fellow countrymen to their cause. They were inclined to be impatient with those who differed from them, and still felt very much on the defensive. Their condescending attitude toward members of other parties co-operating with them in the Fatherland Front was expressed in a comment making the round: "Oh, these other members of the Front are our 'water boys.' They'll carry the water to the top of the hill for us and then we'll take it over."

The next political crisis arose in August, 1945. The government had scheduled an election through which it had planned to obtain a parliament, whose first duty would have been to approve the previous actions of the government and to give the Front broad powers to continue on its way of reform and reconstruction. Because of the claims by the opposition—those who had withdrawn from the Fatherland Front—that they were not being given a fair chance for representation in the elections, the American and British governments insisted that the elections be postponed and threatened to recognize no government coming into power under the proposed arrangements. The elections were postponed. Most Dragalevtsy people again wholeheartedly approved.

But that was the heyday of the opposition. Those who did not like the way matters were moving put their faith in America and expected her to stop further Communistic consolidation within the country. In the taverns of Dragalevtsy the buzzing must have reminded one of bees in a swarm when the Agrarian leader of the opposition, Georgi M. Dimitrov, sought refuge with the American Political Representative, Maynard B. Barnes, and spent part of the time in Barnes's villa near the Sofia-Dragalevtsy highway, with a handful of American soldiers on guard to protect Dimitrov whose life was endangered. The American authorities assumed some personal risks in sheltering him, and eventually secured his departure from the country. Thus, in the minds of the people as well as in the minds of the Bulgarian authorities, America more and more became identified as the chief support of the opposition and as an enemy of the new state being created. Because lines of antagonism had been drawn so sharply, the peasants of the opposition asked, "When will the war between America and Russia take place?" Those favoring the government asked in an uncertain tone, "Will there be a war between America and Russia?"

News of the atomic bomb gave the opposition increased hope since many of them expected America to use the bomb immediately as a threat in the bargaining and jockeying going on between the Western and Eastern powers.

American popularity rode another high wave when Secretary of State Byrnes sent Mark Ethridge to Bulgaria and Rumania to make a study of the situations in these two countries. Mr. Ethridge, a well known Louisville, Kentucky, newspaperman and a keen student of international affairs, conducted himself with such astuteness that he became almost a legendary figure in a short time. In fact, he enters this account in an authentic way because he visited Dragalevtsy quite unexpectedly, ate meat balls at the tavern with the peasants, and endeared himself in particular by treating the crowd to two or three rounds of drinks. "Setting up the house" was a practice none too common in the frugal economy that characterized the village. Most of those present spoke quite freely, but two Russian soldiers, definitely ill-at-ease, remained stolidly silent. One old villager did throw caution to the winds and sidled up to tell the distinguished guest, "We are not satisfied, Mr. Ethridge. Don't believe all of the things these young fellows have been telling you." Mr. Ethridge, upon leaving the tavern, was surprised to see Renaissance Square filled with enthusiastic villagers, who cheered him and presented him with many bouquets of flowers.

Later the Secretary of State's special emissary wrote a critical report on the existing Bulgarian government and pointed out what he judged to be its undemocratic features. The American representatives were unable, however, to persuade the Bulgarian authorities to postpone the elections for a second time, so the voting went off as scheduled on November 18, 1945, with the opposition groups abstaining from the balloting.

In spite of these political developments, the peasants in the Agrarian party (the majority in Dragalevtsy) continued to regard Mr. Barnes and Mr. Ethridge in a favorable light. They like to tell stories of the way these Americans supposedly outwitted the Bulgarian authorities. One of these stories, with no foundation in fact, shows how rumors rise in the Balkans. Mr. Ethridge and his small party were said to have visited a concentration camp for political prisoners near Dupnitsa. Since they were planning to visit the historic and beautifully situated Rila Monastery, they obtained permission to stop off en route at this particular camp. According to the peasants' version, when the party arrived they found comparatively few people in the camp; the place was clean, and the prisoners seemed well cared for. That was that; farewells were said and the party moved on to the Monastery. Late in the afternoon, instead of going to the provincial town of Somokov as originally scheduled, Mr. Ethridge asked his driver when they reached a crossroad to take the fork of the road which circled back past Dupnitsa. Once more at the camp, he asked to be admitted and saw for himself the conditions of overcrowding all too evident when the prisoners who had been sent to the woods for the day were back in their quarters. Without wasting any words Mr. Ethridge merely smiled to the attendants, got back into the automobile, and returned to Sofia.

But stories of camps for political prisoners took my mind back to the 1930's when the government then in power was fearful of Communism and conducted frequent raids upon Communist-operated printing presses. Much doctrinaire literature was seized and the offenders were given heavy prison sentences. A member of an opposition group has never felt very safe in the Balkans. The Zveno group, which has already been mentioned, came into power in 1934 and which still was co-operating with the Fatherland Front, worked out a new wrinkle in the treatment of political prisoners. On March 19, 1935, I wrote in a letter to America:

> Just a little sidelight on political life in Bulgaria. Students who make radical speeches or editors who print little articles opposed to the *status quo* are forcefully invited to leave Sofia for a rest-cure in one of the provincial towns of Bulgaria. They go, for instance, to Karlovo and are "put up" by the government. They are perfectly free with the exception that they must stay in Karlovo, must report to an official at eight each morning, at noon, and must be in their room by eight in the evening, and cannot venture forth until eight the next morning. Such an "invitation" usually holds good for one month, after which the chastened individuals are permitted to return to Sofia, the political cauldron of Bulgaria.

More and more, Balkan governments must be judged not only in terms of the four freedoms which we publicize in America but also in terms of the governments which have preceded them. That is, they must be interpreted, although not justified, in the light of the cultural setting out of which they have sprung.

There was another apocryphal Ethridge story, which illustrated the use of humor as a weapon of the opposition groups to make their life more endurable. The scene was laid around Kyustendil, the chief

fruit-growing area of the country.   Mr. Ethridge, in his search for the
truth, reputedly approached some of the local inhabitants:

"How are you getting along?   Are you satisfied with conditions
as they are?"

"Oh, yes, Mr. Ethridge.   We are quite satisfied, for this is just
like Paradise [the Garden of Eden]."

The visitor was jolted a bit to hear so much enthusiasm after the
many tales of woe which had been poured out to him elsewhere.
"What do you mean?   In what way is this like Paradise?"

"Kyustendil is just like Paradise," came the reply, "because we
have plenty of apples to eat but no clothes to wear."

As time passed, the Communists became more determined to
make their position secure.   To accomplish this, Bulgarian-born
Georgi Dimitrov came down from Russia, where he had once been
Secretary of the Comintern, to take over active direction of party
strategy.   (This Georgi Dimitrov was quite a different person from
the Agrarian leader, Georgi M. Dimitrov.)   Occasionally peasants
would joke about the high board fence around Communist Dimitrov's
yard in Sofia, built to protect him from any would-be assassin.   The
elections of November 18, 1945, revealed to the leaders of the
National Front their relatively weak position.   Great numbers of
people had abstained from voting, a fact commonly interpreted as a
vote for the opposition.   Few foreign observers in Sofia actually believed the highly favorable figures which the government claimed in
the announced election returns.   In the Dragalevtsy district, for
instance, thirteen hundred people had been eligible to vote.   This
number included for the first time all women and all young people
19 years of age and over.   It also included the industrialized area,
called the Mahala, which lies just below the village on the Sofia road.
Approximately 800 votes were cast, of which 200 were against and
600 for the government, or Fatherland Front.   Well informed people
connected with the Ministry of Interior said that most of the five
hundred abstainers had been peasants and that most of the votes cast
for the government had come from the industrialized Mahala, which
was known as a Communist center.   In other words, as one village
man succinctly expressed it, "Our people in Dragalevtsy are not for
the present government."

Granting then that a personal sampling of public opinion, conversation with both Communists and Agrarians in the village, and the rough approximation of election returns all added up to a fair statement of the case, Dragalevtsy would definitely be labeled an opposition village. In fact, before I had even revisited the village a number of people in Sofia had told me that I would find this to be the case. Therefore, as I went around among the people and watched the government in action, I asked myself how it happened that a minority could so easily gain control of all effective governmental machinery. The chief secret lay, of course, in capturing the central government in Sofia, which since 1934 had more and more become a dominant influence in the country. But there were other methods adopted by the Communists which, when multiplied in the five thousand villages throughout the land, would explain to some degree why Communism's knock on the door might be said to have turned into a banging. Some of these techniques of political power were proving successful in Dragalevtsy, while others were not.

Effective party work in the villages would normally be guaranteed and to some extent guided by the organs of the state, such as the controlled militia (police) and the hand-picked mayors and secretaries of the communal councils. But even with this provision all was not smooth sailing in Dragalevtsy for the newcomers back in 1945. The difficulties over the mayor would be a case in point.

In September, 1944, the Central Ministry of Interior appointed a young Communist as mayor. Because local public opinion was either indifferent or unfriendly his work was relatively ineffectual. The following July the members of the Agrarian party, which at that time still participated in the Fatherland Front, held a meeting to protest against their present mayor. They went even further and elected a mayor of their own choosing, with the backing of the mayor of Sofia who was well disposed toward their cause. Although this election was not declared legal, the new mayor took over and began to function. His status remained unclarified because the Communists in the Ministry of Interior did not feel sure enough of themselves to force the issue at that time. By December, 1945, the situation had become further complicated since the incumbent mayor lacked the education necessary

to qualify for governmental retirement benefits and his former supporters were now a part of the opposition. Sofia, too, had a new
mayor. It seemed to the village dignitary that all of his trouble was
becoming a labor of love for which he would receive little financial
return. Upon last report he was seeking a way out of office and was
subject to a great deal of jesting in the taverns. The men all laughed
one day in December, 1945, when a visitor from Sofia addressed him
as "Mr. Mayor," because nobody knew at that time whether he was
the mayor or not.

An office more important, however, than that of the mayor was
that of the Commune Secretary. In Dragalevtsy this man was a Communist and, although he did not take the public limelight as much as
a regular mayor would, he was the key person in the local government.
Communist party matters frequently cleared through him, and he was
in position to inform higher authorities about all phases of village
government. Whereas the mayor's allegiance was primarily to the
people of Dragalevtsy and secondarily to the Agrarian party, a lunch-
eon conversation with the Secretary showed me that his loyalty was
first of all to his party. Through serving it he felt he was best serving
the people.

Part of the secret of Communist control in the local community
lay in the success which the Communists had in enlisting the aid of
many of the young people. In a traditionalistic society, such as one
finds in Dragalevtsy, young people have no place of importance.
Prestige is reserved for the old; and wisdom is the prerogative of the
aged. Therefore a young person is constantly being urged to conform;
and whatever idealism may flare up within him in his late teens
becomes dissipated in the face of his placid parents and the other
apostles of the past. The Communists showed real insight, therefore,
in their glorification of the young people, in giving them a place in
the sun, as it were. One of the first things they did was to get control
of the *Chitalishte,* or Reading-Room Association, and use that as the
core for their young people's program. In the house just back of the
Obshtina they set up clubrooms where members of the *RMS* (Workers
Youth Union) could hold meetings, study up on party doctrines, or
loaf. The members of this particular organization, although not

representing the majority of the young people, had an increasing voice in village affairs and were aggressive in their approach to practical problems. Part of this aggressiveness was directed against the young people at that time still active in the ZMS (Agrarian Youth Society), which was a part of the opposition.

Another means by which the Communists gained support was in the favoritism shown to party members in the distribution of rationed articles. Just as the ward boss of an American city or the prewar mayor of Dragalevtsy learned that gratitude prompts support or that favors done call for favors in return, so the Fatherland Front made good use of its opportunities. Some of its generosity served purely political ends. The mayor of Sofia, so the Dragalevtsy peasants said, gave one million leva at Christmas time to the *Septemvriche,* or National Children's Communist Organization. Opposition groups, of course, received no such largesse.

But many of the criticisms of pork-barrel politics were due to misunderstanding. The peasants of Dragalevtsy could usually procure no clothing coupons if they had wool at home, and most of them did have a small supply which they were allowed to keep. This amount was based on family size and any surplus was requisitioned by the government. Artisans and laborers, however, who had no sheep, who worked in factories or at their trade, received the clothing coupons, for that was the only way they had of obtaining wearing apparel. Wool and cotton, thread, and goods were still so scarce in both villages and cities that no one group was content with what it had, and peasants were inclined to ascribe whatever others received as due to favoritism rather than the merits of the case. The proof that wool was scarce was the relative inactivity of the carding and spinning *sedenki,* the working bees so popular among the women.

"Why don't you have *sedenki* now," I asked.

"We have no wool to work," was the plausible answer.

Communist party members who used their political standing for self-aggrandizement and enrichment were supposed to be severely dealt with by the party authorities. One story making the rounds in Dragalevtsy had done much to discredit the Communists with those in the opposition. Since living in a Balkan village is a great deal like

living in a goldfish bowl, it was not long before the peasants knew
that almost a million leva (notice how rounded or approximate the
numbers are in such stories) had disappeared from local public funds.
There was no official explanation as to its whereabouts, but one Communist had become quite rich and built himself a house better than
the village expected of him.   Later he was expelled from the party,
reputedly because of conversion of funds, but even this action did not
restore the funds to the public treasury.

Unquestionably, a loyal supporter of the Fatherland Front was
able at times to use his political connections for personal advantage.
The peasants would have been surprised if this were not the case, for
they philosophically said, "Whoever sticks his fingers in honey is apt
to lick them."

Mention was made in the last chapter of the phenomenal increase
in radio ownership since 1937.   Now about every third home has a
receiving set and is thus in contact with the propaganda line of the
government-controlled broadcasting service.   Listening to the radio
had become a new recreational pattern for many people.   Over and
over again I asked them what programs they preferred.   The men,
perhaps because they deemed it the proper answer, often said that they
listened to the news.   Quite a few were quick to add, "It's nothing but
lies though."   Many of the women preferred the folk music, and the
young people jazz.   Long speeches claimed few listeners.   The net
effect of radio listening then was recreational, with some political influence exerted upon the devotees of the newscast.   As yet, the radio
had not become a channel for education or raising the standard of
living.   I wondered, too, just when it would, for the peasants had little
hesitation in turning off the set if the program became too serious, and
most educational programs under Communist leadership were inclined
to be serious.

American and British influence was sufficiently strong to force
the Fatherland Front officials to allow an opposition press.   Although
this press was beset with difficulties in 1945, it nevertheless became a
vehement, at times vitriolic, critic of the regime in power.   It took a
strong pro-American, pro-British complexion, though never out-and-
out anti-Russian.   A good check on Agrarian claims of majority sup-

port was the unquestioned popularity in Dragalevtsy of the *Green Banner,* the newspaper published by the opposition Agrarian group. As long as the opposition press continued to circulate throughout the country, the tried and trusted technique of one-sided interpretation could not be brought into full play. Schoolbooks could be rewritten, pamphleteering could be done in the Communist children's and youth organizations, but these activities were much less effective when other groups could print their versions to serve as antidotes. One-party control, such as the Fatherland Front wanted for Bulgaria, was authoritarian. It preferred to have no alternative opinions presented to the people, and felt that as long as it alone could tell the people what they ought to believe, the people would be well off, for they would be indoctrinated with the truth, as the Communist saw the truth.

Another weapon which the Communists hoped to use as a means of penetration was Pan-Slavism, especially among the Bulgarians. The members of the Red Army, however, instead of being missionaries of this mystic racial dogma, did it the greatest harm. Occupying armies seldom become popular, especially when the mass is held accountable for the sins of the few. The peasants were only too prone to fall into the error of the "lumping fallacy," and condemned all Russians on the basis of a few spectacular events which occurred in the village. One happening which Dragalevtsy peasants used in forming their attitude involved two peasant girls whom I had photographed as children several years before. Now that they were in their late teens they proved unusually attractive to two drunken Russian privates who tried to break into their house late one night. Although a noncommissioned officer came to order them away, these soldiers cursed him and kept on pounding against the door of the living-room. The door held fast, and they finally gave up and went away. Had they but known it, the lock had already been smashed; all they needed to do was to turn the knob and enter a room where the peasant family sat in mortal fear. The father knew that to fight for the honor of his daughters would have meant a bullet from a drunken soldier's pistol; the mother sat in prayer before the crude iconostas, while the girls cried softly at the thought of what seemed to be in store for them. In a village where immorality was frowned upon so strongly, this attempted assault was an experience which would be told and retold generation after generation, with some such bitter moral at the end as "And those were our brother Slavs."

Perhaps the most important technique of control was the effective play upon the fears of the people. Fearful people are a paralyzed people, and it was this creeping paralysis which was beginning to wear down the opposition and make possible Communism's eventual triumph. Sometimes events reached such a climax that fear was turned into action, but matters in December, 1945, were not reaching such a climax. Little by little the people were being made more fearful of the future, especially with the decline of British and American prestige. One never knew when the walls might have ears, or whom one could trust, or when one's home would be invaded and searched. One woman Communist spread a story about a neighbor's hoarding; he was twice arrested and his house searched three times, although the rumor was apparently unfounded. Grudges were sometimes "settled" when one of the parties tipped off the authorities to the failure of the other party to follow some unpopular regulation. Accompanying this fear was the belief that one would not have due protection of the law at a trial, since the new law was being written as cases came up, with little reference to prewar statutes or precedents. One was at the mercy of the court where the all-important question too often had become, "Did you or did you not fight against the Fascist German hordes?" Conceivably in the not-too-distant future the "sixty-four dollar question" might be, "Have you ever been sympathetic to Anglo-American interventionists and reactionaries?"*

When I asked my Communist acquaintances how they justified the interpretation of justice which I have been describing, they flashed back, as though well drilled: "But in America does the Negro or the poor man get justice? Don't the courts serve the interests of the rich? Here in Bulgaria our courts do not serve the interests of the privileged, but rather the good of the masses." I already knew that some of these Communist converts had been motivated by the highest idealism, that they felt they had a remedy for the economic and political evils of their country, and that any means they used to correct those evils would

* An observation made in 1946, which has become only too true in 1948.

be justified in their opinion. They argued further that all social change was costly, and they firmly believed that the time was ripe for change, their kind of a change.

Many of them felt confident of the future, but some qualified their anticipation by saying, "It all depends upon America and England. If we are left alone, we can work matters out. We want no interference." And as I reviewed the methods by which they attained their present dominant position nationally in the face of hostile opinion in many quarters, I could see that if left alone for a long enough period, they would succeed in instituting the changes they wanted, whatever might be the cost. They controlled the national government and could rely upon Russia for help whenever needed; they were making headway with the young people; they increasingly directed the chief decisions made by village councils and through these councils and secret police knew what was happening throughout the land; they had control over the radio and were biding their time until they could also control the press completely; education was a function of the national government; economic dependence of the peasants upon the local and national authorities was increasing, and there were both tangible and intangible rewards for Communist party membership; fears could be aroused or played down as the government desired, and courts had become not the servant of abstract justice but the instrument of the state.

The time element was of utmost importance. Before the Russian armies left Bulgarian soil upon the conclusion of the peace treaty, the Communists had to have everything well in hand or face the possibility that dissatisfied cliques in the old Bulgarian army could step in to throw the Communists out and set up a military dictatorship which, while anti-Russian, would certainly have few of the earmarks of the democracy known in the West. It would be a recrudescense of irredentist nationalism, and Bulgaria would be on sale to the highest bidder promising to keep the Russian bear at bay. Without the army the Agrarians, who had a realistic, well-thought-out program, would be powerless; but reliance upon the army for a long period would negate most of their plans and make them the bulwark of a dictatorship which they professed to abhor. Such was the unfortunate dilemma confronting anyone seeking a rational solution to the Balkan impasse back in 1945.

My visits to Dragalevtsy, however, were not for the purpose of involving myself in the weighty matters of Balkan politics. I simply wanted to see how the village had changed, but soon found that an understanding of political events was necessary to an interpretation of the present situation. This became further apparent when I discovered that the three most significant differences between 1937 and 1945 were heightened factionalism, an increased feeling of insecurity, and a shifting of the relative importance of village institutions. Each of these deserves further explanation.

The coming of Communism had fostered factionalism to a degree never before experienced in Dragalevtsy. That, in fact, was its chief sociological effect. During the times when political parties were flourishing with abandon in the late 1920's and early 1930's the competition between party members was more a recreational pursuit than serious political maneuvering. All parties had had considerable backing from their respective leaders in Sofia, and all to that extent were on a similar footing. With the coming of the Germans some villagers ardently supported Nazi ideology and considered Bulgaria fortunate to be allied with the Axis powers; others had their misgivings, but never to the point of splitting up the village on factional lines. Upon the formation of the opposition in 1945, matters were different. No longer was the political competition an internal affair alone, but was one in which outside powers took an active interest. The Communists openly boasted about the might of Russia and spoke with assurance of Russian support; those in the opposition took what comfort they could from British and American actions and speeches but could not claim unqualified aid.

The splitting up of the village into Communists and non-Communists had therefore caused a tear in the total social fabric. For example, children who belonged to the Fatherland Front organization —the *Septemvriche*—received many small favors from the state. Little *Septemvristi* were sent to conferences within Bulgaria and even to Yugoslavia where they performed for their neighbor Slavs. Children who did not belong because their parents disapproved were taunted by the others. They answered back, repeating many of the comments heard around the house, comments definitely unfavorable to Communism and its cause. So the bickering reached into the schoolhouse and the playground, and children early became conscious of political differences not of their own making.

With the young people, as already indicated, the division on the basis of political sympathy was even more marked. The Agrarian young people tended to associate with each other, and watched with dismay the active role that the members of the Communist youth group were playing in village life. Some enamoured couples, where each had differing political loyalties, disregarded political barriers in their devotion to each other, but when broaching the question of marriage to the parents often met stern disapproval. A girl's father would say, "I don't want my daughter marrying a Communist" or "You do what you want, but if you marry a Communist never come back to my house."

The controversy over politics extended also to the various "working groups" which had been such a basic part of village life in the past. A woman who was organizing a corn-hoeing group would invite only those whose political interests were similar. She knew that little work would be done in her fields if she got together women who differed over the present government.

At this stage of accommodation, therefore, factionalism was based on political differences and expressed itself in a separatism which seriously affected village life. People who differed politically simply stayed apart; where they had to mingle, such as on a bus, they made the best of it by teasing and horseplay which seemed to be all in fun but which often gave voice to deeply rooted emotions.

Accompanying the disagreements within the agricultural group itself were disagreements between the Agrarians and the artisans. The peasants of the opposition resented intensely the attempt on the part of the government to classify them with "workers," or men who owned little or no land and who depended entirely upon some skill for a livelihood. The peasant in the past had felt superior, or at least claimed to be more favored in social position than the artisan such as the tailor, although envious of the "easy work" that the tailor had to do. Owing to the Communistic agitation in Dragalevtsy, lines were more sharply drawn between the peasants on the one hand and the artisans on the other. Most of the artisans had learned their trade in Sofia, had been subjected to city influences, and many of them had become acquainted with Communist ideas there before the war. Even Bai Milosh, the village patriarch so frequently mentioned in this account, had a son who had become an ardent Communist. This son was not the one who took over the management of field crops, nor the one responsible for the livestock. Instead he had become a cobbler. He thought of himself as a worker, whereas his brothers thought of themselves as farmers.

Quarreling between the young and old also characterized the factionalism. Although the Agrarian young people opposed the Communists, they were certainly influenced by the actions of their more progressive or radical contemporaries. The older peasants who were opposed to the present regime emphasized time and time again the danger of having young people run the affairs of the land. This displacement of the aged rather than the indifference of Communists to God seemed to be causing the gravest concern to those who had been steeped in the traditional way of life.

But factionalism was not the only pronounced change which I noted. I found everywhere an insecurity which was foreign to the Dragalevtsy I had once known. The opposition supporters could be expected to feel insecure, for they had to face the possibility that Communism would carry the day. But even the Communists who were definitely in the good graces of the party were having many troubled moments. The wife of one Communist was active in the opposition, and when I asked him why he tolerated such political division in his family he simply laughed. I continued to question him: "Aren't you the boss in this family? Why do you let your wife have such independence?"

He then became deadly serious and sought to lead me out of my cloud of ignorance. "You see, it's this way. Suppose the Communists are overthrown. Where would I be then? But if my wife is active in the Agrarian group, she can then speak for me and get me out of trouble."

But some of the peasants who turned Communists were having their days of religious doubt. They asked quite frequently, "Can we be Communists and still believe in God?" They voluntarily sent their children to the priest's class in religion held in the schoolhouse. "And the Communist children know their lessons better than the children of the opposition," was the opinion of a member of the intelligentsia.

The ideas of many new converts to the Marxist doctrine had been rudely shaken the previous summer at the time of the church processional for rain. The drought had been devastating. Corn was drying up; pastures were turning brown. So a band of villagers, with some Communists who went along for old times' sake, accompanied the priest on a circuit of the fields. The boys carried the church relics and the priest walked faithfully along in his hot, black vestments. No rain came and the Communists thoroughly enjoyed scoffing at those who had started out with such bright hopes. Conditions grew worse and worse, so the religious leaders thought another processional in order. The whole performance was repeated, with Communists along again. This time the priest went up high on the mountainside, so as to include village properties not previously visited. His prayers were efficacious, for a shower which later turned to steady rain burst forth upon the band of villagers, wetting them to the skin before they could return to shelter in the village. The religious people thus had the last word when atheism was discussed.

The prevalent feeling of insecurity included more, however, than beliefs and basic attitudes about religion and politics. It stemmed also from the economic uncertainty which characterized the period. Always lurking in the peasant's consciousness was the fear that his holding, his precious acres, would be collectivized as was done in Russia. It mattered not to him that his farming was inefficiently done or that such inefficiency was no solution for the overpopulation which characterized his land. He wanted no part of a great impersonal *kolkhoz* where in the long run he would become a worker instead of an owner, or where he would work land which he could not call his own. That to him was serfdom; it was not freedom. And discussions of these topics trailed off into many beside-the-point objections, which nevertheless seemed important to the peasant. I recall one such discussion which dealt with the idea of a shortened work-week at the factories. The peasants disapproved of the whole plan and used it as a basis for condemning land collectivization because "We want to be able to work as long as we want without having people tell us that we have to stop working."

Peasants were greatly confused, therefore, over the farm policies to be pursued in the next two or three years. They planned and schemed and talked endlessly about what they should plant, what they should do about their debts, or whether the aged fathers should distribute their land to their sons before they died. But always there was the great unknown of government policy which upset their calculations and kept them insecure.

Another important social change was occuring in the institutional pattern of Dragalevtsy. In earlier chapters we noted how the encroachment of the state was making considerable impact upon the traditional familistic patterns, while economic life was becoming more commercialized and religious activities were declining in importance. The coming of the Communists had begun to weaken the family ties even further, for the Fatherland Front had given votes to all women and had thus attacked the dogma of male supremacy; it had honored the young at the expense of the aged; and it had turned brother against brother as the struggle for control grew more bitter. As the representative of the central government, the Fatherland Front was affecting an even larger area of life than the prewar regime did, especially when its economic regulations and its threat to the hallowed traditional system of landownership.

Another disturbing effect was the substitution of Moscow as the center of the universe, for the Communist adherents at least, when formerly Dragalevtsy or perhaps Sofia by courtesy was thought to be the center. These innovations of the present government had done much to prejudice it in the eyes of the people, who made decisions not upon the basic issues which the government was striving to champion, but resisted blindly and perhaps fanatically simply because the new regime spelled the end of their way of life. As they realized this, some of the peasants turned more and more to the church, the institution which had kept Bulgarian nationality alive through the centuries and had become the champion of an independent Bulgaria in days gone by. In Dragalevtsy church attendance had increased and more attention was paid to the forms and ceremonies, although fasting was not gaining any in popularity. Nor were the peasants too trustful of Archbishop Stefan, the politically minded head of their church. But they knew that the church and the family served as mutual supports and that if one suffered the other suffered too. Government which was once tolerated as a necessary evil now had become an active menace to be combated whenever possible. The means of struggling against the government were inadequate, but the peasants had patience and said that they would bide their time. But as they bided their time many of them died and were replaced by men and women who had grown up under the tutelage of the Fatherland Front, who had forgotten about the days of village elders, of large family groups, and no longer reverenced out-of-date superstitions or valued quaintness in contrast to that which was modern.

A new Dragalevtsy was thus being born. Change was nothing new to the village, but this time changes were occurring so fast that the old way of life could no longer absorb the impact of strange traits and differing social values. The transition period was proving painful for those who still wanted to live in the past. Whether it held promise for those gazing toward the future depended upon the decisions or indecisions of men sitting around conference tables in countries thousands of miles away.

RETROSPECT, 1948

As soon as I began to understand what was happening in Dragalevtsy I knew that I was in touch with something tremendously important. Here, in a Bulgarian village which I had once known intimately, I was encountering the same peasant reactions which I had found in many parts of Yugoslavia, a country which also was experiencing political and social upheaval. The Yugoslavs had a National Liberation Front under Tito which paralleled Bulgaria's Fatherland Front under Georgi Dimitrov. Throughout Serbia, in Dalmatia, Croatia, and parts of the Vojvodina I heard Yugoslav peasants complaining about their new regime in the same overtones and undertones as did my Dragalevtsy friends.

What was there about the Communist-dominated governments that the peasants did not like? It was not until I had left the Balkans, and was weatherbound in Vienna, that I had time to formulate the reasons. Some of these have already been mentioned in the discussion of postwar changes in Dragalevtsy, but they can be accurately applied to those other areas in the Balkans where landed peasants are the rule.

The Communists are aware of the peasant's hunger for more land and have instituted land reforms to bring about a greater mass ownership of the farming areas, on the principle that "the land belongs to those who till it." But in the case of those who have land, even in quantities small enough not to be affected by the reform laws, the governments have given little assurance that the land will remain private property for an indefinite period. Constitutions guarantee this, to be sure, but constitutions mean little to many authoritarian regimes. The greatest insecurity in the rural Balkans today, as previously pointed out in the case of Dragalevtsy, is the ever-present threat that one's land may sooner or later be taken over by the state and operated as a government holding. Part of the Communist policy may be the promotion of this uncertainty on the theory that insecure people are more easily controlled. But when one tampers with a relationship as deep-rooted as that of the Balkan peasant to his land, he is also creating the seeds out of which a spontaneous resistance movement could grow. There is little evidence of collectivization at present, but the peasants are not convinced that it is not just around the corner.

Then too, the Balkan peasants, especially in the settled agricultural areas, have not taken kindly to Communism because they characterize it as an urban movement. When seasoned Communists try to converse with peasants about the merits of the Russian system their factory-oriented dialectic falls flat. Nor have they developed an agricultural vocabulary with which to communicate intelligibly with the rural people. The more the Balkan Communists talk, the more the peasants are convinced of the urban orientation of the new government. They consider it anti-Agrarian and anti-peasant. In an attempt to overcome this reserve to their program the Communists organize deputation teams of artisans who spend Sundays out in carefully selected villages helping the peasants repair their wagons, mend their pots and pans, or they even bring along a corps of barbers to cut the villagers' hair. The spirit behind such a move is to have the artisans show by their deeds, "You see, we are your friends. We're all brother Bulgarians [or Yugoslavs, as the case may be]." But it takes more than this to sell such a radical program as Communism to the capitalistic-minded peasant.

The rural villagers elsewhere in the Balkans, as well as in Dragalevtsy, resent the term worker. Newspapers studiously attempt to get the worker ideology accepted by the rural citizens, but the social statuses of the peasant and the worker are such that the government is asking the former to step down a rung, in the peasant's estimation. So Communism is thought to represent a backward rather than a forward move, and is related to the all-important matter of land: the peasant generally possesses it, whereas the worker is usually landless.

Many analyses of the Balkan problems play up rightly the role of the church, whether it be Eastern Orthodox or Roman Catholic, in the peasants' lack of enthusiasm for Communism. Others stress the generations-old nationality antipathies which have some influence. Certainly Pan-Slavism is not paying high dividends in rural areas in spite of heroic efforts by Russian ballet and athletic troupes who tour the provinces of all the Balkan lands. Other writers seek to show that modern Communism is merely a fulfillment of the traditional Communism of the zadruga, but they fail to point out that the zadruga was built around the family and land owned by that family, whereas modern Communism is centered around an impersonal state and ideology. To shift their loyalties from the family to such a state or to replace their religion with a new ideology is asking a great deal of the relatively inelastic peasant mass. State loyalties in the past were built upon joining the army and fighting, even to death, when one's country was threatened, but in times of peace one returned to the native village and had as little as possible to do with the national government after that. But the new turn of events in the Balkans seeks to whip up enthusiasm for the government, morning, noon, and night, when all that the peasants ask is "Please leave us alone."

The future seems to hold little peace for the landed peasants. Russia is in the Balkans to stay. Granting no American armed intervention, only some great upheaval in the heart of Russia itself could weaken the grip of the present National Front governments to the point that the opposition in the Balkan countries could take over the control. Given enough time, the Communists can coerce compliance and can train up a new generation which would enthusiastically repudiate the past, thereby consolidating the Communist position.

The process will, however, not be one-sided. The peasants of the Balkans will in turn influence Communism and indirectly help fashion a type which, like Chinese Communism, is somewhat different from that imported from the Kremlin. (Since this was originally written, Tito's failure to push the collectivization of the Yugoslav peasants has gotten him into trouble with Moscow.)

Americans then must more and more regard the area as Russian-occupied, a conquest of war, which the Reds will continue to dominate because of their advantageous diplomatic and geographic position. Out of their occupation Russian sympathizers have argued that two decided gains would come: the lessening of the nationality and ethnic differences, which have heretofore been such a fertile field of exploitation and manipulation by the great powers; and secondly, the rooting out in some areas of an archaic medieval system of landholding which was the economic basis of whatever Balkan aristocracies existed before the war. A further benefit, under any government would be the elimination of the inefficient strip-farming methods which characterize this area. There is a danger that if this means a complete substitution of a wage economy for the system built around the family farm, new social problems might arise which would prove as great as the problem being remedied. This, like any of the supposed benefits under the Russians, must be weighed against the terrifying, ruthless methods by which their achievement is attempted.

Americans must also recognize the possibility that United States prestige will diminish as the Balkan opposition groups, which had counted on active American intervention, are left to their tragic fates. Furthermore, an active anti-American and anti-British propaganda campaign, sometimes conducted flagrantly, sometimes subtly, will give the Balkan people an eastward rather than a westward orientation. Friendship could turn to indifference and then hostility, illustrating anew the principle that Americans must deal with Balkan questions not just between Washington and some Balkan capital but directly between Washington and Moscow.

Dragalevtsy is a long way from either Washington or Moscow and seems even farther away from the Main Street of any American town. But even now and surely in the days ahead Main Street is going to determine what happens in the Renaissance Square of Dragalevtsy. American foreign policy, which in the final analysis rests upon the informed (or uninformed) opinion of the general American public, more than anything else holds the key to the future for Bai Milush, Yurdan the tailor, and all the other village notables mentioned in these pages. Some of them hope that we will fight Russia soon, drive her out of the Balkans, and set up democratic governments; others hope that we can persuade Russia, though it still remains the dominant power in the Balkans, to give the "four freedoms" a chance to operate so that democracy can become a fact rather than a farce; only a few hope that we will yield to every Russian demand so that present

Russian aspirations in the Balkans can be realized without hindrance or interruption.

But whatever our American foreign policy is, and I hope it will be one of persuasion played more skillfully than in the past, it will not be dealing merely in abstract ideals, ponderous discussions, or complicated financial agreements; fundamentally our policy deals with the lives of millions of people who know that their future rests in American-Russian relations. Only as the average American on Main Street begins to personalize America's world responsibility in terms of something as ordinary as a Balkan village will we as a nation rise to fill the role that the rest of the world, including Russia, is expecting of us.

And the rest of the world is predominantly peasant. I am fully aware of the difference in tone between the bulk of this book and the last three chapters. The first part was a joy to write; the last part, in view of what has happened to the structure of Dragalevtsy, has been painful and difficult to record. I must therefore remind myself, as I remind the reader, that Dragalevtsy on Mount Vitosha is one of the thousands of villages which have survived catastrophes and wars through centuries. The form and substance of their community life is based on change which in the past has come more slowly and gradually, and not as it has recently come to Dragalevtsy with dictatorship and war. Their stubborn spirit, which has given them continuity, has sprung fresh each generation from their close ties with the cherished soil. This spirit, like Mount Vitosha, is subject to erosion but is still strong enough to withstand the buffeting of many storms. Dynamite, however, can change the face of any mountain if the blasting crews stay at the job long enough. It is still possible that the granite of the peasant spirit may in the long run outlast the zeal of reformers— whether under the banner of an impersonal economic system or that of an impersonal state, and thus re-introduce into our way of living at some future date a personal quality which we so sorely need.

APPENDIXES

NOTE ON APPENDIXES

Appendix I consists of tables containing information about Dragalevtsy. Some of the data are based on the 1926 census, since the tabulation for the 1934 census had not been completed at the time of my departure in 1937. Few of the computations were made by machine and there was considerable delay in the publication of detailed analyses for specific localities. Postwar conditions made it practically impossible for me to get more recent statistics from the Central Statistical Bureau on my last visit in 1945.

Appendix II sets forth the kinds of taxes peasants had to pay, and helps explain their attitude of distrust, suspicion, and even antagonism for any centralized government.

Appendix III, by describing the inventory of a grocery store in 1937, reveals the relative self-subsistence of the local economy.

Appendixes IV-VIII are articles, previously published in professional journals, which contain much material not incorporated in the body of the book.

APPENDIX I

A. TABLES ABOUT THE PEOPLE

TABLE 1

FAMILY HEADS BORN IN DRAGALEVTSY, 1934 CENSUS

	BOTH HEADS LIVING		ONE HEAD (SINGLE OR WIDOWED)		TOTAL	
	Male	Female	Male	Female	Male	Female
Total number in village...	252	252	14	10	266	262
Born in Dragalevtsy..........	212	139	9	4	221	143
Per cent born in Dragalevtsy	84.1	55.2	64.3	40.0	83.1	54.6

TABLE 2

NATIVITY OF DRAGALEVTSY-BORN MALE HEADS ENGAGED IN AGRICULTURE AND THEIR FATHERS, 1934 CENSUS

	TOTAL NUMBER IN VILLAGE (MALE HEADS)	MALE HEADS BORN IN DRAGALEVTSY		FATHERS OF DRAGALEVTSY-BORN ALSO BORN IN DRAGALEVTSY	
		Number	Per Cent	Number	Per Cent
Agriculturists..........................	209	191	91.4	184*	96.3
All occupations.......................	266	221	83.1	213	96.4

*184 out of a possible 191

TABLE 3

FAMILY SIZE IN DRAGALEVTSY, CENSUS OF 1934

NUMBER OF MEMBERS IN HOUSEHOLD	NUMBER OF HOUSEHOLDS	NUMBER OF PEOPLE	PER CENT OF POPULATION
1	7	7	0.4
2	13	26	1.6
3	39	117	7.2
4	42	168	10.2
5	46	230	14.2
6	46	276	17.0
7	28	196	12.1
8	21	168	10.3
9	12	108	6.7
10	8	80	4.9
11 and over	18	248	15.4
Total	280	1,624	100.0

TABLE 4

MARITAL STATUS OF THE DRAGALEVTSY POPULATION, CENSUS OF 1926

AGE (YEARS)	MARRIED		UNMARRIED		TOTAL PER AGE GROUP
	Men	Women	Men	Women	
Under 15	0	0	325	307	632
15	0	0	16	19	35
16	0	1	25	20	46
17	0	1	29	18	48
18	1	0	21	11	33
19	3	8	22	18	51
20	4	8	11	7	30
21-25	52	44	22	21	139
26-30	63	66	6	1	136
31-35	36	42	3	2	83
36-40	54	55	0	1	110
41-50	57	55	0	0	112
51-60	47	37	1	0	85
Over 60	27	17	1	0	45
Total	344	334	482	425	1,585

TABLE 5

LITERACY AND ILLITERACY BY AGE AND SEX GROUPS,
DRAGALEVTSY AND THE MAHALA, CENSUS OF 1934

AGE (YEARS)	LITERATE			ILLITERATE		
	Men	Women	Total	Men	Women	Total
15-20	106	85	191	4	10	14
21-25	140	65	205	2	49	51
26-30	101	44	145	4	39	43
31-35	89	35	124	0	41	41
36-40	61	17	78	1	46	47
41-45	47	8	55	4	41	45
46-50	52	12	64	5	45	50
51-55	33	9	42	3	28	31
56-60	17	5	22	2	24	26
Over 60	43	5	48	33	44	77
Total	689	285	974	58	367	425
Per cent of total	49.2	20.4	69.6	4.2	26.2	30.4
Per cent of men	92.2	—	—	7.8	—	—
Per cent of women	—	43.7	—	—	56.3	—

TABLE 6

NEWSPAPER AND MAGAZINE SUBSCRIPTION, DRAGALEVTSY, CENSUS 1934

Newspapers:

Families which buy or receive newspapers ... 21
    Daily newspaper every day ... 13
    Daily newspaper twice a week ... 2
    Daily newspaper once a week ... 1
    Weekly newspaper regularly ... 5
Families which receive no newspaper ... 257
Unreported ... 1

      Total number of questionnaires ... 279

Magazines:

Families which receive a magazine ... 7
Families which receive no magazine ... 271
Unreported ... 1

      Total number of questionnaires ... 279

TABLE 7

LENGTH OF ENGAGEMENT PERIOD, DRAGALEVTSY, 1935*

No engagement .... 1 couple
"Short" .... 3 couples
1 day .... 1 couple
3 days .... 1 couple
1 week ....18 couples
10 days .... 1 couple
2 weeks .... 3 couples
6 weeks .... 1 couple
8 weeks .... 1 couple

* Information gotten from people selected at random. They were of varying ages and had been married for varying periods of time.

B. TABLES ABOUT THE FARMS

TABLE 8

SIZE OF HOLDINGS OF DRAGALEVTSY FARMERS, WITH NUMBER ENTIRELY OWNED, CENSUS OF 1926*

SIZE OF HOLDING (DECARES†)	NUMBER OF FARMS	TOTAL DECARES	NUMBER OF FARMS OWNED	TOTAL DECARES OWNED
0- 10.....................	12	35.2	11	32.2
10- 20.....................	14	237.5	14	237.5
20- 30.....................	27	674.9	26	654.6
30- 40.....................	32	1,147.1	29	1,048.4
40- 50.....................	21	947.3	21	947.3
50- 60.....................	24	1,319.4	22	1,206.3
60- 70.....................	17	1,104.0	17	1,104.0
70- 80.....................	19	1,429.8	17	1,276.2
80- 90.....................	7	589.7	7	589.7
90-100.....................	7	657.3	7	657.3
100-150.....................	37	4,300.2	34	3,950.6
150-200.....................	13	2,191.8	13	2,191.8
200-300.....................	2	492.7	2	492.7
Total...................	232	15,126.9·	220	14,388.6
Per cent owned....			94.8	95.1

* Monastery farm of 1,176.1 decares omitted from table.
† 1 decare is ¼ acre.

TABLE 9

DRAFT ANIMALS OWNED BY DRAGALEVTSY FARMERS, CENSUS, 1926

SIZE OF FARM IN DECARES	HORSES	OXEN	COWS*	WATER-BUFFALO	TOTAL
0- 10	7	0	0	0	7
10- 20	1	4	2	0	7
20- 30	8	10	5	5	28
30- 40	7	11	5	6	29
40- 50	8	16	5	0	29
50- 60	9	32	4	4	49
60- 70	7	27	3	5	42
70- 80	12	20	4	3	39
80- 90	3	6	0	4	13
90-100	5	11	0	0	16
100-150	41	60	6	14	121
150-200	14	16	0	11	41
200-300	5	0	0	6	11
Total	127	213	34	58	432

* Cows includes buffalo cows.

TABLE 10

FARM MACHINERY OWNED BY DRAGALEVTSY PEASANTS, CENSUS OF 1926
(EXCLUDING MONASTERY FARM)

TYPE OF IMPLEMENT OR MACHINE	NUMBER OWNED BY ALL 232 FARMERS
Wooden plow	176
Plows with wheels	157
Metal plows without wheels	5
Harrows	1
Rollers	13
Planters	2
Hay rake	1
Winnowing machines	57
Cream separator	1
Honey separator	1
Others	7

A NOTE ON TAXES (1937)

An item of great expense to the peasant is taxes. The taxes may be divided into two kinds, State taxes and *Obshtina* (local) taxes.

Some of the taxes collected by the State are:

1. An occupation tax, which does not apply to agriculturalists, but to grocers, tavern keepers, milkmen, and teamsters.
2. An income tax on incomes of eighty thousand *leva* (pensions excluded). This tax varies proportionately from two to thirty-six per cent.
3. A construction tax. If a house or building costs 100,000 *leva,* a three per cent tax of its value must be paid after the building is finished.
4. A sales tax on many industrial products which the peasants have to buy.
5. A wagon tax. 25 *leva* annually if the wagon is for home use; 150 to 250 *leva* annually if the wagon is for business use.
6. A road tax. 140 *leva* minimum, with a graduated tax on higher incomes.
7. A railroad tax. 30 *leva* a year if not near a railroad. 90 *leva* a year if near a railroad under repair, which happens to be the case with Dragalevtsy.
8. A school tax for students from the fourth class to the eighth class, which does not affect the Dragalevtsy school (only to the fourth class).

Various local taxes:

1. A land ownership tax. 3½ *leva* per decare (14 *leva* an acre).
2. A land value tax. The village land is divided into first, second, and third categories, and is assessed as follows:

   8 *leva* per decare for the first category
   6 *leva* per decare for the second category
   4 *leva* per decare for the third category
3. A tax on buildings. An assessment is made at the rate of 2½ *leva* for each 1,000 *leva* of value.
4. A pasturage tax of 15 *leva* a year for each work animal.
5. A tax for livestock fund. 15 *leva* per head per year. This covers the cost of keeping a village bull and accumulates a fund for erecting a village barn later on.
6. A wood tax. 20 *leva* per cubic meter if purchased from the government.

AN INVENTORY OF STOCK CONTAINED IN A DRAGA-LEVTSY GROCERY STORE IN MARCH, 1937

Actual Value: $160

100 grams black pepper
200 grams ground cloves
1½ k* bicarbonate of soda
20 liters sunflower oil
150 eggs (taken in exchange for goods)
3 k homemade bread
2 k ground coffee
1½ k powdered sugar
4 liters vinegar
20 k granulated sugar
40 envelopes cinnamon
50 envelopes vanilla
3 boxes sardines
3 cans beans
100 labels
12 packages cookies
7 packages macaroni
7 packages cake flour
4 papers of pins
3 k loose cookies
bottled soft drinks, in season
60 pairs horseshoes
60 pairs oxen shoes
60 k nails (5 sizes)
3 k wagon bolts
7 k small bolts, nails
4 kerosene lamps
10 sheets wrapping paper
40 liters kerosene (near foods)
50 boxes matches

30 balls lace thread
2 k cleaning soda
¼ k black wool dye
15 balls cobbler's thread
18 boxes shoe polish
12 boxes of icon wicks
5 boxes of crayons
10 boxes Sunlight Soap
12 packages glass cleaner
50 packages special bluing 3
30 pairs shoestrings
60 spools sewing thread and darning cotton
15 k lentils
1 k dried peppers
12 k potatoes
11 k onions
3 k red pepper
1 k garlic
15 k prunes
2 k olives
3½ k *halva* (candy)
1½ k fish
10 k cream cheese
1½ k sausage
1½ k butter
2 k cheese (yellow)
2 dozen rolls
5 k plum jam
2 k zwieback
100 grams tea

*k—kilogram, or 2.2 pounds.

3 k wheat
10 k lard
9 k spaghetti
3 k sea salt
½ k alum
14 k lump sugar
½ k sage
½ k linden tea
3 boxes cocoa
4 cans honey
11 lemons
9 bungs
100 candles
6 k beeswax
1¼ k sulphur
2¼ k glue
¾ k ink
1 liter Flytox
½ k starch
200 grams resin
7 lamp chimneys
2 k hand soap
30 erasers
30 packages needles
15 nipples
3 curry combs
60 copy books
$4-$5 candy (6 kinds)
3 dozen pencils
135 packages cheap cigarettes
lamp wicking (45 meters)
6 big cans shoe blacking
2 dozen handkerchiefs
15 meters garter elastic
1 dozen key chains
1 pair red earrings

2 dozen knives
10 packages razor blades
1 flashlight battery
12 boxes thumb tacks
12 pairs cuff links
8 boxes hair pins
3 dozen bachelor's buttons
300 grams spices (3 kinds)
6 cigarette holders
6 penholders
100 packages milk biscuits
20 packages pipe tobacco
5 cards of snaps
15 electric bulbs
4 padlocks
1 bottle cleaner
6 brooms
2 balls string and cord
2 jars honey
1 k parchment
90 feet rope
2 boxes toothpicks
80 packages abrasives
2 k naphtholene
¼ k tartaric acid
1 k epsom salts
¾ k dyeing salt
300 grams incense
¾ k bluing
50 k washing soap
6 wick holders
50 crochet needles
200 hair clips
2 scrubbing brushes
4 pacifiers

NEIGHBORHOODS AND NEIGHBORLY RELATIONS IN A BULGARIAN VILLAGE*

During my first three years in Bulgaria, 1929-1932, I became generally acquainted with its rural life. When I returned to Bulgaria in 1934 for another three-year period I chose for special study one village, Dragalevtsy by name, whose 1,669 inhabitants live in houses clustered near the foot of Mount Vitosha four miles from the outskirts of Sofia. I visited the village on frequent occasions and lived there for weeks at a time. Although my investigations led me to consider many things such as the basic institutions, the formal and informal groupings, customs and folklore, along with the operation of the social processes, social control, and social change, one of the most difficult of the social phenomena for me, an outsider, to understand was the *mahala*, or neighborhood.

THE MAHALA. Dragalevtsy, like the majority of European agricultural villages, is a compact settlement of farmers whose land lies around the village in strips, numbering approximately 16 per Dragalevtsy farmer. The village is at least four centuries old and has grown but slowly during that time. Until three or four generations ago all life was organized around the patriarchal *zadruga,*[1] or joint-family. The members of such a family owned everything in common and worked in harmony under the administrator or *domakin,* the acknowledged head of the *zadruga.* Although their dwellings were crude and overcrowded each *zadruga* needed a large plot of land around the houses for the flocks of sheep and other animals kept at home during the winter months. With the liberation of Bulgaria from Turkey in 1878 forces were let loose which hastened the break-up of the joint-family system.[2] Brothers moved away from the paternal home into dwellings of their own, these usually being

* This article appeared in *Social Forces,* XVII, No. 4, May, 1939. Reprinted by permission.

[1] Ivan Evstatiev Geshov, *Zadrugite Vv Zapadna Bulgaria,* Per. Spisanie, God. V. Kn. xix i xx, str. 426, Stredets, 1886.

St. L. Kostov and E. Peteva, *Selski Bit i Izkustvo Vv Sofiisko,* Sofia, 1935, str. 58.

[2] Some of the factors contributing to this break-up: (a) individualization following Bulgaria's liberation in 1878 and the spread of popular education; (b) fashion of small, individual families in the West; (c) disagreement between the wives of brothers living together under the same roof; (d) unwillingness of men working outside the *zadruga,* either as laborers or professional men, to hand over their whole earnings to the common treasury; (e) woman's newly-acquired right of inheritance.

constructed on a part of the large plot of ground belonging to the dissolving *zadruga*. It therefore happened after a generation or so that six or seven houses whose heads all bore the same family name were located in a particular section of the village. Such clusters of houses in Dragalevtsy were called a *mahala* and often bore the name of the oldest living member of the family such as "Grandfather Grigor's *Mahala*." This usage of the term grew up quite unconsciously on the part of the peasants, and even today they use the term *mahala* without any clear conception of just what they mean by it.

At first glance it seems that *mahala* means a certain section of the village because it is often referred to in giving directions, but it is more correct to say that the peasant really means "over there in that particular section of the village where all of those related Manchevi live." This means that the *mahala* has both a geographical and kinship nature. On the other hand, if one of the Manchev men should for any reason move to another section of the village, he would still consider himself a Manchev, while admitting that he lived in a different *mahala*, and that the Mancheva *mahala* would not be extended to include him. In other words, the *mahala* is not identical with the term *rodstvo*, which means the large family connections. It applies only to those large family connections living in close proximity plus any other families dwelling among them. And this latter element is becoming of more importance. Today traces of kinship are beginning to vanish because the origins go back too far and because outsiders are slowly moving into Dragalevtsy.

The *mahala* never acts as a unit about anything, because its geographical character is its predominating aspect. Every villager can give the names of the other homes in his particular *mahala* and can even plot the *mahala* boundaries on a map of the village. But this does not mean that he feels any psychological bond connecting him with each of those homes any more than would the people who live on the same street in a small American town. Yet the very fact that they live near one another means that they will tend to interact more with one another than with people living on the other side of the village. This is why the *mahala* becomes important in a sociological analysis: it locates an individual in a given environmental setting.[a]

[a] Louis Petroff in his article "Peasant Primary Groups in Bulgaria" (*Sociology and Social Research*, 13, p. 557) thinks of the *mahla* (so he transliterates the word) as one of the important primary groups of the Bulgarian village. In his article he does not attempt to explain the origin of the *mahala* but thinks of it rather as "A section of the village separated by a small stream, a hill, a main road or a similar boundary. Or it may be a cluster of houses around a centering place, such as an inn or a store, but most commonly around a water fountain or a well." In Dragalevtsy the *mahala* originated as a kinship group, though the land originally owned by a *zadruga* was doubtless determined largely by geographical factors. The kinship origin is also shown by the fact that all the *mahali* in Dragalevtsy bear family names rather than those based on topographical or economic features.

Furthermore, the *mahali* (plural form) differ in size and prestige as well as in location. If the fortunes of two or three homes in a *mahala* rise, then the prestige of that *mahala* rises too. Land values go up in that place and the choice residential sites tend to shift there. This is illustrated in the case of the Daneva *Mahala* where the Danev men because of shrewd business methods have been able to accumulate considerable capital. Just the reverse is true in *mahali* where the families are very poor.

But the general use of the term *mahala* by the Dragalevtsy villagers is that applied to the smaller neighborhood of from seven to twelve houses. This use will be best understood if we briefly consider one of the village *mahali*: for instance, the Stoiova *Mahala* which consists of eight families living in the following spatial relationships and identified by the names of the family head as follows:

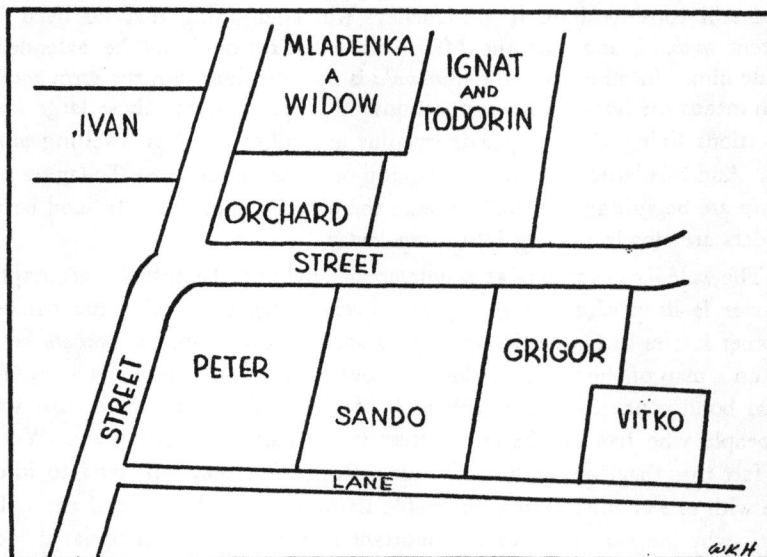

THE STOIOVA MAHALA*

Seven family heads are men, one is a woman.

Ignat and Todorin live with their families in separate divisions of the same house.

The kinship nature of the *mahala* is shown by the fact that Ignat and Sando are brothers and are nephews of Peter, and uncles of Todorin. They

* Subsequent investigation showed this *mahala* to be representative of others in the village.

TABLE 11

INTERACTION BETWEEN FAMILY HEADS OF STOIOVA MAHALA, DRAGALEVTSY,

SUMMER OF 1937

(Positive Interaction, +; Negative, —; Neutral or None, O)

GIVEN NAMES OF HEADS	MLA-DENKA	IGNAT	PETER	SANDO	GRIGOR	VITKO	TOD-ORIN	IVAN
1. Mladenka,* a widow................		+	—	O	—	—	O	—
2. Ignat, a "peacemaker".............	+		—	O	+	O	+	+
3. Peter, an elderly man...............	—	—		—	O	+	—	+
4. Sando, bro. of 2.......................	O	O	—		+	O	+	+
5. Grigor, an outsider..................	—	+	O	+		—	O	O
6. Vitko, now retired...................	—	O	+	O	—		O	O
7. Todorin, nephew of 2, 4.........	O	+	—	+	O	O		O
8. Ivan, a landlord......................	—	+	+	+	O	O	O	

* The predominance of conflict in Mladenka's relationships may be attributed to the fact that she is a woman and thus at a decided disadvantage. The peasants think of Bulgaria as still being a "man's country," and so it is.

are very distant cousins of Vitko and of Grigor's wife who persuaded Grigor, an outsider, to move to Dragalevtsy. Mladenka moved in from another *mahala,* while Ivan came from some other part of Bulgaria. Further light is thrown on the nature of the *mahala* by an analysis of the interaction between the family heads of the Stoiova *Mahala* as shown in table 11. The positive interaction[4] took such forms:

Ignat plowed Mladenka's garden plot for her and received in return permission to keep his sheep in her yard during the winter.

[4] I made no attempt to work out a complicated classification of social interaction with these simple, peasant folk. I soon learned that a rule-of-the-thumb method *similarly* applied in each case got results which checked with my own observation as well as that of the best informed people in the village. Eliminating from consideration here assimilation, competition, and accommodation I used merely the concepts of co-operation (Positive interaction) and conflict (Negative interaction). Where there is little trace of either positive or negative interaction I used the term Neutral. My description is based on the following questions: Which of the family heads co-operate regularly? Examples. Which have difficulties or quarrel more than they co-operate? Examples. Which have little to do with each other? Why?

The examples presented by the villagers to justify their statements were common knowledge in the whole neighborhood. Therefore, I was little surprised to find that once I had tentatively jotted down the prevailing interaction as given by the first informant every subsequent interview confirmed it. It is the case of anybody's business being everybody's business. Indeed, there is little doubt in the "public's mind" as to the relationship between any two people. I even suspect that two people wanting to better their relationship, for instance, would find the public a handicap due to the fixed conception of their respective roles.

234 BALKAN VILLAGE

Families of Ignat and Grigor work together in the field and at home throughout the year. Their children are of similar ages.

Sando and Ignat draw wood from the mountain for Ivan and in return borrow money from him occasionally.

Peter and Ivan, both elderly men, are drawn together by common interests.

Negative interaction can be illustrated as follows:

Peter's dog attacked Mladenka's sow which was about to bear young. As a result the litter was stillborn. Mladenka unsuccessfully tried to recover damages from Peter. Now she says of Peter: "He only speaks to me between his teeth."

A quarrel between Mladenka's daughter and Vitko's daughter, formerly the best of friends, over the question of employment as a domestic.

Mladenka is engaged in a lawsuit with Ivan over the question of property. The dispute arose when a new street was constructed between their houses.

Grigor quarrels with Vitko, and Ignat; Sando, and Todorin quarrel with Peter over land.

A count of the bonds between the family heads shows that the three categories are approximately equal in number: Positive—nine; Negative—eight; Neutral—eleven. Of course, we have not attempted to analyze bonds between the wives of the family heads, but we can be sure that if two men are in a quarrel they will forbid their wives to associate with members of the other's family.

In other parts of Bulgaria I have found that the word *mahala* has a slightly different significance and is used to describe some large section of the village which is separated because of such physical limitations as a river or a hill.[8] This means that other places would not have the twenty-two *mahali* which we find in Dragalevtsy. However, the Dragalevtsy people themselves use this broader term to describe an industrial community which is springing up between the village and Sofia and which has been assigned to the Dragalevtsy commune. Whenever any resident from there comes to Dragalevtsy to pay

[8] "The *mahala* (Dorfviertelschaft) is an enlarged neighborhood, which is usually determined by the physical features of the village. A river, a hill, or a strip of woods divides the village into two or more parts, localities, 'house complexes,' even *mahali*. If, however, there are no geographical lines of demarcation, 'calling-distance' determines the extent of the individual 'house complexes.' If two inhabitants of separate or distant 'house complexes' greet each other, each speaks when the conversation turns upon it of his *mahala* as of something individual and independent, distinct from the others. To each his *mahala* is a sort of miniature *Heimat*. Every man in the whole village is identified first as a native of his *mahala,* then as a member of his neighborhood, finally as a native of his own home. Neighborhood, *mahala,* and village are three gradually increasing entities, of which only the last two exhibit outwardly defined boundaries." (Wasil Handjieff: *Zur Soziologie des Bulgarishen Dorfes,* pp. 35-36.) Also see Note 3 in this connection.

taxes or to attend some social function, the villagers say, "Oh, he's from the *mahala*." In this sense, therefore, they are thinking not at all of any family relationship between the people of that settlement.

NEIGHBORLY RELATIONS: THE *Susedstvo*. For a clearer picture of social interaction we must turn to a smaller unit than the *mahala*: namely, the *susedstvo* [6] which is a complex of houses whose yards adjoin or face each other across a narrow street. The peasants say, "Without neighbors life is impossible," or "God help those who have bad neighbors" and they are thinking of next-door neighbors. Bulgarian writers especially in reminiscing about their childhood tell of the free interchange of goods between neighbors. In any time of need, whether it be of food, garments, or work, the neighbors were always called upon to render aid. That is still true today, though there are two tendencies setting in: first, many villagers prefer to go to relatives living elsewhere in the village for aid rather than to go to a next-door neighbor; second, nowadays neighbors when they lend live more in expectation of financial remuneration. In other words, the commercialistic spirit is pervading even neighborhood contacts. Some villagers feel this more keenly than others.

The *susedstvo* therefore, like the *mahala*, is a geographical unit which is the scene of intense social interaction, though this interaction takes place through ordinary individuals and groups rather than through the *susedstvo* itself, thought of in terms of a psychical entity. It is an interesting fact that personal friendships and preferences sometimes carry women outside of the neighborhood for even the ordinary needs of life. For example, Anna may live next to Gorka but may prefer the companionship of Mara who lives four or five houses down the street. Sometimes this friendship goes to such an extent that Anna will draw water from a more distant fountain in order to meet there with Mara.

However, no number of exceptions can do away with the fact that women who are neighbors depend greatly upon one another. Not only in times of crisis such as birth, death, or marriage are the neighbors' services invaluable, but are especially useful in varying the tedium of everyday life. If a woman has half an hour to spare, she is apt to pick up her knitting or spinning and go to a neighbor's house for a chat while doing her handwork. After a while, visits of such a sort become so habitual that a woman would find it difficult to get along without them. It must be remembered that the Bulgarian woman has no magazines and no radio to entertain her at home. Her only source of entertainment is to share some other neighbor's company.

Newcomers to a neighborhood (and these are usually women) have to go through a period of assimilation. Not only must they bear the embarrassing

---

[6] Many of the peasants still use for neighbor the word *komshia*, a Bulgarized form of the Turkish *koms*.

scrutiny of the neighbors and answer hundreds of questions, but they must also be quick to appreciate the social values and interests of the women of the surrounding houses. This is always so difficult that the villagers have a proverb: "One can't even drink the water from a different village," which they use in the social as well as physiological sense.

In a *susedstvo* we likewise find that there is often a family tie because the yards of married brothers or cousins frequently join. (See diagram on page 232.) If there is harmony between the brothers, such relatives are the closest of all because they are also neighbors; between such houses most of the borrowing takes place.

Since at least three-fourths, if not more, of a woman's recreation is provided in the neighborhood, this unit forms the basis for most gossiping groups. Men cross neighborhood lines because they can go to the tavern, but their wives must stay at home.

In comparing the *mahala* and the *susedstvo* we may conclude that the *mahala* once was the scene of the intimate interaction now characterizing the *susedstvo*. This was back in the days when the *mahala* was a family circle because of *zadruga* ties. As the number of houses increased and the feeling of kinship weakened or became extinct the *mahala* was superseded by the *susedstvo* as an important basis of interaction.

THE SOCIAL CONTACTS OF A BULGARIAN VILLAGE*

It seems an anomaly that the peasants who live in the Sofia region are among the most conservative in Bulgaria. One often hears the statement from Bulgarian and foreigner alike: "Surely the fact that a peasant lives near Sofia, a city of almost 300,000 inhabitants, should have some pronounced effect upon his attitudes and lower his resistance to social change." But there is universal agreement that these peasants are backward, though there is divergence of opinion as to the reason why. An early writer [1] advanced the theory that the *Shopi* [2] stock had been weakened because of the frequent "calls to arms" answered by the peasants. Living as they do on the edge of the important Sofia plain these peasants have been drafted for military service much more frequently than their fellows in the distant mountain recesses. In the little village of Dragalevtsy, four and a half miles from the outskirts of Sofia, more than forty fruit trees grow near the War Memorial, a tree for each son fallen on the field of battle since 1885, the date of the Bulgarian-Serbian War.

Another explanation for the *Shopi* conservatism is the fact that close proximity to the city makes it easy for the most intelligent and the most ambitious villagers to break with the village and establish themselves in Sofia. One of Dragalevtsy's most brilliant young men now resides in Sofia and visits the village only occasionally. But during his early days in the village he was a dynamic spirit: serving as president of the School Board at the time of negotiations for and erection of the handsome new school building; as chairman of the Committee on the Erection of a War Memorial, carrying the project through to successful conclusion where four previous committees had failed and the funds collected mysteriously disappeared; as president of the Reading Room Association, a "cultural" organization which has become an uplifting force in villages throughout the land. But now that he is gone, no native has arisen to lead as he led.

The *Agronom* for that district explains the conservatism in part by the poverty of the soil. Unproductive soil forms a poor basis for an enlightened,

---

* This article appeared in *Rural Sociology*, IV, No. 3, September, 1939. Reprinted by permission.

[1] Irechek, Konstantin, who traveled extensively in Bulgaria in the latter part of last century.

[2] *Shopi*—the term used of the peasants in the Sofia region. Formerly it was derogatory in content.

up-to-date type of farmer. Coupled with poor soil is the dividing up of the farm among all the children upon the death of the family head, with the result that farms become smaller, strips of land more numerous and scattered, and the occupation of farming a less remunerative enterprise.

Other theories take into account the descent of the *Shopi* from stock differing from that of Bulgarians in other parts of the country and their lack of educational facilities under Turkish rule (14th to 19th centuries). Then, too, we should remember that Sofia was nothing but a small provincial town— not much more than an overgrown village at the time of Bulgaria's liberation in 1878.

Part of my purpose in selecting one village for investigation was to determine as far as I could what contacts these villagers had with the outside world. I knew that I would probably arrive at no single all-embracing explanation of *Shopi* conservatism, but I did feel that I could suggest to those interested in overcoming this conservatism the proper modes of attack.

The analysis of Dragalevtsy's[3] social contacts falls naturally into two divisions: (A) the peasants' contacts outside the village, and (B) the peasants' contacts with the "outside world"[4] within the village.

THE PEASANT VISITS THE "OUTSIDE WORLD"

1. TO SELL AND BUY; TO WORK. Thirty-eight milkmen go from Dragalevtsy to Sofia every morning. Eight walk beside a donkey; thirty ride in the high two-wheeled horse-drawn carts. The majority of milkmen cover a milk route, knocking at the doors of the regular customers and waiting patiently for the maid to bring a container into which to pour a quart or so of milk from the large cans they carry. The rest, perhaps less energetic and content with a lower price, leave their milk at a milk-station just inside the city limits. They are paid weekly and do not have the bother of making collections from housewives; furthermore, they do not have to rustle out of bed so early in the morning. Some of the milkmen buy newspapers to read on the return trip, some like to go farther into the city for a glass of wine or brandy, but most hurry back home to aid in the work on the farm, especially if a busy season is on.

Besides the milkmen there are sixteen workmen and ten students who make the daily trip and serve as a bond between the village and the outside world. These two groups are usually less opinionated and better trained than the other villagers to whom they attempt to interpret the puzzling aspects of western culture manifested in Sofia.

[3] Population, December 31, 1934: 1,669 inhabitants.
[4] The peasants often speak of Sofia as "the outside world" and people from Sofia as "the people from the outside world," thus showing that a pronounced psychological barrier exists.

TABLE 12

FREQUENCY OF TRIPS TO SOFIA, MALE AND FEMALE FAMILY HEADS,
DRAGALEVTSY, 1934 CENSUS*

FREQUENCY	NUMBER		PER CENT	
	Male	Female	Male	Female
Daily:..	37	1	13.9	0.4
Weekly:				
4 times..........................	7	1	2.6	0.4
3 times..........................	9	2	3.4	0.7
2 times..........................	17	4	6.4	1.5
1 time..........................	113	99	42.5	37.5
Monthly:				
3 times..........................	8	9	3.0	3.4
2 times..........................	14	26	5.3	9.9
1 time..........................	35	58	13.2	22.0
Yearly:				
4 times..........................	7	16	2.6	6.1
3 times..........................	1	3	0.4	1.1
2 times..........................	3	2	1.1	0.7
1 time..........................	0	4	0.0	1.5
No times........................	15	39	5.6	14.8
Total........................	266	264	100.0	100.0

*Unreported: 3 male, 3 female.

The above table, based on the trips of the family heads, reveals the frequency of trips to Sofia:

The table[5] shows that thirty-three male heads go to Sofia oftener than once a week. The great exodus comes on Friday, the market day. The peasants' childlike anticipation of market-day is best symbolized by the wagons which stand already loaded in front of the gates on Thursday evening. All that is necessary in the dim light on Friday morning is the yoking of the sleepy oxen, before the families start on their way to Sofia. I went with the villagers on these expeditions and saw their "ports of call," each visited via back streets and not by any handsome boulevards.

[5] At the time of the government census in December, 1934, I received permission to add to the regular census blanks a questionnaire of my own dealing chiefly with social contacts. Every family head was required to appear before one of the local clerks and answer all questions on the blanks, the writing being done by the clerk. Many of my statistics in this article are based on these questionnaires which, in the person of family heads, represented 97 per cent of the population.

Cattle market: The cattle market and the sheep market, located not far away, lie on the other side of Sofia from Dragalevtsy, back of the railroad station toward the municipal cemetery.   It is there a peasant goes if he wishes to dispose of, or purchase, an animal.   At this market a nice young bull costs $25-$30, a fresh buffalo cow, $50-$60; ordinary milch cows, $35-$45; horses, $12-$60; donkeys, $12-$18.   In the sheep market a pair of sheep sell for $3.60. The cattle market is a colorful place.   There is much excitement in the horse section where gypsies ride their not-so-fiery steeds up and down to show how sound they are.   But the peasant does little visiting with others in the market; he is not the kind to strike up an acquaintance with just anyone.   He does deal with the nimble-witted cattle-buyers whose crafty ways stand for city ways in the peasant's undiscerning judgment.   In other words, the peasant's contact with "the outside world" in the cattle market helps build up a psychological barrier against the city since the peasant seldom leaves feeling that he has made a good bargain, unless he has concluded a trade with another peasant more rustic than himself.

The mill: A second place the peasant is likely to visit is the mill, not far away from the general curb market.   In spite of the fact that there are many mills in Sofia the people of Dragalevtsy have chosen this as their favorite one, with another ranking as second choice.   If they are tired out after their trip to the mill, the villagers lie down on sacks of grain until their turns come; if not sleepy, the peasants form talkative groups near their unyoked animals in the mill courtyard.   But here again we find peasant talking with peasant, much of the conversation condemning the modern times, some government policy, or the sad effects of the World War.   A talk with a conservative peasant from another village merely heightens the conservatism in the Dragalevtsy peasant.

Curb market: After finishing at the mill the peasant will perhaps go to the General Curb Market where his wife, squatted on the sidewalk, has been crying her wares for hours in the hope of selling a few bunches of vegetables or several "pairs" of eggs.   She has seen many enticing objects in the vendors' pushcarts, observed the styles [6] worn by city housewives accompanied by peasant servant girls, the strut of the military, the bizarre appearance of a foreign tourist in knickers taking pictures of the scene.   She must also have talked to other peasant women who, like herself, return to a favorite spot week after week.   But the question arises: Do all the men usually take their wives along? Is it usually a family affair, this trip to market?   The answer is that between fifty and sixty per cent of the female heads go to Sofia on a typical market day; fifteen per cent never go at all.

___

[6] The chief tailor in Dragalevtsy says that styles in dress reach the peasants from other villages.   The women, for instance, imitate what a peasant from another village wears, but not what a city woman wears.

Flower bazaar and tavern: It is around the fourth destination on Fridays that fondest memories cling, because this is the spot near the Sofia flower bazaar where young people from surrounding villages go upon completing their morning duties in town. It is here that romance blossoms and young men from one village are introduced to girls from another. While the younger people are amusing themselves here the older people, especially the men, gather at the tavern called *Dulgata Mehana,* the particular establishment to which Dragalevtsy peasants are loyal.[7] They lunch and drink here, they rest here, and here they swap their stories. Nor is it without pride that they tell how Fiodor Chaliapin, the celebrated opera singer, in 1934 spent a very merry evening in this *Dulgata Mehana,* enjoying its drink and atmosphere. Seldom, however, does the peasant get to converse with the Sofia citizenry in this tavern. Here again he is in a peasant world; if he were not, he would feel decidedly uncomfortable. Should he decide to see a movie, in the afternoon he would go to a cheap theater on a side street and guffaw with his fellow peasants.[8]

2. TO SERVE HIS COUNTRY. The *trudova* system, or that of compulsory labor for the young men of Bulgaria, has received much attention in the West. It served a magnificent purpose, taking as it did young men from villages throughout the land, mixing them up in labor camps, and providing them with picks and shovels for the construction of highways, bridges, and other public works. But now the young Bulgarian citizen is given military training instead. This is not in keeping with the Treaty of Neuilly, which limited Bulgaria's armed forces to 33,000, but what nation in Europe, the Bulgarians ask, has been abiding by the treaties? The trend from *trudova* to military service is shown by the fact that in 1935 not a single youth was called from Dragalevtsy to do *trudova* service, but sixteen went to be trained as soldiers.

The effect of life in a labor camp or a military barracks upon the young men is apparent upon their return to the village. They have gone out from a family system where each member works unquestioningly as a part of the whole; they return, in spite of military discipline, often very conscious of their own individuality, and have to pass through a process of reconditioning before the early customs, habits, and patterns of thought again close in about them. However, before the returning young men are reabsorbed by the community, reverberations of struggle are felt throughout parts of the social structure. There are some who never again fall completely into line and who naturally

---

[7] Every village over a period of years has tended to select one tavern where peasants from that village spend their leisure time while in Sofia.

[8] Fifty-five per cent of the villagers (babies, children, and adults) have never seen a cinema. Out of 265 families reporting, *all* members of 73 families had seen a cinema; *no* members of 78 families had done so.

turn to Sofia for employment and sympathy. But the significant fact is that most young people do submit to the process of resocialization and as they grow older adopt the conservatism of their elders. In other words, no attempt is made in the army experience to teach them new farming methods, bee-keeping, animal breeding, or anything else which they might apply in a useful way upon their return to the village.

3. FOR THE GOOD OF HIS SOUL. When asked "Why do you go on pilgrimages to various Bulgarian monasteries?" the peasants often answer: "We go for the good of our souls." No mention is made of the enhanced social status that is theirs as a result of such a trip or the excitement of being sped on their way at the edge of the village by the priest and a flock of relatives or welcomed back far outside the village by the same relatives two or three days later. The most popular place to visit is Rila Monastery, the historic, magnificent establishment in the heart of the Rila Mountains to which thousands come at Easter time. The Dragalevtsy peasants (only thirty-five from the village went in 1934) mix with the assembled multitudes at Rila, attend the services, buy sacred objects, and snatch what sleep they can before starting on the return journey. If they are walking, the pilgrimage requires five or six days; if they go by automobile from Sofia, they spend one day en route each way. In olden days pilgrimages played a great part in creating social contacts between the villages and the outside world. Now we can safely conclude that as other means of making social contact increase, the importance of making pilgrimages decreases.

4. TO VISIT SOCIALLY. Once a year a Bulgarian village has an "At Home Day." This event always falls on the name day of the saint, angel, or member of the Trinity for whom the local church is named and is commemorated by the preparation of immense quantities of stews for the few hundred guests from outside. Many of these guests are old residents returning with their families for a visit. There is a special service at which bread and boiled corn is blessed, the priest in return receiving a portion of the food. At the meal afterwards, to which all guests are invited, pledges are made for the upkeep of the local church. Many guests would rather go to the homes of friends and relatives than partake of the common meal; this makes more intimate visitation possible. These "At Homes" of neighboring villages are the chief attractions drawing the peasants from Dragalevtsy to other villages. Table 13 on the following page shows us how often Dragalevtsy family heads visit other villages (for the "At Home" as well as other purposes).

Combining the data in this table with other information obtained we can make the following conclusions regarding the social visits of Dragalevtsy people to other villages:

TABLE 13

FREQUENCY OF TRIPS TO VILLAGES, MALE AND FEMALE FAMILY
HEADS, DRAGALEVTSY, 1934*

FREQUENCY	NUMBER		PER CENT	
	Male	Female	Male	Female
Monthly:				
6 times	2	0	0.8	0.0
5 times	0	2	0.0	0.8
4 times	2	4	0.8	1.6
3 times	3	2	1.2	0.8
2 times	8	9	3.1	3.5
1 time	68	52	26.4	20.3
Yearly:				
6 times	4	8	1.5	3.1
5 times	2	3	0.8	1.2
4 times	14	8	5.4	3.1
3 times	21	17	8.1	6.7
2 times	13	19	5.0	7.4
1 time	8	8	3.1	3.1
No times	113	124	43.8	48.4
Total	258	256	100.0	100.0

*Unreported: 11 males, 11 females.

Roughly speaking, about half of the family heads (men and women) do not go to other villages in the course of a year. For those who go, the greatest frequency of visitation is once a month.

Men born in Dragalevtsy visit the other villages more than do their fellow-villagers not born in Dragalevtsy; however, women born in Dragalevtsy visit less than those born outside. [9]

Children seldom go with their parents to other villages, though certain young men make numerous visits to parties during the year.

There are other contacts which the peasant makes with the outside world away from the village, but these are not important enough for separate consideration. There is, for instance, "the iron grip of the law." Since the mores of Dragalevtsy are still strictly observed, no criminals were led off to prison from the jail-less village during the three-year period in which I studied Dragalevtsy. Annually there are four or five lawsuits, involving about thirty people and taking on an average ten days' time for each person. For those

[9] Eighty-three per cent of the male family heads but only 55 per cent of the female heads were born in Dragalevtsy. The 45 per cent of non-native wives come from villages ranging in distance from two to ten miles.

involved, the trial is a big, important event, but the effect upon the village is slight. What does have an effect is the quarrel which leads to the lawsuit, but that is an internal and not an external matter.

THE "OUTSIDE WORLD" VISITS THE VILLAGE

1. THE MOUNTAIN AND THE MONASTERY. The "white-collar" people of Sofia are enthusiastic hikers. On sunny days, both winter and summer, they start out on an extended hike, usually in the direction of Vitosha, a majestic mountain which towers seven thousand feet above the Sofia plain. If very active, they climb to Hizha Aleko, the mountain hotel below the summit, there to spend the night. Or if interested only in a Sunday afternoon stroll of ten miles, they visit *God's Consecrated Spot on Vitosha,* a historic monastery from which they get a magnificent view of the Sofia plain, the city, and the Balkan peaks twenty miles to the north.

Dragalevtsy, hugging as it does a shoulder of the mountain, is on the main road leading from Sofia to the monastery (twenty minutes' walk above the village) and the mountain hotel far above the monastery. Dragalevtsy's taverns serve, therefore, as resting places for the weary, hungry, and thirsty trampers. Especially in Bai Penko's tavern is there mingling between the village "elite" (intelligentsia and richer peasants) and these Sofia visitors—"people of the world." The peasants laugh at the sight of the women dressed in winter in ski trousers or in shorts in summer. No one ever explains to the peasant that sport styles are extreme.

One evening in Bai Penko's tavern I was with a group of peasants who chortled when they saw a fat betrousered woman attempt unsuccessfully to get her loaded knapsack off. Turning to one of them I asked what he thought of such women, "Oh, we know what they are like," was the answer. When I pressed him further as to what he meant, he said: "They are the worst kind." Then I could not resist asking: "What would you do if your daughter came home dressed like that?" and the retort flared back, "Why, damn it, I'd kick her out of the house."

Estimates vary as to the number of *turisti,* as the Bulgarians call them, who pass through the village each year. Suffice it to say that on holidays and week ends there is a steady stream pouring through unless the weather is too forbidding. On August 28th, the Day of the Virgin, thousands flock to the monastery for the special services there as well as for the setting. Many of these hikers visit Dragalevtsy, whose square has been changed overnight into a lively market lined with temporary restaurants and a ramshackle merry-go-round.

The chief influence that these visitors have upon the villagers is to make them think that life in the city is as gay and carefree as the singing groups who stop to spend money in a generous manner.   This is one reason that the peasants complain so bitterly of their dull, monotonous life and long to have their children counted among the white-collar class.

Recently Dragalevtsy has become a mountain summer resort.   Twelve families have little villas in or near the village, while as many more live in the monastery.   These seasonal guests buy most of their produce from the villagers, and patronize Bai Penko's tavern daily.   Some, especially the twelve families with summer houses, are counted as real citizens of Dragalevtsy, though the peasants do not try to assimilate them into their informal groups.   These summer guests are in a position to do much in the way of village improvement if they cared to seize their opportunities.

2. FAMILY GUESTS.   Another important influence from outside comes in the form of guests entertained by the family during the course of a year.   The numbers of guests from Sofia, from other towns, and from villages are shown in Table 14 below:

TABLE 14

GUESTS IN DRAGALEVTSY HOMES DURING THE YEAR 1934, CLASSIFIED
ACCORDING TO DOMICILE (CENSUS OF 1934)

NUMBER OF GUESTS	NUMBER OF FAMILIES ENTERTAINING GUESTS			TOTAL NUMBER OF GUESTS*		
	From City	From Town	From Village	From City	From Town	From Village
0	96	249	62	0	0	0
1-10	125	8	135	786	36	824
11-20	34	0	58	555	0	888
21-30	3	0	14	75	0	380
31-40	4	0	1	150	0	35
41-50	5	0	0	250	0	0
Over 50	1	0	1	100	0	65
Total	172	8	209	1,916	36	2,192

*Computed from actual figures and not from class midpoints.

Out of the 268 families that reported, 96 families do not have any guests from Sofia during the year.   The guests visiting the 172 remaining families total 1,916 people.   In other words, if all the people who come from Sofia to visit stayed in the village and did not return home, the village would little more than double its present population, ignoring the possible natural increase. Of course, the total of 1,916 does not necessarily include that many people, but certainly over 1,000.   These visitors are relatives or friends, generally of peasant origin, who have gone to the big city and succeeded.   As one stands in the main village square and sees these visitors arrive, averaging 36 each Sunday, one marvels at the grotesque bundles with which their arms are loaded. A christening, a wedding, and, to a less extent, a funeral, call them back to the village. Conveniently for them, christenings and weddings take place on Sundays; funerals, unfortunately for them, cannot wait for Sunday but occur a day or two after the death.

There are no towns within forty or fifty miles of Sofia, and therefore very few guests from other towns visit the village. Only 8 families report such guests, the total number of the visitors reaching 36.

Out of 271 families reporting, only 62 do not have guests from other villages during the year. This means that 209 families do. The total number of outside villagers is 2,192, many of them coming to Dragalevtsy's "At Home Day" on the Day of the Holy Trinity.

Only a few of these guests originally came from Dragalevtsy but it is of interest to notice how many leave the village permanently in the course of a single year, why, and where they go. These facts are shown in Table 15.

TABLE 15

MEMBERS OF FARM HOUSEHOLDS WHO PERMANENTLY LEFT DRAGALEVTSY
DURING 1934, CLASSIFIED ACCORDING TO REASON FOR LEAVING AND
DESTINATION (CENSUS DATA)

LEFT TO BECOME:	DESTINATION:			Total
	Sofia	Town	Village	
Soldier	3	1	0	4
Student	4	0	0	4
Coffee house proprietor	1	0	0	1
Cabman	1	0	0	1
Watchman	0	1	0	1
Laborer	0	0	2	2
Wife	1	0	4	5
Husband	0	0	1	1
Unreported	1	1	0	2
Total	11	3	7	21*

*These 21 persons came from 19 of the 279 families covered by the census questionnaire.

3. VILLAGE GUESTS. During the course of a winter several *vecherinki*, or community parties, are staged in the schoolhouse by some organization for the purpose of raising funds. These are usually followed by a dance at which the thirty-five guests from Sofia (that being the average) mix little with the peasant folk. These guests are entertainers or friends of the intelligentsia.

Three or four lectures, dealing with topics related to the elevation of village life, are given each year by men from outside. Each government inspector from the various departments is required to visit the village once a year and some in the course of this visit take occasion to give an educational address to the people. I do not feel, however, that the peasants take a very vital interest in these talks unless they get into the realm of politics, always a fascinating subject.

From the 15th of May until August 1st soldiers in training are encamped in and about Dragalevtsy, but it is only occasionally that they mingle with the young people of the village. Every year, however, three or four village girls become engaged to soldiers and subsequently upon marriage move elsewhere.

The outside world is also represented by a few salesmen and speculators in land and cattle, these numbering about fifteen a week. They transact their business with the interested party, perhaps break bread with him, and then go on their way.

4. TELEPHONE, RADIO, LETTERS, PRINTED MATTER. There are two radios in the village, one belonging to the priest and the other standing in the window of the mayor's office to blare forth its music and messages to passersby in the main square. The first program I heard from the public radio was the aria, "My Heart at Thy Sweet Voice," from the opera *Samson and Delila* as played by an orchestra in Amsterdam, although music like this is soon turned off in preference to the folk-music periodically broadcast from the Sofia station.

There is one telephone in the village in the office adjacent to the mayor's. There is great pomp about the use of this instrument since one pays two cents and receives a receipt of payment from the telephone operator. Making a telephone call is a serious affair, so serious, in fact, that few peasants ever do so.

The post arrives around one o'clock each week-day afternoon, but there is little excitement attached to its coming, for not more than ten personal letters, usually for the intelligentsia, arrive daily for the whole village. A peasant family receives no more than one or two letters a year. Twenty newspapers and twenty magazines come each day for the 279 families. According to data furnished by 279 questionnaires, 21 families bought or received newspapers [10] to 257 who did not; and 7 families received magazines to 271 who did not. In both cases, 1 family failed to report.

[10] Of these, 13 families received a daily newspaper daily; 2 received a daily paper twice a week; 1, once a week; and 5 received a weekly paper regularly.

CONCLUSION

The concept "social contact" implies both the possibility of contact as well as psychic interaction.[11] The quantitative measurements of this study deal chiefly with the possibilities which the peasants have or create for social interaction, since these were sufficiently clear-cut for the village officials and peasants to measure. But when it came to the more intangible element of psychic interaction I had to rely on direct personal observation. Therefore, the following conclusions are based in part on statistics and in part upon observation:

1. Proximity to a "city-culture" and frequent trips to the city on the part of the villagers does not necessarily mean psychological contact with that "city-culture." For the most part, the peasant moves in a peasant world even while in the city. It is quite natural for him to attach himself to the familiar.

2. Proximity to the city may in itself be a deterrent to the ready acceptance of "city ways" on the part of the villager, since he constantly confronts fashions, habits, and viewpoints which clash decidedly with his own. This leads me to wonder whether or not "modernization," granting that it is desirable, might not come more quickly through a small, provincial town which is more in keeping with rural thought and life than through direct contact with the city. The hikers who visit Dragalevtsy, although causing dissatisfaction, make the mature peasant more resistant to city influences; these visitors do seem to have an influence upon the young; but it would be hazardous to guess to what degree, because so often the seemingly liberal young people become conservative when they have children of their own.

3. Government leaders in their attempt to raise the peasants' standard of living visit the village systematically for lectures and some demonstrations. They seem to be overlooking the fact that thousands of peasants regularly visit the city where, if some Peasant Center could be established, methods of improved living could be interpreted in a favorable light. Some such approach would lessen the peasant's negativism toward the city, a negativism which has been built up as a defense or as a result of genuine disapproval.

4. The statistics relative to the reading matter which comes into the village weekly show how little is being done effectively to influence the peasant by letters, journals, and other publications, although the literacy rate for males over fifteen years is 92.

[11] At first I had in mind the formulation of a contact Index such as Kulp used in his Chinese study, *Familism in South China.* I soon found that the various contacts were of varying intensity, concerned different types of people, and would, therefore, require separate weighting. My methods were not refined enough to make such weightings feasible. Furthermore, aside from the methodological interest, the value of such an index would be limited to the study of other Bulgarian villages in the same cultural setting.

5. This study of one village can be merely suggestive and does not afford the basis for any sweeping conclusions, but it can serve as a pattern for those who wish to measure the social contacts of villages which are similar in many respects to Dragalevtsy.

6. In considering the social contact which the peasants have with the city and its implication for social change, we must not overlook the sheer enjoyment derived by the peasant from the very fact of contact itself, whether it be from the thrill of a new experience or the more intimate association with friends from other villages. Because recreation is not yet commercialized and impersonalized, face-to-face contact is the chief form of amusement. Of course, this need is usually met within the village, but a talk with someone from the outside world does possess a novelty not afforded by everyday association.

SOCIOMETRIC WORK WITH A BULGARIAN WOODCUTTING GROUP[1]

In the late autumn, when all other farm work has been completed, the villagers of Dragalevtsy[2] turn their attention to the gathering of the winter's supply of wood. The scene of their activity is a wooded section of the mountainside, three or four miles from the village, determined in advance by a forester's decree. Most of them toil gladly, since all winter long they must continually feed the wood into the ever-devouring gullet of the sheet-iron stove standing in the center of the living room. No twig is too small to find its way there.

It would be wrong to imagine that the villagers were doing any lumbering, even on the simplest scale. Most of their activity centers around the task of cutting down brush as high as a man's head, or of felling trees so small that a pair of hands could include the trunk in its grasp.

I. MEMBERSHIP OF GROUP. There are ten wood-gathering groups in the village. Before 1931 individual families went to the section of the forest opened up for the people of Dragalevtsy and took all the wood they could get in the time allowed. This system had two chief faults, according to Yurdan Chalukov, the assistant mayor at the time: in the first place, the members of the political party supporting the mayor learned beforehand at what time the forest would be opened to the villagers and stole the march on the others by going there on the day assigned, although the other villagers did not learn about the opening until two or three days later, by which time the best wood had been collected.

The second chief fault with this system was that families with more able-bodied workers gathered the most wood, although they paid perhaps less taxes than those who got less. In order to eliminate these evils, a new system which is peculiar to Dragalevtsy alone was inaugurated. The near-by villages, for instance, still use the older method of permitting each family to "grab while

---

[1] This article appeared in *Sociometry: A Journal of Interpersonal Relations*, **II**, October, 1939, pp. 58-68. Reprinted by permission.

[2] Dragalevtsy, a village of 1,669 inhabitants, located four miles from the outskirts of Sofia, Bulgaria's capital city. The peasants of that region are generally regarded as very conservative by educated Bulgarians.

the grabbing is good." Now, the *Obshtina*[a] divides the village into ten groups; the part of the forest made available to the villagers is likewise divided into ten sections; each group thus has a limited section in which to work. The *Obshtina* usually divides the village according to neighborhoods, though sometimes one family from a larger neighborhood is assigned to the group of a smaller neighborhood in order to make the number of families average about thirty for each group. The only case of this kind in Group X, which we are studying, is that of Krustan Arnaudski, who lives across the river from the others.

The *Obshtina* lists the names of the family heads in making out its divisions; theoretically these family heads are supposed to go collectively to get the wood for their households. In other words, they are supposed to constitute the group. However, variations occur. Some of the family heads are too old or too busy or too lazy to go. In that case they do one of three things: (1) they send their married sons who live with them, these sons performing the work more capably than the older men could; (2) they hire village youths from other neighborhoods to go and gather the wood for them; or, (3) they send weaker members of their own family, such as younger boys, the older girls, wives, or—in the case of one lazy man—a mother.

Thus, in reality, the group of wood-gatherers varies from day to day as regards the actual personnel of those working in the forest. We might say that most of those working there are family heads or able-bodied married sons, though mixed with them are women, girls, and younger boys. Before sending a substitute the family head is supposed to get permission from the group leaders. The failure to do this results in many quarrels and, as one leader says, "makes a man quarrel with his best friend."

The reason why the presence of women and children is frowned upon lies not so much in the objection to women and children working, as it does to the fact that women and children cannot do as much work in a day as a man. Since all the cut wood is piled into thirty different piles, one for each family, and the piles later distributed by lot, those who work hard each day get no more wood than those who do less work or who send weaker substitutes.

The question arises as to the classification of this type of group. On the basis of admission to membership, we can conclude that it is chiefly involuntary since the family heads are assigned by the *Obshtina* and since the family head can order members of his family to replace him in case he does not care to go. Only in the case of outsiders gathering wood for pay does the group seem voluntary. The group is secondary as far as function is concerned, but partakes of certain primary group characteristics when we notice that the *Obshtina*

[a] *Obshtina*—used here in the sense of the local governmental unit under the direction of a mayor appointed from Sofia.

usually divides the village up according to neighborhoods. Thus we have many persons accustomed to associate as neighbors interacting along economic rather than social lines.

II. DURATION OF GROUP. The group is temporary, since the *Obshtina* lists have varied from year to year. However, for thirty days the wood-gathering continues, halted in bad weather but energetically pursued in good weather, even on Sundays. During this period there is constant interaction between the members of the group, who get to know the working qualities of the others in an intimate way. The most exciting day of all is the day when the wood has been piled up, the piles numbered, and the family heads take their turn drawing lots for the piles. It is then that the whole family comes in the ox-cart to haul the wood home. There is joy as though a harvest were being gathered. Each family usually takes home from four to five ox-carts full of wood, most of which consists of branches or scrub-growth. After the wood is stacked in the yard, the group is ended; its existence is terminated by the completion of the job it set out to do.

III. STRUCTURE OF GROUP (RELATIONSHIP). With thirty individuals, unequally divided as to ability or inclination to work, there must be some sort of leadership to keep the group functioning effectively. The nominal leaders are two men appointed by the *Obshtina,* one as superintendent and the other as his assistant. Leaders appointed by the *Obshtina* usually serve even though they profess an unwillingness to do so. Some members of Group X point out that those who do the most talking against the way the present leaders discharge their functions are themselves loath to accept the responsibility if it is offered to them. The leaders of Group X this year were Stoyanche Chalukov and his god-son (almost his equal in years) Yurdan Chalukov.

The leaders of all ten groups gather on an appointed day to visit the forest with the forest policeman, who shows them how the forest has been divided into ten sections. The leaders then draw lots to see which section will fall to their particular groups. On the day of the visit this fall neither leader of Group X went because each one thought, or at least hoped, that the other leader would go. It so happened that Group X got what its members considered the worst part of the forest, though the leaders maintain that their absence had nothing to do with the section allotted. Upon seeing the state of things, the leaders of Group X went to the mayor and asked that some re-distribution be made on the grounds that the forest had not been equally divided. As such re-distribution seemed out of the question, the mayor suggested: "You go ahead and cut down the wood in your section, and the priest and I will come and visit the forest and see whether people in other sections have bigger piles than you. If they do, we'll re-distribute then." But the mayor and the priest never made this visit with the result that the members of Group X have nothing but complaints as consolation.

The duties of the leaders are burdensome. They must decide whether the weather permits work in the forest or not; they must accept or reject some family head's proposal for substitution; they must argue with those who do not work well; they must direct the making of the piles and the equal distribution of the wood among these piles; furthermore, they must keep a record of those who come to work and those who do not. The only authority vested in them is the right to report to the mayor the name of any man who they think should not be given any wood for failure to do his share of the work. However, no such instance occurred this past year.

Quite often a group has a formal structure in addition to the actual structure. This formal or theoretical structure corresponds to the plan of a house; the actual structure corresponding to the shape, relationship of the parts, etc., which may be quite different from the original plan in even so definite a field as architecture.

The woodcutting or wood-gathering Group X has two leaders appointed by the *Obshtina,* under whom the family heads are supposed to work. This is the plan, but we notice that there are variations since many family heads send substitutes. Our first problem is to see whether the appointed leaders are the actual leaders: that is, to see if the plan of the group corresponds with the structure as we discover it.

In order to accomplish this I followed Moreno's method as explained in his book, *Who Shall Survive?* namely, to ask each member of the group which five men he preferred and which five he would eliminate if he were choosing a group of his own with direct reference to one activity—the gathering of wood, and with no interest at all in the question of the friendship involved.

Each of the family heads on the *Obshtina* list furnished us with the information desired. Where some family heads had sent substitutes, we interviewed the substitutes instead. A few people, neither full-time substitutes nor family heads, who worked in the forest from time to time in the place of someone who stayed away were interviewed if they were mentioned twice by others. The only exceptions were numbers 19 and 30, both of whose fathers we interviewed. Some family heads who did not go to the forest were mentioned either as desirable or undesirable, and their names were included on the list which formed the basis for the diagrams.

There was no way of cross-checking to see whether the answers were correct; nor was there any reward to hold up to them in order to identify their emotions with their answers. In this respect, one might consider the method open to question. However, each man was told: "There will be no reward for you in answering these questions, nor will any harm come to you as a

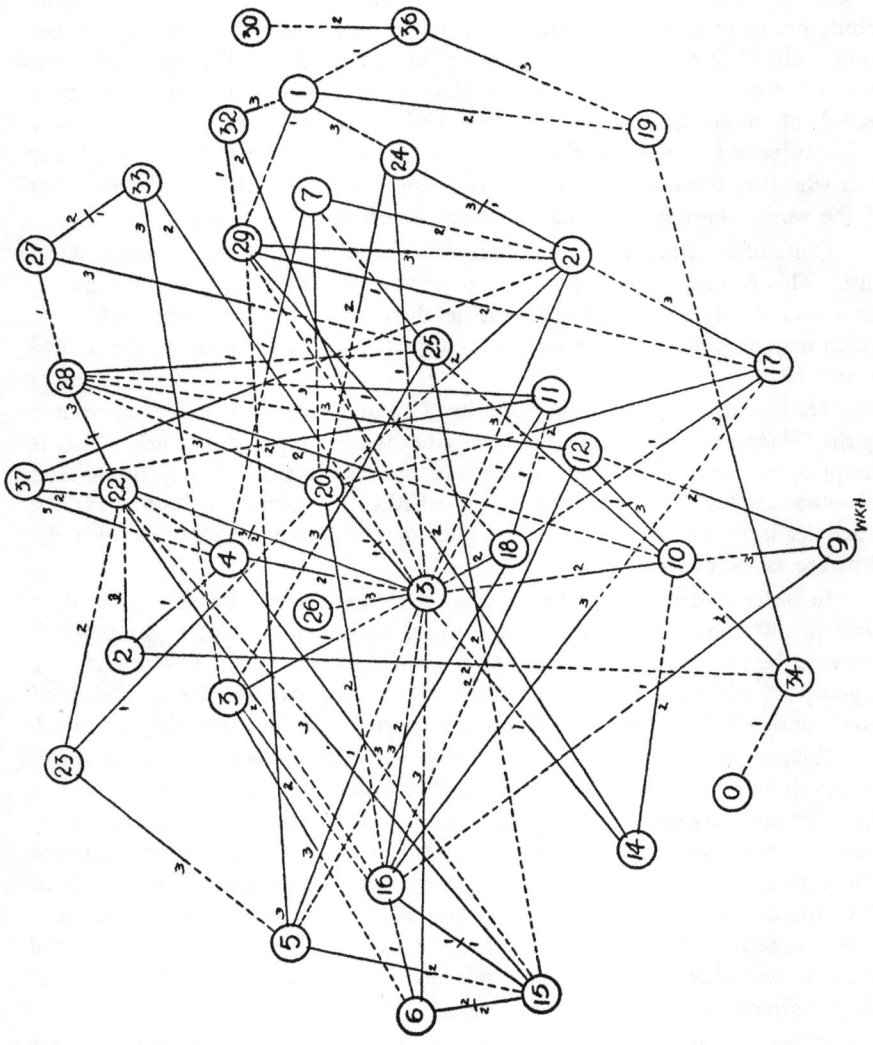

SOCIOGRAM I. Woodcutting Group, Dragalevtsy, Bulgaria—34 men, first three choices

result. If you answer, it will be simply out of kindness and because of your desire to help me." Such an approach met with a splendid response, since practically all of the villagers knew that a "book" was being written about their village and were eager to help in its preparation. I am inclined to believe that in most cases this desire to help on the part of those interviewed has an emotional content, though it is something hard to measure or estimate.

While these interviews took place over a two-day period during the Christmas holiday recess, I visited the village several times when the wood-gathering was taking place to make family interviews and received considerable incidental material about wood-gathering which seemed to be on everybody's mind. Group X was selected by chance. Since the groups were all equal in size there was no reason to choose any one more than another for the study of the group *per se*. (See Sociogram I.)

An analysis of Sociogram I, which is based on the first three choices of each man, shows us how weak is the leadership of the two men appointed by the *Obshtina*—namely, numbers 4 and 7. At no time do they come out as important leaders but this may be due to conflict situations which arose between them and group members during the course of the wood-gathering. The predominant choice is 13, a hard-working retired railroad man, who is close-mouthed and has the reputation of "minding his own business." He was mentioned 15 times: 6 firsts, 6 seconds, and 3 thirds. This sociogram shows that when the mayor appointed the leaders he did not consider the same qualities which the peasants themselves thought essential. He appointed men who had been former political figures on the assumption that they could also lead capably in the task of woodcutting.

The other leader individuals besides 13 are 10, 15, 16, 20, 21, 22, 28. An interesting concentration of leadership is shown by the reciprocal bonds existing between some of these eight leader individuals: namely, 15-16, 13-20, 13-22, 22-28. (Notice again the strong position of 13.) The leaders also have the following reciprocal bonds with non-leader individuals: 10-12, 15-6, 21-24. That is to say, every leader individual has at least one reciprocal bond, while three of them have two reciprocal bonds—the majority of these being with other leader individuals. *Furthermore, there is only one other reciprocal bond in the whole group in which a leader does not figure*—namely, 27-33.

Perhaps the quadrilateral 13-20-28-22-13 sums up the concentration of leadership best of all. The only gap is the failure of 28 to reciprocate the choice of 20. But both 28 and 20 are joined by reciprocal bonds to 22 and 13 respectively, who in turn are connected reciprocally. This, it seems to me, demonstrates the value of a sociogram in an analysis of group leadership, for in no other satisfactory way could this quadrilateral be illustrated and its implications manifested.

WORK-SHEET FOR SOCIOGRAM I

Individual Number	Chose	First	Second	Third
1	—	29	19	24
2	—	4	34	22
3	—	13	16	6
4	—	22	13	15
5	—	13	15	29
6	—	16	15	13
7	—	4	21	20
8	Did not go.	Sent Number 4 instead		
9	—	16	12	10
10	—	25	13	12
11	—	12	37	28
12	—	10	28	16
13	—	20	22	26
14	—	13	10	29
15	—	16	6	22
16	—	15	13	17
17	—	18	20	21
18	—	11	13	5
19	Did not go.			
20	—	13	16	28
21	—	24	20	13
22	—	28	16	13
23	—	29	22	5
24	—	13	20	21
25	—	7	15	3
26	Did not go.	His brother, 33, went instead		
27	—	28	33	25
28	—	25	10	22
29	—	18	17	21
30 and 31	Did not go.			
32	—	29	13	1
33	—	27	13	3
34	—	outsider	10	19
35	Did not go.	No. 3 went for him		
36	—	1	30	19
37	—	21	22	4

IV. Effect of Kinship on Choices. Twenty-seven of the thirty-four individuals comprising this group are related to some other individual in the group. Therefore, the question naturally arises as to the influence of such relationship upon the choices that the men made. Sociogram II, on the following page, shows seven clusters, each cluster made up of related individuals bearing the same family name. Of course, some of the individuals within a cluster are only distantly related because the joint-family names in Dragalevtsy have a place connotation in addition to the one of relationship. But just the same, the village usually thinks of the Pachevi or the Chalukovi as a definite group in the community bound together by kinship as well as geographical proximity. The sociogram also shows the choices made by each individual for other individuals in the same cluster. A few in-law relationships are not shown in this sociogram, but an examination of the data showed them to be relatively unimportant in this woodcutting group.[4]

I was interested in my analysis of the group to see what effect a feeling of insecurity on the part of an individual might have upon his choice of a relative. The best measure of this feeling of insecurity seemed to be the failure to receive favorable votes. It does seem significant that every individual[5] shown on Sociogram II who received only one or else no favorable votes from the group at large selected some relative, with whom he naturally felt on more intimate terms. When an individual received as many as two votes from the group at large, then the chances were about fifty per cent that he would name a relative among his first three choices. Of course, the unwanted individual does not know definitely the opinion, expressed on the questionnaire, which the general public has for him, but in a face-to-face society like Dragalevtsy every individual has a rather clear picture of his social status. This was illustrated forcibly when 23, who received the largest number of negative votes, refused to name any individuals which he would reject from a woodcutting group of his own formation. He co-operated in naming those he would like (two of the first three being relatives), but lacked the hypocrisy necessary to name any others as being undesirable; he knew where he stood in the opinion of the community.

Not only was I interested in the position of the person choosing relatives but also in the position of the relatives chosen. I wondered, for instance, if relatives out of kindness or a sense of loyalty would list some kinsman whom the group at large might reject. This did not prove to be the case because only one person named by a kinsman was not listed by someone outside the

[4] The *svatovshtenie*, or in-law relationship, is very important in Bulgarian villages— so much so that two brothers cannot marry two sisters, since the second brother by marrying a sister-in-law would be marrying a relative, something taboo.

[5] The Voynishki (Numbers 36 and 37) are exceptions here, but since they are not on speaking terms one would not expect them to choose each other.

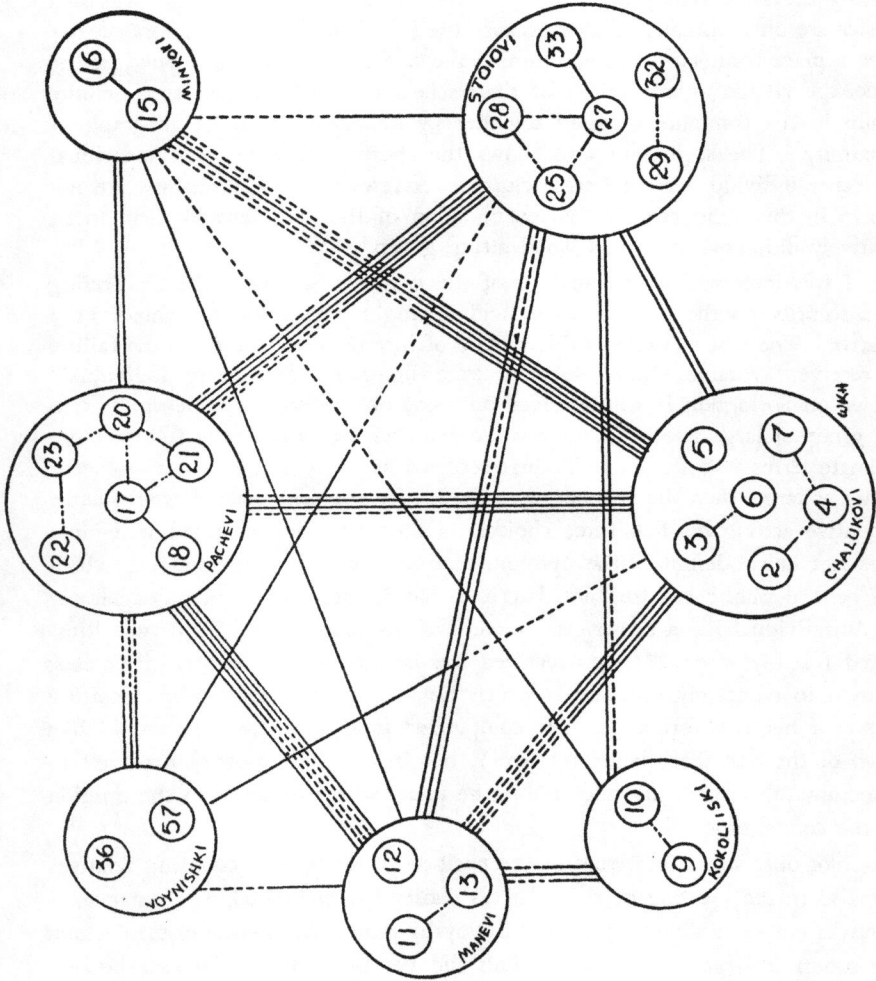

SOCIOGRAM II—EFFECTS OF KINSHIP ON CHOICES. Each cluster is made up of related individuals bearing the same family name. Lines between clusters show the number of times members of one cluster mentioned those in another cluster (first three choices)

kinship group. That is, individuals who chose relatives chose those upon whom the group at large likewise placed approval.

Sociogram II likewise shows us the status of the different kinship clusters as far as the woodcutting activity is concerned. The Pachevi, Stoiovi, and Chalukovi, each consisting of six members, are comparable in size but received 16, 9, and 6 votes respectively. The other clusters, made up of two or three members, are similarly comparable but vary considerably: Voynishki, 1; Koko-liiski, 3; Minkovi, 10; Manevi, 15. The size of the cluster has little to do with the number of votes received; it is rather the popularity of certain individuals within the cluster which determines the voting.

My conclusions regarding the effect of kinship as far as this one group is concerned are: (1) the choices of unwanted individuals included a relative with whom they felt some security; (2) the persons chosen were usually those upon whom the group as a whole set its stamp of approval; and (3) family clusters can be said to have a status in the same sense that individuals do, and are rejected or mentioned favorably through the medium of the individuals comprising those clusters.

THE FOLK APPROACH IN EXTENSION WORK

A BULGARIAN EXPERIENCE*

THE INCIDENT. One day in Dragalevtsy, a Bulgarian village of 1,600 people, the mayor's courier went from house to house to inform all expectant mothers of a meeting to be held in the schoolhouse the next afternoon. The public health nurse from Sofia wanted to tell them about prenatal and postnatal care. Attendance, according to the courier, was compulsory. As he made his rounds, comments such as these flowed in his wake: "What does that mayor think he's doing? Making a public spectacle of pregnant women!" "I've already had more babies than that nurse will ever have. She can't tell me anything I don't know." By nightfall the women of the village, after discussing it over the stone fences between the yards, had decided that the expectant mothers should not attend the meeting.

The next afternoon two or three women did appear, women whose families felt under obligation to the mayor and consequently supported all of his programs. The mayor and the nurse were much disappointed, but dared not invoke the compulsory part of the courier's invitation. The nurse went ahead with her demonstration for the faithful few, but even these left the meeting much bewildered and quite disappointed. They told their friends, "We couldn't buy all the stuff she told us to buy, even if we should want to do everything she suggested."

THE PROBLEM. Incidents similar to this occurred so frequently during my three-year study of that village that I tried to discover what more effective approach could be used to bridge the gap between the scientific and the folk knowledge. The mayor and those assisting him were well-intentioned, but the people never seemed to apply the suggestions that the outside lecturers made. Accordingly, the lecturers became more convinced that the peasants were stupid, and the peasants became more self-satisfied with the ways that they already had. What was supposed to be *extension of the new* really became *extinction of the new* before it had time to take root.

The "uplifters," who frequently used the phrase *izdigane na seloto* or "the raising up of the village," were unnecessarily complicating their task.

* This article appeared in *Journal of Applied Anthropology*, II, No. 4, September, 1943. Used by permission. This also appeared later in *Autonomous Groups Bulletin* as Vol. I, No. 3.

"The . . . purpose of the *sedenka* is to help some woman card her . . . wool." *See page 261.*

Instead of concentrating on the improvement of home-making and the encouragement of hygienic practices, which were their primary aims, they were also trying to change the women's meeting habits, or their ways of getting together. They insisted that the women leave their homes and come to the school for an artificially assembled meeting of a stiff, formal sort where they would be on the "receiving end," without the give-and-take of informal conversation to which they were accustomed.

As I sensed this difficulty I became convinced that the folkways already provided an avenue to the village women: namely, the *sedenka,* or "sitting," which is the name the villagers have given to the women's working groups.

THE SEDENKA. Allegedly, the main purpose of the *sedenka* is to help some woman card her fluffy, newly-washed wool or to help her spin some of the wool into thread. Actually, it is recreational as well, for the women thoroughly enjoy sharing the gossip, the songs, and the food which accompany such get-togethers. Although these *sedenki* (pl.) seem at times to be hit-or-miss affairs, certain unwritten rules govern their activity. If a woman, for example, wants to have the help of her neighbors in carding her wool there are procedures she must follow.

1. She will select the guests quite carefully, inviting those who owe her work in kind or those to whose houses she wants to be invited when they card their wool. She rejects from the number those who cause ill-feeling, who stir up trouble, or who are at odds with each other. Similarly she rejects those whose houses she does not want to visit in a "return engagement" either because their food is poorly prepared or because they are dirty and slovenly in their housekeeping. At times she is prevailed upon by a close friend or a relative to invite some individual who is not popular enough to receive many invitations but who is anxious for the social intercourse that these occasions provide.

2. She will issue the invitations in the time-honored way. Although she may have seen two friends the evening before at the fountain and learned from them that they definitely plan to attend, she nevertheless goes to their homes before daybreak to call out in the crisp autumn air, "Anka, Anka." The dogs set up a terrific roar, and Anka finally appears at the door. "I'm having a *sedenka* today and I hope you can come." Anka accepts most graciously, while the walking alarm clock moves on to issue the next invitation.

3. She will prepare quantities of special food. There are certain dishes that are *sedenka* favorites. In the fall, one of these is *banitsa,* a soggy pumpkin pie two feet in diameter. A stew of beans or one of meat and vegetables is often popular.

4. She will see that the activities at the *sedenka* flow along normally. There must be enough of the comb-like affairs, long spikes set in a small

wooden frame, through which the wool is drawn. The women in all parts of the room must be kept supplied with wool. Mealtimes must come at the prescribed intervals, and the good conversationalists must be urged to repeat some of the latest news, while those who consider themselves singers must be encouraged to start a song. And so the day passes. The women have arrived in the morning as soon as they completed their morning tasks, and they stay until midafternoon. At other times, however, a smaller group assembles in the evening for four or five hours of enjoyment and spinning.

Needless to say, these *sedenka* groups are powerful agencies in the dissemination of news and in the formation of village opinion. After a day spent in one of these sessions a woman has a supply of "small talk" sufficient to last her for two or three days in conversations with those who did not attend this particular gathering.

GOOD EXTENSION PRINCIPLES AND THE SEDENKA. The specialist who uses a *sedenka,* whether especially arranged for her or not, would be following good educational and sociological practice.

1. *She would be bringing people together in a familiar environment:* that is, one of the village homes. There would not be the strangeness of the schoolroom nor the distractions of completely new surroundings. Instead of having to adjust to a new place and a new person (the speaker) the women would play the role of hostesses and expect the speaker to adjust to them.

2. *The people would already be accustomed to meeting with each other.* Any newly-formed group needs an exploratory period in which the bolder individuals try various things on the group to see what meets with favor and what with stony indifference or frank disapproval. In a *sedenka* group, people already know how their remarks and their questions will be received, which is a matter of much importance in a learning situation. Among people who do not know each other well an ill-advised laugh at a sincere question can kill the chances of a lively, helpful, wholehearted discussion. The congeniality of the group is further assured by the fact that the hostess is able to use a selective technique which weeds out the incompatibles. Fortunately, these "incompatibles" are usually compatible in other groups where they have much in common with their associates in these groups. Therefore, every village woman could be reached in some *sedenka* grouping.

3. *The demonstration agent could use the artifacts of the village home to good advantage.* As far as possible the demonstration should be built around what the women already have, for that is what they must use if they follow the speaker's suggestions. The average village home would not spend more than four or five dollars a year on furnishings, utensils, and the like, nor could one expect them to spend more than this out of the meager budget

on which they operate. Demonstrations then should be worked out not so much to illustrate the ideal but to show how present practices can be improved with the utensils already at hand. If this is done the village women no longer could say, "Oh, I can't do that, for I don't have all those things the stranger had."

4. *Local leadership would be recognized and used.* A great mistake, too often made, is the assumption that the mayor[1], an outside governmental appointee, is the leader of the village in all respects. Every activity has its own local leaders. By skillful questioning the outsider can learn which women are most respected in their particular neighborhoods. Each of these could be asked to call a *sedenka* together for her neighborhood at a time convenient both to the specialist and the women. Before they sponsored any such novelty the leaders must be convinced of the worthwhile nature of the activity; and can then be taught to assume an important part in the demonstration.

5. *The new proposals could be fitted more easily into the fabric of everyday life.* Not only must the women be given the techniques but they must be given an ideology to accompany those techniques. They must have an answer ready for the doubting husband, the curious neighbor, the pooh-poohing mother-in-law. They must see that what they are asked to do bolsters up rather than tears down those social values which they consider essential to their way of life.

To illustrate, we may return again to the matter of postnatal care. Expectant mothers in Dragalevtsy hesitate to prepare layettes for the infants in advance. They feel that such behavior, presuming as it does that the baby will survive, would anger the powers that be; women must expect the worst because the worst so frequently occurs. This is a fundamental fact to be reckoned with in the teaching of infant care. Most public health nurses recognize this difficulty, but many try to eradicate it by telling the women how superstitious and how silly they are. The more positive approach would recognize the limitations and try to do at least these two things:

a. Insist that clean cloths, soap, and all other available equipment needed at childbirth and in early infancy be prepared and set aside in advance. None of these cloths should require sewing, since all pregnant women are forbidden to sew.

b. Tell the mothers-to-be how they can make simple, hygienic garments as soon as they recover sufficiently from the delivery, for there is no *tabu* against such action then. Once they understand how to make and use such special garments in place of the unsanitary swaddling clothes, some of them

---

[1] The national government which came into power in May, 1934, sent engineers and lawyers and other educated people into key villages as mayors to supplant the local peasants, who had been elected by their fellow villagers.

will prepare them in advance in spite of the *tabu*. A few of the up-to-date mothers-in-law may also prepare these garments in advance, at the same time forbidding their daughters-in-law to sew.

The value of such an approach lies in the avoidance of a sharp break between the old and the new; instead, the two are blended. Social changes occur without the people feeling that such changes threaten their mores. A most important point, then, in fitting the new proposals into the fabric of everyday life is the scrupulous forestalling of a clear-cut issue between the old and the new whenever that is possible. There are times, to be sure, when some champion of the old challenges the new, and the specialist must meet the challenge with everything at his command. However, the specialist must never seek to destroy the old because it is old; nor should he initiate an "either-or" choice for the peasant.

APPLICATION AND EVALUATION. I used the *sedenka* to serve a purpose of my own in an experimental fashion but the Bulgarian extension people to whom I broached the matter were a bit reluctant to use the *sedenka* for at least three reasons:

1. They had their eyes turned to the west and mistakenly thought that what they *imported* was better than what they *already had*. In other words, making use of the local groups would have seemed a step backward rather than a step forward. It just was not the modern way to do things, and they were out to "modernize" the village.

2. They had been "bitten" by the attendance bugaboo. They had to get a big "turn-out" so they could add up impressive figures when they reported the event; their supervisor had to use figures to impress the one above him; and so it ran up the whole hierarchy. Then, too, the workers themselves began to measure their own success in terms of attendance. Of course, if such a measure is used it is ridiculous to get twenty or twenty-five women together in a home when you could get fifty women together in the school. Unfortunately, such individuals are bewitched by the fallacy that exposure means education and the more people exposed the greater the education.

3. A few extension workers realized that they would not be as much the master of a *sedenka* gathering as they would of a number of people arranged in chairs, all ill-at-ease and everybody afraid to speak up. Those who lacked self-confidence in their own training, or in their ability to handle questions did not want to be put in the position of having to say that they did not know the answer to some query. This was partly the fault of their training, as well as a failure to evaluate properly the goals for which they were striving.

One day I asked a woman named Sandra if she would let me come to a *sedenka* at her house. She made all arrangements, invited her friends, and prepared some food. All the women brought their own handwork. Because

I was investigating at this time the relationships of the Bulgarian family, a Bulgarian woman teacher and I spent about four hours guiding the discussion around the roles of the husband, the wife, the child and the in-laws. Over and over again, I thought of the excellent educational opportunities such an occasion offered. In fact, I had to answer almost as many questions about America as I asked about Bulgaria, and the teacher was asked many questions which would never have been raised in a schoolroom. The topics covered ranged from how men treated their wives in America to what one did for a bad sore in a child's mouth. There were many informal conversations going on much of the time among pairs or trios of the twenty-five women, but when some particular question proved of general interest the conversation would stop and all would listen attentively.

I know that this gathering at Sandra's home was not a fair test of the *sedenka* as an extension aid; however, this experience and experiences with at least twenty-five other *sedenka* groups convinced me of the rich possibilities these groups afford.

For those interested in the problem of finding a way through cultural barriers this particular study can be merely suggestive. What succeeds in Bulgaria will not necessarily succeed elsewhere, but surely some of the principles will apply. Few of us utilize sufficiently the avenues a culture affords; instead we want to travel pathways of our own blazing, often leaving our followers lost far behind. It is much better to start where the people are already, and move with them down familiar paths, pointing out ways the old paths can be improved. Sometimes drastic alterations will be necessary, but these should only be decided upon after the possibilities of the "blended approach" have been carefully considered.

BULGARIANS AND SOUTHERN RURAL WHITES

IN CONTRAST*

The Bulgaria of which I speak is three-fourths rural, definitely peasant. The group of Southern whites to which I limit myself in this analogy is made up of the small farmer, whether he be owner, tenant, sharecropper, hillbilly, or cracker.[1] My discussion, centering as it does upon what the political columnists so fondly and not inaccurately term the "little people" of each region, therefore excludes the comparatively well-to-do urban industrial and professional groups of both Bulgaria and the South. In comparing rural Bulgaria and the rural South I was reminded of a question which has been often raised recently: Are we to have an American peasant class?[2] While I cannot answer this question to my own satisfaction I recognize its implications. If we are to have a peasant class there is much we can learn from the agricultural sections of Europe where a stable, organized life has gone on for hundreds of years through the intensive use of all available natural resources in the midst of turbulent political changes, plagues, and famines.

Just as visitors in writing of the South misuse the word "poor white"[3] so we in considering the European scene often misuse the word "peasant," giving it a connotation of reproach as though a peasant were a serf.[4] The

* Read before the Fifth Annual Meeting of the Southern Sociological Society in Knoxville, Tennessee, April 5, 1940. Appeared as an article in *Social Forces*, XIX, No. 1, October, 1940. Reprinted by permission.

[1] "The South today, especially the Southeast, is essentially a land of hillbillies and other ruralites, whose chief contact with the commerce and culture of the world is through hick towns (p. 8).

"The South is a land of farms and farmers." . . . To appraise the South is to appraise farmers, whether for the art of living or for the lack of a living" (pp. 10-11). H. C. Nixon, *Forty Acres and Steel Mules* (Chapel Hill, 1938).

[2] " . . . Such are the beginnings of peasantry in the New World—The Collapse of the Black Belt plantation system is a preface to American peasantry." A. F. Raper, *Preface to Peasantry: A Tale of Two Black Belt Counties* (Chapel Hill, 1936), p. 4.

[3] W. T. Couch, Editor, *Culture in the South* (Chapel Hill, 1934). See chapt. 20, The Tradition of "Poor Whites," by A. N. J. Den Hollander. M. R. Mell, "Poor Whites of the South," *Social Forces*, December, 1938, pp. 153-167.

[4] " . . . With this transformation (that is, the peasant becoming an entrepreneur) have come changes in the connotation of the word 'peasant.' He is no longer a rustic of inferior status too ignorant and dull to take advantage of commercial opportunities;

Bulgarian peasants whom I knew intimately for six years are independent farmers who dwell in their own homes, subsist on their own land⁵ and form a folk, in the anthropological sense.

Bulgaria, a Balkan country the size of Ohio with a population of six million, was for five hundred years under Turkish rule, becoming independent in 1878 as a result of a Russo-Turkish War. Bulgaria's reconstruction period therefore covers approximately the same time as ours.[6] The few large land-owners in Bulgaria fled to Turkey after the Liberation. This means that the Bulgarian farmers own their land; tenancy is very uncommon; the employment of farm laborers even less common.[7] As the farm population has increased, the already small holdings have had to be further divided, until now the average farm totals 15 acres scattered in 17 strips around the picturesque villages in which the people live.[8] The heart of Bulgarian peasant economy is the agricultural village[9]; the heart of life in the village is the home and the family system. Each farm of 17 acres must support, in addition to all dependents, four or five adults of working age. The fact that women and children

it is increasingly recognized that the really important characteristics peculiar to the peasant are his sentiments and attitudes, the intense attachment to his native soil and family tradition, which, even in the economic sphere, take precedence over the desire for individual advancement and gain. This peasant ethos is common throughout continental Europe." *Encyclopedia of the Social Sciences,* Article on Peasantry by C. von Dietze.

[5] Peasantry, of course, is not synonymous with farm ownership everywhere in Europe, but the governments there (notably in Ireland and Denmark) recognize the importance of a landed peasantry as shown by recent attempts to lessen tenancy. See *Farm Tenancy, Report of President's Committee,* 1937, Section III, Some Tenure Programs of other Nations.

[6] The crises through which Bulgaria has passed have much in common with those of the South as listed in H. W. Odum, *Southern Regions of the United States* (Chapel Hill, 1936), pp. 13-14. Nikola Stanev, *Istoria Na Nova Bulgaria, 1878-1928* (History of the New Bulgaria), Sofia, 1929.

[7] Ian C. Mollov and T. E. Bakurdjiev, *Organizatsionnata Struktura Na Zemedelskoto Stopanstvo Vv Sofiiska Okolia* (The Organizational Structure of the Farms in the County of Sofia), Sofia, 1931, pp. 6-7. (95.3 per cent of farmers work their own land, 4.7 per cent rent their land; only 3.2 per cent employ hired labor.)

[8] *Ibid.,* p. 5. For the country as a whole see the *Statesman's Year Book, 1939*: "According to the census of 1934, eighty per cent of the active population were engaged in agriculture, most of them being small proprietors holding from *one to six acres.*" This is understood more clearly when it is remembered that only thirty-nine per cent of the total area is arable and that this is divided into 750,613 farms. (*The New International Yearbook, 1938,* article on Bulgaria.)

[9] H. C. Nixon, *op. cit.* "Farm ownership or a sounder lease policy is not enough to enable Southern hillbillies to live in decency. It is essential to provide by public effort for social and economic co-operation among small farmers, to make possible a better system of farm villages" p. 61.

work outdoors with the men means an abundant labor supply but also requires close co-operation, planning, and division of labor.[10]

Peasant economy is based on a self-subsistence principle in which a satisfactory balance between plant and animal life is maintained.[11] Since cash income is low the plane of living is low.[12] That is, the peasant cannot buy from the outside world much in the way of clothing, machinery, conveniences, or recreation. On the other hand, he does eat well according to his own standards. Furthermore, he maintains his self-respect. There is security in land which nothing else affords unless it be a family large enough to work the land one owns. No matter how much one discounts that sort of economy, history has shown it to be the most enduring man has yet devised.

The picture is different in the South.[13] Although our farms average 71 acres they are operated by tenants in 54 per cent of the cases,[14] usually on a cash crop basis.[15] Only in the Appalachian-Ozark area, which by the way is most like the Bulgarian, do we find subsistence-farming as the prevailing principle.[16] There, however, it is blighted by isolation and lacks the co-operative features found in most agricultural villages: a swineherd caring during the day for all pigs in the village, communal pastures, or neighborhood corn-hoeing groups. To be sure, there is mutual aid and co-operation in the highlands but these tend to be confined to periods of crisis rather than to the performance of ordinary daily tasks.

[10] *Ibid.*, p. 14: "In fact, excessive ruralism has caused an unusual amount of labor to fall to the lot of women in this region of chivalry [the South]."

[11] Oxen, water-buffalo and horses, in the order of importance, are the work animals in Bulgaria. The government is trying to persuade peasants to replace oxen with dual-purpose cows as an economy move.

[12] Ian C. Mollov and H. K. Kondov, *Dohodnostuta Na 57 Zemedelski Stopanstva Vv Bulgaria* (1932-33). (The Incomes of 57 Bulgarian Farms for 1932-33.) This study gives some indication of the level of living possible.

[13] Standards of living are low in the South. See C. C. Taylor, H. W. Wheeler, E. L. Kirkpatrick, *Disadvantaged Classes in American Agriculture*, Washington, 1938. Good bibliographies on pp. 8 and 9; description of the Old South, pp. 115-119.

[14] *Report of the President's Committee on Farm Tenancy*, 1937, p. 35. Figures cited here are for sixteen South Atlantic and South Central States and the District of Columbia. The percentage would be even higher for Southeastern States alone.

[15] Odum, *op. cit.*, p. 391. On pages 489-491 Odum quotes Rupert B. Vance: "Until recently in this country no critical theory of tenancy has been developed which takes into consideration the fact that while the United States is drifting into tenancy, certain European countries with semi-feudal backgrounds, notably Denmark, Ireland, and France, have made the transitions to peasant proprietorship."

[16] Couch, *op. cit.*, p. 25. "This section [Appalachian-Ozark] is responsible for the fact that the South has a larger number of practically self-sufficing farms than any other important section in the United States." C. P. Loomis and L. S. Dodson, *Standards of Living in Four Southern Appalachian Mountain Counties*, Washington, 1938.

The failure of the Southern whites to co-operate for economic ends is tragic. A Southern adaptation of co-operative patterns found successful elsewhere, if generally accepted, would afford a fuller, richer existence for the thousands of families which go their individual, poverty-stricken ways in the mistaken belief that co-operation is incompatible with independence. European peasants are renowned for their independence as well as for their co-operation.[17]

The Southern population is mobile, one out of every three Southern tenant families moving yearly.[18] The Bulgarian population is permanent, as shown in the study I made of the farmers of one Bulgarian village where 91.4 per cent of the male family heads and 96.3 per cent of their fathers had been born in the same village.[19] We would expect this contrast because of the differences in the economic system.

But there is an interesting similarity between Bulgarians and the Southeast in those population characteristics which are dependent upon biological factors. The Southeast is often called the "nursery of the Nation" with a natural increase of 9.5 (birth rate 21.7, death rate 12.2),[20] whereas Bulgaria is one of the leaders of Europe in this respect with a natural increase of 10.5 (birth rate 23.9, death rate 13.4).[21]

Homogeneity is characteristic of Bulgarian people as it is of the Southern white, not only in respect to similarity of racial strain but in respect to religion as well. Most Bulgarians are adherents of the Eastern Orthodox Church; most Southern whites are Protestants.[22]

The Southern whites share the region with a numerous minority; Bulgaria has no significant minority problem, for the Turks who comprised 11 per cent

[17] This co-operation can be expressed on an informal basis as well as through a formal organization. Carl C. Taylor, Head of the Division of Farm Population and Rural Welfare, in addressing the American Association of School Administrators in February, 1940, said: "Self-help is no new doctrine in rural areas, and the best approach to the improvement of rural life on all fronts is to utilize the capacities for self-sufficiency and to expand self-help from an individual to a community and co-operative basis. To do otherwise is so completely to urbanize farming and farm life as to lose nationally the unique contributions which country life always has made and always should make to our civilization."

[18] *Report on Economic Conditions of the South,* National Emergency Council, 1938, p. 47.

[19] The Sociology of a Bulgarian Shopski Village, doctoral dissertation, Cornell University, 1938.

[20] Odum, *op. cit.,* p. 492 (evidently includes both Negro and white rates).

[21] *The New International Yearbook, 1938, article on Bulgaria.* Note the decline since 1926 when the natural increase was 20.1 (birth rate 37, death rate 17) D. Kostov, *Geografia Na Bulgaria i Susednite i Durzhavi* (Geography of Bulgaria and Neighboring States), Plovdiv, 1928.

[22] Odum, *op. cit.,* p. 15.

of the population in 1926 have been returning to Turkey at a greatly accelerated pace.

There are striking anthropological contrasts between the Bulgarian peasant and the Southern white. The most marked of these is the peasant's close identification with a folk culture which is characterized by a consciousness of kind, established patterns of habit and thought, artifacts identified with that culture alone, and a strong exercise of social control. There is also uniformity of dress, agricultural method, and social values.

Among the Southern whites the Appalachian-Ozark area alone possesses the characteristics of a folk, for its people are closely knit together, have mountain handicrafts of which they are proud,[23] and, although differing in economic status, tend to conform to cultural patterns handed from the past. On the contrary, the tenant farmer may have his share of superstitions, folk remedies, and traditional attitudes, but he lacks "consciousness of kind" which would identify him with a folk culture.[24]

The four social institutions which I wish to mention briefly but which I shall not compare in detail are the family, education, religion, and government.[25]

The Bulgarian family is patriarchal, children are valued as economic assets; there is a strong kinship feeling even unto the third and fourth generation. Marriage is still an arrangement between two families under the sole control of the church. Family disorganization in the form of desertion or divorce is practically unknown; illegitimacy rare.

There is compulsory education to the fourteenth year in Bulgaria. However, the law is seldom invoked because the parents have recognized the economic value of education. That is why Bulgaria is the most literate country in the Balkans, a testimony to the high value the peasants place upon education and the rigid social control at work in the compact villages. If some

---

[23] W. T. Couch, *op. cit.*, chapter 15—The Handicrafts by Allen H. Eaten; chapter 19—Appalachian America by J. Worley Hatcher; chapter 26—Folk and Folklore by B. A. Botkin.

[24] The folk culture is quite different from a regional or Southern culture such as Odum describes at length in his Chapter IX in *Southern Regions* on Institutions and Folkways. The Bulgarian peasant is primarily identified with the village culture and secondarily with newer national culture in process of development. The Southern white is identified with a regional culture but not with a folk culture.

[25] Because of space limitations I omitted a section dealing with Psychological Comparisons. This would have compared the race prejudice and regional "inferiority complex" of the Southerner with the nationalism and sensitiveness to criticism of the Bulgarian. Bulgaria, defeated in the World War, has its Lost Cause as does the South. Bulgarians, like Southerners, have gained the reputation for conservatism and hospitality. On the other hand, industry is more a Bulgarian than a Southern trait.

poorer peasant wanted to keep his children home from school he would have to face the withering scorn of his neighbors. I cannot help contrasting this situation with that found in the South where truancy is a major educational problem arising from the mobility of the population, the distance between home and school, and the low place afforded education in the scale of social values.

Most young Bulgarian men after their eighteenth year are called upon to serve their country as *trudovatsi* (members of the Labor Corps) or as soldiers. The time they spend in the barracks not only widens their social contacts and broadens their outlook but also educates them in the formal sense to the extent that they take advantage of courses offered. In America the Civilians' Conservation Corps is roughly analogous, differing in that it is on a voluntary basis, pays the youth for work done, and is restricted to those young men from families of a low economic level.

The Bulgarian peasant has a dualistic view of the universe. First, there are the forces of good which must be propitiated. The priest is God's intermediary and can intervene with him in the event of a drought, serious illness in the family, or sterility in the wife. The priest christens the baby and sanctifies the marriage tie. In the event of death he performs the liturgy to insure the soul's passage into a heaven thought of in very realistic but not enthusiastic terms.

There are also the forces of evil whom it pays well to placate. A few old women in every village are the "priestesses of superstition" whose incantations work wonders and drive off the Evil Eye. Peasants do not discuss this white magic when the priest is around, so complete is the dichotomy between the Good and the Bad. Religion as represented by the church consists of form and ceremony rather than a challenge to daily living. Furthermore, the Bulgarian peasant derives little emotional release from an "other worldly" rapture indulged in on Sundays. He is too secure, too stolid, too practical for that. On the contrary, the insecurity of the Southern white is attested to by the increasing numbers adhering to the excitable Pentecostal type of religious expression.[26]

We hear much in the South today about suffrage reforms, abolition of the poll tax, government paternalism, and the failure of democratic processes. Since the same problems are being faced in Bulgaria a comparison may prove helpful.

Fifty years ago the villages were governed by elders, the influential heads of the larger families. After Bulgaria's Liberation from Turkey in 1878 the

[26] John B. Holt, Religious Secession and Class in the Southeast. A paper read before the Section on Sociology of Religion, annual meeting of the American Sociological Society, 1939.

right to vote was gradually extended to the village men before these men had had the advantages of an adequate school system. They like ignorant people the world around were more influenced by personalities than by principles, thus becoming an easy prey to politicians who played upon their emotions, catered to their prejudices, and took advantage of their credulity. But vote they must or be fined approximately five dollars for staying away from the polls.

With an electorate so inexperienced in the democratic tradition, great confusion arose. For instance, there were sixteen political parties in a nation of six million, making it impossible for any party to get a clear majority. The only way government could go on was by a bloc composed of several parties, but even this was inefficient. Therefore in 1934 Bulgaria had a New Deal, a *coup d' etat* headed by some military men who initiated numerous agrarian reforms. No longer did the peasants vote and thereby control government policies; instead they were told what to do. Gradually those who had engineered this *coup d' etat* were displaced from power by the King, a dictatorship was averted, and two years ago[27] a semblance of democracy was again restored when the vote was given back to peasant men and mothers. Instead of allowing party affiliations the government organized the electorate on the basis of occupation, following the corporation system in Italy where parliamentary members represent an economic rather than a geographical constituency.

Watching the failure of democracy in Bulgaria has made me gravely concerned about the future of democracy in the South. I am strongly in favor of giving our disenfranchised groups the right to vote, but so many advocates of suffrage reform seem to forget the necessity of training these groups in the meaning and proper use of the ballot. Democracy is not a quantitative process which is better guaranteed by increasing the number of voters; it is a qualitative process which requires increasing understanding of the obligations of citizenship as well as extension of the franchise. Ignorant voters pave the way for demagoguery[28]; demagoguery creates a situation ripe for the dictator; dictatorships doom democracies.

Since 1934 the Bulgarian political philosophers have been floundering between democratic and dictatorial procedures but the peasant has been handed over to a new type of paternalism which has its analogy in the South. The central government in Sofia is represented in the village by a professional man, usually a lawyer, as mayor. This mayor acts as local justice of the peace; he takes advantage of every public occasion to tell the peasants in a fatherly way what they ought to do and think about matters of national importance.

---

[27] Parliamentary elections were held on the four Sundays of March, 1938 (*The New International Year-Book, 1938, Bulgaria*).

[28] A. F. Raper, *op. cit.*, pp. 165-169.

The mayor has some influence with the Debt Commissions coming from government banks to relieve the debt burdens of the farmers, he distributes whatever relief is available for needy families, and he has a prominent part in the administration of the school, public health, and village improvements. Because of this he is gradually displacing the priest as the most important personality in the village. In other words, the paternalism of the church is now being supplanted by that of the state.

We find a similar situation in the South where white farmers are beginning to depend less upon landlords, banks, and advancing merchants, and more upon the grants from governmental units, whether in the form of relief or credit facilities. Plantation or small-town paternalism is yielding to governmental paternalism.

The Bulgarian peasant is not a joiner. He does not use the organizational approach in attacking a problem but prefers to work through informal groups. There are two chief reasons why he avoids membership in the numerous formal groups seeking the villagers' support: first, he is penurious and will pay no membership fee unless he sees some prospect of personal advantage; secondly, he does not understand the purpose or program of the organizations, since most of them originate in the cities and are promoted by the *intelligentsia*. There are no church organizations claiming his support as in the case in most Southern neighborhoods. Living in a village as he does the peasant can visit with friends and neighbors without the necessity of having an organization to provide a rallying place.

The Southern white thinks vertically; the Bulgarian peasant horizontally —a difference in mental pattern which accounts for the difference in social process.

By "thinking vertically" I mean that traditionally the Southern white is dominated by the attraction of the American ladder of opportunity, although for him it has often proved mythical.[29] That is, success in life is determined by the extent to which one approximates the plane of living enjoyed by those of a higher economic level. Climbing means competition rather than co-operation.[30] Frustration seems to be displacing the traditional, optimistic view among many of the Southern whites. They look up the ladder, but say, "What's the use of starting the climb!" As individuals they are pitted against forces over which they have no control.[31]

[29] H. C. Nixon, *op. cit.*, p. 9. Shows the traditional nature of this mind-set in speaking of the Old South: "Nonslaveowners expected to become small slaveowners, and small slaveowners expected to become large ones." The mythical aspect is shown nowadays by the phrase "once a sharecropper, always a sharecropper."

[30] Odum, *op. cit.*, pp. 585-586, emphasizes the need for county and/or community co-operation.

[31] Perhaps Populism in the late 19th century came as near creating a consciousness of kind among the rural whites as anything else has ever done.

The Bulgarian peasant in thinking horizontally identifies himself with other agriculturalists and accepts their culture as a heritage of which he is proud. He derives strength as an individual from his consciousness of kind. His attitude was forcibly demonstrated when I tried to get answers to a questionnaire on occupational attitudes. I could not get a single peasant to answer one simple question: If you were not a farmer, what would you most prefer to be? It was inconceivable to them that they should be anything other than farmers. Although the Bulgarian peasant rides frequently in a bus or automobile it never occurs to him to want one of his own. If given an additional sum of money to spend he would buy more of what he already has— land, a new house, or animals. Because he thinks horizontally he co-operates with his fellows. As a matter of course he submits to stern social control for the common good.

I would like to say in conclusion that the lot of the Bulgarian peasant is not an enviable one; his plane of living is low, but the improvement that will take place can occur in the social organization already in existence. The Bulgarian does have security for which he has had to pay the price of class distinction, at least as it exists in the minds of others; whether the disadvantaged groups of the South are becoming typed as a class without gaining security in exchange is a matter for serious consideration. In the South we are faced with the fact of disorganization among our rural population and a consequent reorganization. It has not been my purpose to map the plan this reorganization should follow, but to present a comparison which may help to clarify and stimulate our thinking as we search realistically for a solution.

A NOTE ON METHODOLOGY AND BIBLIOGRAPHY

1. CHOICE OF A VILLAGE: One of the first problems to be faced in this study was the choice of a village as a unit for investigation. Dragalevtsy was finally chosen on the basis of the following criteria:

   a. It seemed representative of the villages of the *Shopski* region with respect to culture patterns and plane of living.

That the government authorities, notably the agricultural economists in the Ministry of Agriculture, considered Dragalevtsy representative along this line was shown by the fact that they selected it as one of the twenty-five villages throughout the country for a farm-income study. Another indication of its representative nature was the testimony of people who had moved into Dragalevtsy from other *Shopski* villages; they saw little difference between the culture patterns and plane of living to which they had been accustomed and those in Dragalevtsy. Officials consulted in connection with the choice of village were very quick to state that the *Shopski* region was one of the most conservative parts of the country, a point which has been borne in mind throughout the study.

   b. Large enough to contain a significant number of formal groups and institutions.

Dragalevtsy was a medium-sized village, but did have all the institutions and most of the groups found in villages throughout the *Shopski* region.

   c. Near enough to the American College to make possible frequent visits throughout the year.

Work at the College precluded the possibility of choosing a village on the other side of Mount Vitosha, even if that had seemed desirable. Because it fulfilled the first two requirements so well, Dragalevtsy was chosen in preference to two villages nearer the College and to others more readily accessible by automobile.

2. BECOMING EN RAPPORT WITH VILLAGERS: After being assured of the co-operation of the mayor and other officials, I cultivated the acquaintance of the peasants for a five-month period before introducing any intimate questionnaire. During this period of "acquaintance," I attended a dinner for

Dragalevtsy people at the monastery as the mayor's guest, where, after a warm introduction by him, I spoke briefly to the people in their native language as to my reason for being with them and my desire to know all of them better. On special occasions such as Christmas and name-day celebrations I visited the people in their homes and shared their common meals. I spent a day at a "carding-bee," where thirty women were working. Not only did I visit with the women informally but also took several pictures. These were distributed gratis to the women, after which I had a ready entree into all their homes. In the course of the study, at least 250 photographs were given to the people and proved a source of much delight to them. By the end of the five-month period I was known to the whole village, and in turn could give the family names of a considerable number of men and women. Proof that these methods were successful in gaining the confidence of the people was the fact that during the three years I had only one instance of non-cooperation, that individual being a moody tavern-keeper. Other indications that I did establish a *rapport* with many of the villagers were (a) the peasants' use of *nash chovek* ("one of our very own") when speaking of me to visitors; (b) the message sent the year after my departure to the effect that, if I returned to live in Dragalevtsy, the villagers would give me land for a house.

3. COLLECTION OF DATA:

a. *Personal observation*: Much of the material, especially of a descriptive sort, was obtained by personal observation during the three-year period of study. My quarters were on the Main Square, which was the center of village life. During two Christmas, and one summer, vacations I lived in the village; at other times I went there for the day or the afternoon, making such a trip on the average of once every two weeks.

b. *Questionnaires*: At the time of the census at the end of 1934 I prepared a questionnaire on social contact and social mobility for the villagers to fill out along with all the government blanks.[1] Then, I sent to the Central Bureau of Statistics a questionnaire dealing for the most part with population characteristics. A third questionnaire was used as a basis for the study of various village organizations. In addition to these I prepared a list of questions covering the material to be embodied in every chapter. These served as the basis for interviews.

c. *Interviews*: I soon learned that no peasants would fill out questionnaires left with them for that purpose. All information had to be obtained through personal interviews, though schedules were useful in guiding the

---

[1] Such questionnaires were really filled out by village clerks, who read off the questions and wrote in the peasants' answers.

discussion and in making the interviews standard in character. In every formal interview I had the assistance of a native English-speaking Bulgarian with a village background to ask the questions in a way the peasant could grasp. I took all the notes since I could understand the responses, writing while the assistant was asking the next question. In many cases I made notes only after the end of the interview. In seeking interviewees I followed the practice of going to those whom observation and village opinion pointed out as knowing most about the particular subject. In getting information about organizations[2] I interviewed at least two officers and at least one-half of the members, guiding myself by a membership list obtained for each organization. The survey of family groups included thirty homes chosen with respect to size, economic status, and location in the village. A careful reading of the study has doubt-less shown to what a great extent information has been drawn from all elements in the population.

d. *Printed sources and official records*: With the exception of some of the material contained in the earlier chapters nothing especially pertinent to Dragalevtsy could be obtained from printed sources. Any generalizations about other villages or Bulgaria as a whole had to be tried out in the village before they were accepted as applicable. For instance, ethnological works of forty years ago mentioned Dragalevtsy but their evidence could not be accepted as of current significance without an investigation to see if the old conditions still held. Official records in the *Obshtina* and in the Central Bureau of Statistics proved of considerable help in specific sections, though this informa-tion was limited in character.

e. *Rechecking data*: Any divergent answers were always checked with reliable informants in order to see which answer was more representative of the village as a whole. Personal observation and tentative conclusions were constantly checked with the *intelligentsia* and villagers capable of "sizing up" the situation.

[2] The following examples of patterned relationships were studied in detail: Mer-chants Association, buyer-seller groups, Insurance Association, cornhoeing groups, Agricultural Zadruga, Animal Husbandry (dairy Cooperative), artisan groups, four merchant groups, neighborhoods, threshing ring, spinning and carding groups, wood-cutting groups, children's play groups, young people's *sedenki,* women's gossiping groups, men's tavern cliques, *vecherinki,* Younak Sports Association, *Chitalishte,* the teacher group, adult folk school, christening groups, wedding groups, mourning groups, Association for the Orthodox Christianization of Youth, Temperance Association, Village Council, School Board, Church Board, Red Cross Association, Village Court, Union for the Protection of Children, Association of the Medal for Valor.

For fuller discussion of these see the author's Ph.D. dissertation, "The Sociology of a Bulgarian *Shopski* Village," Cornell University, 1938.

4. ORGANIZATION AND SYNTHESIS OF DATA: Before starting the study I had already delimited the field and had made a tentative outline for each proposed chapter. This was possible because of a previous three-year acquaintance with Bulgarian villages. The original plan was altered to the extent of including an additional chapter, combining others and some shifting of material. The study of the data collected led to definite conclusions in connection with every chapter, although no attempt was made to generalize regarding Bulgarian villages as a whole from the study of a single unit.

★ ★

The above statement about methodology was written ten years ago and is the basis upon which the research techniques used in this study must be evaluated. Within the past ten years a number of significant refinements in social research have been developed, but these did not appear in time to be applied to the Dragalevtsy study, which was one of the very few comprehensive sociological studies of village life under way in the 1930's. World War II postponed the publication arrangements already agreed upon, but in doing so gave an opportunity for the concluding chapters on social change. The information for these chapters was collected from numerous interviews in Dragalevtsy and in Sofia during November and December, 1945, a period which I spent in Bulgaria in connection with my official duties as Agricultural Attache, with headquarters at the American Embassy, Belgrade, Yugoslavia.

★ ★

BIBLIOGRAPHICAL NOTE

Since most of the publications used in the preparation of this book were in Bulgarian and are also relatively inaccessible to the American reader, no bibliography is included here. Anyone wishing to read more widely on Bulgaria or the Balkans in general is referred to the excellent bibliographies prepared by the Library of Congress in Washington. See especially THE BALKANS: Part I. General and Part III. Bulgaria, both sections published in 1943.

GLOSSARY OF BULGARIAN WORDS USED
MOST FREQUENTLY

agronom—agricultural extension worker

baba—grandmother; old woman; midwife

Bai—prefix of respect

banitsa—native pie, usually pumpkin or white cheese

Chitalishte—a cultural organization with a reading room

decare—unit of land; approximately one-fourth acre

dedo—grandfather

den—day

domakin—master of the house; *domakinya*—mistress of the house

haidutsi—guerrillas; bandits

horo—Bulgarian national folk dance (plural, *hora*)

icon—picture of saint or Virgin Mary

iconostas—household shrine

intelligentsia—educated class; "white collar" people

kaval—native shepherd flute

Koleda—Christmas

kozhuh—fleece-lined sheepskin coat

kruchma—tavern

leva—Bulgarian monetary unit

mahala—neighborhood, quarter of the village

maistor—master craftsman

Obshtina—small political unit (commune); municipal building

pazar—market

rakiya—plum brandy

rodstvo—blood relationship

sedenka—recreational working-bee (plural, *sedenki*)

Sekretar-Birnik—chief clerk and tax collector of the *Obshtina*

Shopi—those dwelling in the region around Sofia; *Shopski*—the adjective describing the region

smes—wheat and rye mixture

sofra—low, round dining table

stopanin—same as *domakin*

subor—village reunion, "at home"

sukman—woman's black jumper dress

surmi—boiled cabbage or grape leaves filled with meat or rice

susedstvo—small neighborhood (one's immediate neighbors)

svatovstvo—in-law relationship

trudova—compulsory labor for the state; *trudovak*—one doing such labor

Tsar—King; *Tsaritsa*—Queen

tsarvuli—pigskin sandals worn by the villagers

vecherinka—public evening entertainment

vodosvet—ceremony at which holy water is sprinkled

zadruga—old joint-family; modern association of farmers

INDEX

INDEX

Fasts, church, 10, 22, 108, 110-111, 215
Fatalism, 30, 32, 34, 80, 142
Fatherland Front, 197-216
Ferdinand of Bulgaria, 67
Fire, 23, 25, 32, 58, 61, 109, 111
Flag, Bulgarian, 88
Food and drink, *banitsa,* 45, 47; at festive occasions, 22, 86-88, 98, 106-108, 111, 124-125, 186, 242; at inns, 193, 241; at market, 103-241; at *sedenka,* 261; food shops, 148, 228-229; for children, 114; of Pechenegi, 61; permitted pregnant women, 29; preparation and utensils, 25-28, 53; pure food laws, 172-173; school lunches, 170. *See also* Liquor, *Rakiya*
Forest, village, 10, 23, 40, 169, 191, 250-259
France, 122, 268; diplomacy, 183; Revolution, 65
Fruit, 40, 45, 59, 107-108, 139
Fuel, 23, 40, 115, 250-259
Funeral customs, 10, 34-38, 142, 190, 197-198, 246

G

Germany, 9-10, 66, 74, 183-187, 192, 196-197, 210
Geshov, Ivan Evstatiev, 230
God, and crops, 43-44, 136; and father's authority, 66; and human laziness, 39; and illness, 33-36; as creator, 27; as giver, 77; Communists and, 212; priest as intermediary, 51, 271. *See also* Dualistic conception of universe, Priest, Religion
Godparents, 4, 70, 86, 89, 128-132, 190
Government, local, after Liberation, 68-69; after 1937, 191-192; and justice, 163-170; in peasant societies, 146-148; ordinance about grazing, 56; under Communists, 203-205; under Turks, 65
Government, national, after Liberation, 67-69; *agronom,* 154-155; and Communists, 197-215; and education, 134-136; Debt Commissions, 52-53; impress upon village life, 161-181, 271-272; mayor as representative, 9-10; pensions, 51; regulations about building, 21
Greece, 12, 61, 65, 184
Greetings and leavetaking, 6, 25, 46, 111, 178

Groups. *See* Kinship groupings, Social groupings
Guerrillas, 66
Gypsies, 16-17, 24, 71

H

Handjieff, Wasil, 234
Health Committee, 10, 174
Health practices, and prayers, 33; icons, holy water as cures, 32, 129; in familistic society, 147; medical care, 172-174, 192, 260; "night air," 23; personal cleanliness, 24-25; sobering drunks, 98. *See also* Childbirth, Funeral customs, Sanitation
Holidays, 12, 24, 28, 79, 106-111, 118, 124-129, 190-191. *See also* Christmas, Easter, Epiphany, St. Dimiter's Day, St. George's Day
Holy water, 22, 24, 31, 32, 127. *See also* Christening, Epiphany
Horo, 3-4, 8, 19, 36, 74, 77-80, 87-88, 90, 108, 125-126, 190
Hospitality as social value, 27
Household arts, 29, 53, 75-76
Housing, construction, 21-22, 72; furnishing, 23-25, 99; in zadruga, 230-231
Hungary, 184
Husband-wife relationships, 95-112; coming of first child, 92; Communism, 212; equalitarian, 189-190; happiness, 99, 101, 112; in commerce, 147-148; in-laws, 102; interdependence, 96-97, 99, 101-102; quarreling, 98-99; role of husband, 92, 95; role of wife, 93, 95; separation and divorce, 96, 100-101; shared activities, 102-112; terms of endearment, 97-98. *See also* Courtship Patterns, Parent-child relationship

I

Icon, 23, 32, 38, 43
Iconostas, 6, 24, 39, 106, 207
Illegitimacy, 83, 190, 270. *See also* Chastity
Immortality, beliefs about, 34-35, 83-84, 142
Income, 40-41, 52, 187, 268
Infant mortality, 32, 113
Inheritance, 55-56, 230
In-law relationships, 28-29, 58, 70, 93, 99, 102, 114, 190
Institutional competition, 180-181, 273

www.ingramcontent.com/pod-product-compliance
Lightning Source LLC
Chambersburg PA
CBHW020336270326
41926CB00007B/200